BELIEF AFTER FREUD

Belief after Freud confronts the psychoanalytic experience and the experience of faith. A purified vision of faith, so many times disfigured by infantile or neurotic dynamics, can emerge through the crucible of psychoanalysis. The work contributes to the dialogue between psychoanalysis and faith, based on the respective lived experiences, rather than from theoretical positions only. The book is divided into three parts:

- Part I centres on Freud's position on religion. After an introductory chapter assessing Freud's present validity, the following chapters critically examine Freud's position and interpretation of religion.
- Part II examines how people of faith experience psychoanalysis, including the role played by unconscious feelings of guilt, and the ideas of sin and salvation.
- Part III explores ideas of sexuality, power, and obedience, including the unconscious and pathological roots of the relation with money, and the sense of evangelical poverty.

Now in its fifth edition in Spain, *Belief after Freud* has also been published in Argentina and Brazil. Many readers say the book has opened a new form of belief for them. The book has also been of great interest to non-believing psychologists.

Carlos Domínguez-Morano (Huelva, Spain, 1946) is a Doctor in Theology and Sciences of Education and a Licentiate in Psychology. His psychoanalytic training took place in Paris and Madrid. He is Professor of Psychology of Religion and he works as a psychotherapist and trainer of psychologists and psychiatrists. He has served as President of the International Association for Medical-Psychological and Religious Studies. He is a Catholic Jesuit priest. His publications revolve around the relations between psychoanalysis and the Christian experience, affectivity, and interpersonal relations.

BELIEF AFTER FREUD

Religious Faith through the Crucible of Psychoanalysis

Carlos Domínguez-Morano

Translated by Francisco Javier Montero
Translation reviewed by Verónica Polo Torok

Routledge
Taylor & Francis Group
LONDON AND NEW YORK

First published in Spanish in 1998 as
Creer despues de Freud
by San Pablo Comunicacion SSP

First published 2018
by Routledge
2 Park Square, Milton Park, Abingdon, Oxon OX14 4RN

and by Routledge
711 Third Avenue, New York, NY 10017

Routledge is an imprint of the Taylor & Francis Group, an informa business

British Library Cataloguing-in-Publication Data
A catalogue record for this book is available from the British Library

Library of Congress Cataloging-in-Publication Data
A catalog record has been requested for this book

ISBN: 978-1-78220-643-9 (pbk)

Cover: Miguel Pérez

Typeset in Palatino
by The Studio Publishing Services Ltd
email: studio@publishingservicesuk.co.uk

CONTENTS

ACKNOWLEDGEMENTS

As mentioned in the Preface to the present edition, my deep thanks go to Francisco Javier Montero, my translator and friend, for his work of translation, advice, and friendly backing all along the way. I also thank the SAFA Modern Languages Centre, University of Jaén, at Úbeda, and Verónica Polo Torok, in charge of the revision of the present translation. Teresa and Victoria Montero helped Mr Montero in the translation work. My friends Arturo Sandiano and Mónica Cabieces also rendered great service in the revision for the style adjustment. Very special thanks also to my great friend Miguel Pérez for his generous contribution of the original painting for the book's cover. I cannot omit my appreciation and gratitude to the Library of the Granada Faculty of Theology for the wealth of their bibliographic material and their willingness to provide me with any text I might be interested in throughout the development and revision of the present work. The advice of Professors Juan A. Estrada and José M. Castillo on theological matters has been invaluable. Finally, I wish to express especial gratitude for the support I had from that great figure of psychoanalysis and religion, Ana-Maria Rizzuto, in the drive towards publication of the book in English.

To Francisco Javier Montero,
a really good man,
a profound believer,
and a very dear friend.

ABOUT THE AUTHOR

Carlos Domínguez-Morano is a Doctor of Theology and Sciences of Education, and Licentiate in Psychology. His psychoanalytic training took place in Paris and in Madrid. At present, he is Professor of Psychology of Religion at the Faculty of Theology of Granada (Spain), and he works as a psychotherapist and trainer of young psychologists and psychiatrists. He has been President of AIEMPR (International Association of Medical-Psychological and Religious Studies and Director of the University Center Francisco Suárez of Granada. He is a Catholic priest and a member of the Society of Jesus. His publications revolve around the relations between psychoanalysis and Christian experience (believing, the mystic experience, popular religiosity, the Spiritual Exercises of St Ignatius, etc.), and also feature affectivity and interpersonal relations (friendship relations, couples, homosexuality, etc.). He has a particular interest in art in general, and in film in particular.

Among his main publications are: *El psicoanálisis freudiano de la religión* (1991); *Creer después de Freud* (1992); *Psicoanálisis y Religión: diálogo interminable* (2000); *Los registros del deseo* (2001); *Psicodinámica de los Ejercicios Ignacianos* (2003), *Experiencia Cristiana y psicoanálisis* (2006); *El "Otro" de los místicos. Reflexiones desde el psicoanálisis* (2016).

Professor Domínguez-Morano has been visiting professor in several Spanish and Latin American universities, such as Universidad Iberoamericana of Mexico, Universidad Católica of Buenos Aires, Universidad Católica of El Salvador, Universidad Complutense of Madrid, Loyola-Andalucía of Sevilla, and Universidad Ramón Llu'll of Barcelona.

PREFACE

Belief after Freud was born of an inner demand. After some years of doctoral thesis work on Freud's texts in their critical view of religion (*El psicoanálisis freudiano de la religión*, San Pablo, Madrid, 1991), I experienced a double need. On the one hand, the need to respond to the questions posed to religious faith by psychoanalysis's founder in a more personal and vital way than that allowed by doctoral research. In effect, during the thesis work, I harboured a very special resolve to transmit Freud's position with the highest possible objectivity, avoiding any personal defences that could interfere with the exposition of his acid criticism of religious belief. After this restraint, necessarily imposed by academic rigour, the need to express in a freer and more personal way what that criticism meant for me became an inescapable inner demand. On the other hand, I felt a profound desire to revisit a series of basic aspects in our faith that seemed to require deep reassessments, both in their practical connotations and in their theoretical formulations. So I took up (I do not know how wisely) reflection on such fundamental themes as the image of God, the communication with Him in prayer, the experience of guilt and salvation, and others. The problems around the religious vows in consecrated life, concerning three basic dimensions of any life of faith, those of sexuality, power, and money, also played an important part in the revision of the most intimate experiences that psychoanalysis has unravelled from their deepest roots and motivations.

Thus, I tried to contribute to the already long dialogue between psychoanalysis and faith, doing so from lived experience rather than from purely theoretical positions. I have the conviction that such a dialogue can be rewarding and fertile only at the level of experience, avoiding the temptation to reach a definitive, final, and complete answer, as has so many times been attempted in both the psychoanalytic and the theological fields. As I have been able to express elsewhere (*Psicoanálisis y religión: diálogo interminable,* Trotta, Madrid, 2000) it seems certain that psychoanalysis and religion are doomed to exist under a permanent, reciprocal question mark; interrogations that emerge in a radically new way every time somebody speaks to formulate his *Credo,* no matter which. By its essence and not by chance, the dialogue between psychoanalysis and faith appears thus as a never-ending endeavour. Not an easy dialogue, to be sure, and not without good measures of anxiety and resistances, because it involves in-depth matters in terms of both beliefs and praxis, which should be reassessed with the determinants from the unconscious. The final answer to these questions cannot be anticipated, either from theology or from any psychoanalytical theoretical position. Yes or no will have to come only from the unique and inescapable experience of each questioned individual.

The present work, appearing now in English, has caused effects, reactions, and echoes of all kinds throughout its relatively long life in Spanish and Portuguese. It has questioned, comforted, unsettled, and upset as well. Because of this, it is the work that I feel is more alive and dear to me among all those I have produced. Opening it to such a wide and important public as the English-speaking readership gives me great satisfaction and new opportunities for interchange and reflection, for which I am deeply grateful to Francisco Javier Montero, my translator and very good friend. Without his effort and determination, the present edition would have never seen the light. I equally thank the prestigious Routledge publishing house for allowing me to reach the wide English-speaking public. The present edition has been restructured and updated in various ways, while preserving the original spirit and ideas.

INTRODUCTION

CHAPTER ONE

The validity of Freud

The assertion "We are far beyond Freud" has become commonplace. You hear it on the street or in the classroom, although, perhaps prudently, toned down to "Freud will be obsolete in the course of fifteen or twenty years".

Yet, today, Freud remains. His relevance, at least as a presence, is undeniable. Just by looking at any bookstore's psychology section, we can see that his works continue to sell. His image appears time and again in newspapers and magazines, in films and television fiction series. In scientific publications concerning psychology, in defiance of the desires of many, he continues to appear as the most influential figure at the heart of this field. In the psychiatric hospital or at university, Freudian psychoanalysts obtain positions as professors and department chairs. We could concur with Pontalis: "everywhere, even between prudent Jesuits, Freud is welcome with open arms" (Pontalis, 1968, p. 26, translated for this edition).

Freud is, we might say, everywhere. Even to the point of triggering the suspicion that this Freudian presence is a topical subject but not a valid reference. We would be in front of the ghostly presence of a dead man who speaks to a reality: Freud is present everywhere so that he is, in fact, operative nowhere.

The question has been raised, and certainly not in vain: "From delirium, fashion and exploitation, psychoanalysis has become . . . indeed, what has it become?" Pontalis asks (1968, pp. 26–27, translated for this edition). There are serious reasons to question whether Freud's topicality has been the precise cause of his loss of relevance, his operating power, even in his own domain, the psychoanalytic community.

Freud's name is indivisibly bound to the fundamental concept in psychoanalytical research: the unconscious. What, by definition, is marginalised, rejected, what cannot be seen. Hence, paradoxically, the desired phenomenon of superseding Freud, and the reality of his widespread diffusion, might have quite a similar outcome: defence against that unconscious, either from the belief that it is obsolete, or from having tamed it and made a theoretical or technical adaptation object out of it. Perhaps there was much truth in a professor's words when he denied his students the possibility of an introduction to psychoanalytical theory, since, according to him, "the more you know about psychoanalysis, the less you are experiencing psychoanalysis".

Is Freud irrelevant or simply omnipresent? Such is the question I try to address in this introductory chapter. To this end, we will ask ourselves about Freud's validity at three different levels, or, put another way, we will observe his impact within three concentric spheres of influence. First, we shall analyse Freud's position within the world of psychoanalysis, second, we shall approach the wider realm of psychology and, last, we shall try to assess Freud's relevance in general culture.

Freud in psychoanalysis

Freud "works" inside the world of psychoanalysis. We could say that ninety per cent of presently valid psychoanalytic principles are originally Freudian concepts. This can be confirmed by leafing through any psychoanalytical dictionary (Laplanche & Pontalis, 1973; Roudinesco & Plon, 1997).

There is no doubt that this is an indication of the creativity and multi-dimensionality of Freud's work, for which subsequent psychoanalysis has had no option but to build upon. But, at the same time, these observations may indicate the degree to which Freud might have been appropriated, tamed, and castrated by what could be called the "dynamics of Freudian orthodoxy".

The International Psychoanalytical Association, in effect, has frequently become the jealous guardian of an orthodoxy that, in the manner of the magisterium of the Church, preserves "the sacred deposit of the faith". To this end, they have built up rigid defences against anything they have considered to be deviation or heresy. In this way, magnificent psychoanalytical insights, such as those of Ferenczi or Reich, have been wholly set aside in order to safeguard the untouchable core of "Freudian truth". Such authors have been rejected *en masse*, leaving out important theoretical elaborations, including many among them that could be considered, after an impartial analysis, equally orthodox.

It is not uncommon to feel that, in the end, psychoanalysts become infected by the object of their study, the unconscious, by dint of their long-time handling of it. Psychoanalytical circles seem too often shrouded in mysticism, irrationality, childish omnipotence, and even some striking neurotic guilt in front of "god the father Freud". The pseudo-religious and sectarian environment of psychoanalytic schools of thought, their conflicts and splits, their claims and anathemas, are well known, and amount to one of the most shocking alienation stories in human relations, precisely among those whom we could call "masters in listening" (D'Amore, 1978; Fages, 1976; Munroe, 1955; Wyss, 1973). Freud imprisoned by orthodoxy!

But we find also a Freud who is quoted and spread to the last corners of the universe, a Freud who, we could say, has been turned into another consumer goods item. We can see this demonstrated in Woody Allen's films, where having access to a lawyer and a psychoanalyst are necessities for prestige and social status in the USA.

"We are bringing them the plague . . . and they don't even know it," said Freud to Jung when they were arriving in the USA to make psychoanalysis known at Clark University. However, Freud did not realise that, in the USA, they were ready to turn his "plague" into cologne for daily use. He was unaware that psychoanalysis would be transformed there, as important sociologists have well shown, into an instrument that would constrain individuals to the dominant thought structures, preventing any deviation (Parsons, 1951). Freud himself feared that, in effect, because of its fast diffusion in the USA, psychoanalysis could suffer "a great deal from being watered down" (Freud,

1925d). Psychoanalysis is, thus, infected, by way of excessive love, with a mortal disease. This Freud is far from the one who, at the start of his initial psychoanalytic conception, was marginalised by the Vienna Medical Society and condemned to painful isolation in the scientific and cultural communities (Gay, 1988; Jones, 1958; Roudinesco, 2014).

However, not everything translates to suffocating orthodoxy or sweetened diffusion. Facing the "therapy healers" or the "soul managers", obsessed in their analytical practice more by mere "effectiveness" than by the search for truth, it is necessary to show "another psychoanalysis" in which Freud is present and valid as a source of inspiration and a channel for new technical and theoretical developments.

Within this context, we have to place the masterly figure of Melanie Klein and her English school of thought. Faithful to Freud, she was willing and able to expand on his ideas. Her research on the early stages of life has brought to psychoanalysis the most fruitful explorations in the world of psychosis, along with deep and lucid perspectives that address the problems of those early stages. We shall refer more than once to these insights, for instance, when dealing with matters such as the image of God, guilt, interpersonal relations, etc. Clinical practice was also enriched by Klein's contributions, particularly on the psychoanalytical approach to childhood. However, it was only with reluctance that this woman's important technical and theoretical innovations were accepted by the International Psychoanalytical Association (Brown, 1964, pp. 56–87; Fages, 1976, pp. 126–144).

We also see how the toned-down and distorted Freud in most of American psychoanalysis has been denounced by one of the most polemical and original figures of French psychoanalysis: Jacques Lacan. By proclaiming his "come back to Freud" motto and conducting a deep and original reading of Freudian text, he has given it back all its intensity, offering a reformulation (from an adult perspective, as opposed to childish fidelity). This is a much better fit to Freud's discoveries. The physical models, which the founder used to translate his new findings (according to the ideas of the time for all scientific disciplines) have been replaced in Lacan by linguistic models, better suited to the understanding of the mechanisms driving the unconscious. This change from the physical to the linguistic is, for Lacan, his main difference from Freud:

> You asked about what distinguishes me from Freud: well, the answer is right here, in the fact that I know linguistics. . . . I can say this because linguistics arose a few years after psychoanalysis. Saussure began it shortly after Freud, in *The Interpretation of Dreams,* had written a full-fledged treatise of linguistics. This is my "distance" from Freud (Caruso, 1969, p. 112)

Lacan will be present more than once as we reflect on some of the important questions in the experience of faith. This, however, does not translate to a full Lacanian positioning in relation to this complex and polemical figure in psychoanalysis. Lacan's genius, unfortunately, is not apparent in many of his followers.

These figures, Klein on the one hand and Lacan on the other, portray not only a presence, but also a valid and functional Freud within the psychoanalytic realm. Klein, like Freud, always knew how to progress by questioning all of her earlier assumptions. She represents the call to progress and development in psychoanalytical concepts and techniques. On the other hand, Lacan's psychoanalytical reformulations are an incentive to go back to the discipline's roots and save it from becoming too diffused and domesticated into just another technical theory helping to control the system.

Freud in psychology

The relationship between psychoanalysis and most of the rest of the world of psychology has not been too good. Before looking to the present situation, let us make a tentative approach to the problem of psychological methods.

The diversity of material, orientation, and methodology offered by present psychology is such that it poses the question of whether any psychological knowledge is at all possible. All schools of thought agree to define psychology as science of behaviour, but each one of them has a very different understanding of what that behaviour is and of the methods to be employed to approach and understand it. As Pinillos asserts, psychologists seem to be more concerned about making sure that what they do is seen as science rather than defining the object of that science, a fundamental goal for a discipline to establish itself as such (Pinillos, 1979).

To simplify a very complex picture, which obviously exceeds the goals of this introduction, we could say that there are two main approaches in the present terminological and methodological psychology jungle. Two approaches, as shown by Lagache, which reflect two ways of being and knowing, two basic attitudes in front of human reality: one with a naturalistic profile, the other with a humanistic one (Lagache, 2013). These two attitudes towards the study of behaviour lead, in turn, to two great streams in contemporary psychology: the experimental–psychometric stream, which is of naturalistic character, and the clinical–dynamic stream, the humanistic one. The first seeks to understand *what* happens and *how* it happens, wanting to explain and measure. The second would rather understand *why*; it wants to understand and heal. In order to situate psychoanalysis within the context of these two currents first requires a short exploration of history.

Psychology, in order to position itself as a science, had to make a huge sacrifice, giving away the metaphysical context in which it was born and where it remained for centuries. That step was very abrupt. Perhaps there is nobody better than Watson to incarnate that break away from the past. In his famous "behaviourist manifesto", he declares the need for psychology to cast off any concept that might have even a minimal philosophical connotation. In this way, consciousness, feelings, emotions, personality, or instincts were removed from the realm of psychology. It seemed that psychology had the natural science model, in particular that of physics, as the only one fit to serve as its scientific basis. "Psychology, as the behaviorist views it," writes Watson,

> is a purely objective experimental branch of natural science. Its theoretical goal is the prediction and control of behaviour . . . The behaviorist . . . recognizes no dividing line between man and brute . . . The time seems to have come when psychology must discard all reference to conscience. Psychology needs introspection as little as do the sciences of chemistry and physics. (Watson, 1913, p. 176)

The beginnings of psychology in the twentieth century are, thus, marked by a methodological reductionism, which, as Wolman asserts, is "a childhood ailment, common to all new-born sciences" (Wolman, 1973). At the same time, psychology went into a period of childish dependency on "adult sciences", especially on physics, which became the only valid reference for psychologists at that time. We have a telling example in that of Hartley (1749), who undertook the task of laying the foundation for all psychology of "association" in Newton's studies of the pendulum.

Freud fell into this positivist and materialistic movement. His first project does indeed coincide with the reduction of psychology to neurology, conforming to the physical sciences model. We have proof of this in his work *Project for a Scientific Psychology* (Freud, 1895). However, either chance or his own background is going to turn him, in Miller's paradoxical expression, into "a loyal rebel" against that very tradition in which he framed himself. Although he always saw himself as a faithful follower of the positivist principles of his time and maintained its somewhat illusory hope for scientific achievements, he became, much to his own regret, a transgressor of the positivist principles of his environment.

Freud was as much a neurologist and materialistic positivist as Pavlov, but, in the laboratory corridors, he met not a salivating dog but Anna O faking a hysterical pregnancy, the fruit of her emotional fixation on Dr Breuer. Here, a difficult course begins for Freud, a bitter fight between his loyalty to, and his defiance of, the positivist principles he had proclaimed as his scientific creed. Total loyalty, however, was no longer possible. Therefore, when he sees hysterical symptoms as symbols that cry out for what cannot be put into words, he is establishing the basis for a totally different view of behaviour, and, hence, of psychology. From this moment on, he will be unable to build a psychology based just on natural science principles, even if he keeps trying to express his psychoanalytical findings in language borrowed from physics (condensation, displacement, principle of inertia, etc.). Much to his own regret, he could not prevent embarking on a road in which he had progressively to ignore everything else in the experimental and positivist psychology of his time.

Thus, the clinical–dynamic stream in psychology was firmly consolidated by Freud. From then on, behaviour is no longer presented as just a given element to be tested and explained, but also as a symbol that must be decoded, reconstructed, and interpreted by a sense. Obviously, finding a scientific principle for such a procedure is more complex, causing unending controversy, but the fact is that, from Freud and psychoanalysis onwards, there has been a proliferation of attempts, with diverse methods but identical inspiration, which have approached behaviour from the perspective that places *the subject* in the forefront.

Inside the clinical–dynamic stream itself, there was no absence of critical positions against Freud and psychoanalysis. However, the origin of many of these criticisms had a psychoanalytical footprint that would not fade in spite of all attempts to disown it. In any case, it is generally accepted that schools such as Lowen's bio-energy, Schultz's relaxation methods, Moreno's psycho-drama, Rogers' non-directive therapy, Bion's group psychotherapy or Perls' Gestalt therapy, etc., would be difficult to understand without psychoanalysis.

As for the other great stream in present psychology, the experimental–psychometric one, it begins to suffer from experimentalist suffocation with severe consequences. As an example, it needs a new theoretical body of its own in order to answer the requirements of psychological research, instead of continuing to borrow from the physical science model. In addition, we can see a trend towards revisiting issues that had been side-lined in mainstream research, such as conscience, emotion, thought, and, above all, subjectivity, which had previously been exiled. As reflected by Pinillos, from the day that psychologists from the Palo Alto school of thought realised that the multiplicity of psychological processes studied had no proper explanation without a subject which would unify them, things started to change in the psychology panorama of the day (Pinillos, 1980, p. 580).

The question is whether the time has come to try a certain unification of the knowledge of psychology in which experimental approaches do not necessarily exclude the views of the clinical–dynamic stream. In other words, to have an understanding of psychology in which the assertions of unconsciously inferred behaviour will not be automatically dismissed, and, therefore, will make psychoanalysis a necessity for explaining what we call *behaviour*.

At the same time, it would be appropriate for psychoanalysis, so long turned away from the rest of psychology, to question whether its discourse has not taken on a certain omnipotent tone, being too dismissive of the scientific methodology that characterises psychology itself. It is good to look for the hidden and concealed meaning of particular conduct, but, sometimes, by dint of so much search for hidden meaning, the object under observation becomes distorted. Hence, a fall into a kind of "interpretative delirium", which should be cured by the proper analysis offered by the rest of psychology's more rigorous methodology. This is not a call for an eclectic methodology that would obfuscate results, but for a respectful attitude towards the approaches of different methodologies. It is not a matter of mixing the laboratory with the clinic, or the microscope with the couch, but of initiating a fruitful dialogue on what is found from each approach and both approaches. At least, it would be a better use of time which is now spent in futile controversy or disqualifying insults. Meehl enumerates some of these disqualifications: that statistical methods are dead, pedantic, trivial, superficial, academic, blind, etc.; on the other hand, the clinical methods are said to be mystical, otherworldly, nebulous, crude, sloppy, wordy, stupid, etc. (Meehl, 1954, pp. 4–5).

To summarise, then, what has been written so far in this second section, we can state that psychoanalysis stands as the strongest force of the clinical–dynamic stream, as an inspiring source for other schools of thought within that stream, and as a challenge to the experimentalist suffocation that so-called "scientific psychology" suffers.

Freud in culture

Psychoanalysis, as a research method for the unconscious processes, has had its major growth and impact in the clinical world. As Freud says, "psychoanalysis was born out of medical necessity" (Freud, 1919g, p. 259). However, it should be recognised that psychoanalysis is something more than a simple psychotherapy method. It could even be that the attempts to reduce it exclusively to that clinical dimension entail one of the most telling examples of defence against the unconscious that has ever existed.

Psychoanalysis broke down the walls between health and pathology and went on to transform itself from psycho-pathologic theory to general psychology. That is why it had to "invade" all the areas considered "healthy", such as art, religion, and philosophy, since the paths that can lead to artistic creation, religious practice, or philosophic system are, to a certain degree, analogous to those that lead to hysteria, obsessive neurosis, or paranoia. So, the step from the clinic to culture was, for psychoanalysis, a "scientific imperative and an irresistible temptation" (Freud, 1919g, p. 259). A similar step was the one from a purely individual psychology to a collective one, as also, as expressed by Ricoeur, was the step from the field of dreams to the field of the sublime (Ricoeur, 1970, p. 178).

Furthermore, it should be understood that this step cannot be considered as something marginal and incidental in the aggregate of Freudian thought. If this step were omitted, Freud's whole theoretical construction would be seriously affected because, in effect, the entire hermeneutical concept, which was born out of the interpretation of dreams and neurosis, was affected through a sort of rebound effect in this transfer from clinic to culture. This gave rise to important theoretical changes. Thus, for instance, the model which divided the personality into conscious, preconscious, and unconscious systems was shown to be lacking after the analysis of cultural formations, in this way causing the creation of the "second topography": the division of the personality into the new framework of id, ego, and superego.

There is also another relevant factor to take into account: it was precisely the analysis of the religious phenomenon that took Freud beyond the clinical frontier. As we shall see in the next chapter, he was pushed in this direction when he detected the analogies between the language of obsessional neurosis and that of religious rites. Later on, Freud's language analogy led him to believe he could speak about a structural identity in the respective bases of neurosis and culture. So, in *Totem and Taboo* (1912–1913), Freud puts forward what we could consider a "basic universal structure" which would support neurosis as much as religion, morality, or social formations.

From then on, starting from the model of neurosis and dream interpretation, Freudian text spills over, time and time again, into the psychoanalytic reading of the most diverse realms of civilisation: jokes, drama, the novel, poetry, painting, biographies, etc. (Freud, 1905c, 1907a, 1908d, 1908e, 1910c, 1913f, 1914b). These were successive steps in the extension of the hermeneutic field. But art and religion occupied prevailing places in his interest as objects of applied psychoanalysis. More globally, in his *Civilization and its Discontents* (1930a), Freud left us an amazing, dramatic interpretation of our life in society as the result of both an unavoidable repression and a required introjection of aggression as unconscious guilt. Rarely has the critical problem of the difficult search for happiness been approached so pointedly.

Freudian constructions on the interpretation of culture have given birth to multiple theories and works by psychoanalysts and thinkers.

In this way, it can be truly said that Freud remains present and valid in our culture through the creations of personalities from many different backgrounds who have felt inspired and challenged by the work of psychoanalysis's founder.

The full image of man has been deeply shaken since psychoanalysis appeared, to the point of impeding the view of the human subject in the same way as before. Psychoanalysis has caused, as Freud himself said, the third and deepest wound inflicted on human narcissism. The first occurred when science demonstrated that our planet, far from being the centre of the universe, was only a lost and insignificant body inside the cosmic system. The second wound was inflicted when biological research showed that man was nothing special or unique in the animal hierarchy: Darwin relegated us to another link in the physical evolutionary chain. But, if Copernicus and Darwin dealt deadly blows to man's lust for uniqueness and power, psychoanalysis has caused perhaps the deepest wound, by showing us that we are not even masters of our own house. The unconscious, as a realm excluded from our knowledge, will, and control, dwells in us and determines us, without our being able to know exactly when and how it does so (Freud, 1916–1917, pp. 284–285). From here on, an anthropological revolution takes place, the dimension of which we have yet to comprehend. Quite certainly, many things have started to change.

We could say that psychoanalysis has given us a new way to understand the world of values, bringing what we could call a "revaluation of the rejected", and, from there, a new way of thinking about important areas of our society, such as education, psychiatry, or art. Psychoanalysis has greatly contributed to a thoughtful approach to children and their upbringing and education, through the pedagogic approaches of people like Vera Schmidt in the USSR during the early years of the Revolution, A. S. Neill in the UK, or systems such as institutional pedagogy in France (Barande, 1973; Bettelheim, 2006; Pfister, 1927; Rinaudo, 2009).

In a way, psychiatry has not been able to avoid the impact of Freudian psychoanalytic theory. It is this theoretical base that has provided a framework for manifestations such as antipsychiatry, which has had such an impact, for example, in Italy, France, and the UK (Basaglia, 1969; Foucault, 1972; Laing, 1971). Also, the field of psychosomatic medicine conducts research based on Freudian concepts, in cases such as the Psychosomatic Institute in France (Marty, 1998) and Rof Carballo and his team in Spain (Rof Carballo, 1972).

This "revaluation of the rejected" has been especially potent in the arts world. We all recognise that the surrealist movement saw Freud as their master and main inspirer. Art, cinema, and literature all seemed to find a world of creative possibilities in the unconscious. Works by those such as Dalí, Ernst, and Magritte in painting, Hitchcock, Buñuel, Kazan, Pasolini, and Bertolucci in cinema, Arrabal and Miller in theatre, Joyce and Zweig in literature, tellingly illustrate the impact of psychoanalysis on artistic creation (Ruitenbeek, 1962, 1964; Domínguez-Morano, 2012).

If the psychoanalysis concept of "revaluation of the rejected" has worked for education, psychiatry, and the arts, it has caused a commotion for philosophy, ethics, and religion by introducing the "false conscience" problem. As masterfully exposed by Ricoeur, Freud has become, alongside Marx and Nietzsche, one of the grand "masters of suspicion". With Descartes, one could doubt how things appear, but not how consciousness appears to itself. After Marx, Nietzsche, and Freud, we start to doubt consciousness itself (Ricoeur, 1965). From here on, an open question is created for philosophy, ethics, and religion.

Philosophic thought seems to have had certain difficulties in facing the challenge that psychoanalysis introduces. The concept of the unconscious did not have a good reputation among philosophers, who, in general, did not greatly appreciate it. In either case, examples such as the thinkers from the Frankfurt School (Adorno, Marcuse, Fromm), or Foucault, or, particularly, Ricoeur, lead us to think that philosophic thought will not be the same after Freud (Assoun, 2009; Ricoeur, 1965).

The same thing could be said about the fields of social sciences or anthropology in the light of contributions by figures such as Mead, Bastide, Devereux, or Lévi-Strauss (Ruitenbeek, 1962).

And what of ethics and theology? How have they adjusted to the challenge that psychoanalysis introduces? In general, moralists and theologians have not appeared too ready to investigate the "false conscience" problem. A problem, we should make clear, which is not presented by Freud, but by his discoveries, by the way in which psychoanalysis is used as a research method for the unconscious processes.

Regarding the issue of the relationship between psychoanalysis and faith, to which we shall return later, it is necessary to differentiate between how those dwelling in psychoanalytical territory have reflected on their faith, and how those that, from a theological background, have approached psychoanalytical methods. In the former group, those who are deeply rooted in psychoanalysis, and who, because of their belief, have carried out a theoretical reflection on their faith, we generally find a deep, sometimes dramatic, but always balanced view of the psychoanalytical dilemma. Along these lines, we should point out contributions by practitioners such as Beirnaert, Vergote, Meissner, Rizzuto, De Saussure, etc., whom we shall frequently refer to in this book.

Quite another situation is when the reflection starts exclusively from theology and approaches psychoanalysis as a particular stage of its own work. In these cases, the impressions can be disappointing sometimes. Defence mechanisms are triggered automatically, even compulsively. We have seen that in detail elsewhere (Domínguez-Morano, 1991, pp. 476–483) and we will have the opportunity to come back to it in Chapter Four when analysing theological echoes and resonances. However, we could already say that either all of the problem is set in a useless dispute, or all the lines of argument are fixed on Freud's ignorance of any authentic religious experience. Or, sometimes, a series of psychoanalytical concepts are brought in, but, one suspects, just to integrate them in their own belief structure, stripped of any uncomfortable content. Defensive rationalisation, not the honest attempt to answer the problem, has become all but the norm. There are, however, notable exceptions to this sombre scene. For instance, the contributions from theologians such as Bellet, Plé, and Duquoc, in some excellent publications and, in an outstanding way, Pohier, even at considerable cost: the publication of his *Quand je dis Dieu* (Pohier, 1977) led to his being prohibited from teaching, preaching, and celebrating the Eucharist. The impact of these sanctions on his life and thoughts have been described by Pohier himself in a dramatic and disturbing work entitled *God in Fragments* [*Dieu fractures*] (Pohier, 1985).

However, this answer should not be understood as a forced confession before a Freudian or psychoanalytic tribunal. It is not about faith having forcibly to explain itself by way of an intellectual terrorist attack. It is a matter of faith presenting account of itself within a society and a culture that Freud has had an impact on, and in which faith must be revealed and proclaimed.

This present work is conceived as an attempt to contribute to that confrontation between psychoanalytical experience and the experience of faith. In a way, it stands as a sequel to a former work, *El psicoanálisis freudiano de la religion* [The Freudian Psychoanalysis of Religion] (Domínguez-Morano, 1991), of which we offer a systematic synthesis in Part I of the present work, after removing its more technical elements. It is intended as a tool for faith practitioners regarding the more decisive and valid contents that we find in Freudian text.

In Part II of the book, we reflect on prayer, the image of God, and the guilt–sin–salvation triad to test faith's response to the psychoanalytical challenge. In Part III, we look at specific aspects of the believer's relationship with sex, power, and money as three essential elements in his relation with the world, three elements that have even qualified, as vows, the core of religious life.

However, before starting to describe Freud's challenge to faith by means of his writings and then the attempt to respond, it is worth ending this introductory chapter by looking at Freud's validity with some general character reflections.

Man, an animal of illusions

We have already seen that the mere presence of Freud, or psychoanalysis, does not guarantee its current validity. Furthermore, an excessive presence of Freud raises suspicions of being a means of defence against what was his discovery: the unconscious. That is why we could say that Freud's validity will be proportional to the measure in which his contributions denounce individual or collective false illusions.

Xavier Zubiri, the Spanish philosopher, said "Man is an animal of realities". After Freud, we should add, "an animal of realities condemned to become ill through illusions". And it is hard to cure oneself of the unavoidable force that drives one to deceitful illusion time and time again without progress. Psychoanalysis has highlighted that, in man's heart, there is a void, a desire, a want which nothing and nobody can fill. A want that, despite driving our actions, our seeking, and our longings, is also the origin of the inescapable alienation that, through many phantasies, is always ready to be revived. Phantasies of having found that true object of our longing (as happens when falling in love); phantasy that generates the erroneous belief in "eternal love", even if reality shows that it is not necessarily so; phantasy of finding again the "innocent child", of having recovered the safe guidance of a perfect father; phantasies of revolution that are fed exclusively from the rebellion against an old paternal ghost; phantasies of salvation and eternal life as displaced targets of infantile narcissism and omnipotence.

Only from the place of emptiness, however, is it possible to access the truth of reality that, as bad as it can be, will always be preferable to the best phantasy. Only from the death of illusion can religious hope, not just childish escapism, be born. Only from the truth of loneliness is it possible to experience freedom and an authentic encounter with the other as other, and not as a ghost born out of our indigence.

Psychoanalysis as an exercise in suspicion and as an instance of truth does not halt in front of any type of frontier. Nobody, conservative or progressive, is assured of any type of immunity against self-delusion.

> The psychoanalytical revolution is not satisfied just dividing old and new. Everybody is affected at a more radical level, one in which his defences coincide in sheltering behind a ground marked by its absolute and idealised character: morality, science, and absolute itself. Such subjects are the ones that are less likely to let themselves be driven to the goal of the psychoanalytical revolution: to be called into question. (Bertolus et al., 1971, p. 104, translated for this edition)

Finally, we would have to conclude that the assertion that "Freud is obsolete", both by its frequency and by the ignorance it bears, provides grounds for us to suspect it masks a profound wish. A wish that can be understood as a wish to reawaken the overlooked meaning within ourselves: the one hidden in the language of the unconscious.

Obviously, Freud's understanding should never be taken as the last word. That is the great mistake that psychoanalytical institutions have made so many times. In this sense, it can and should be possible to speak of building on Freud. But then it would be a collaboration driven precisely by the movement he set in motion and not a denial, as is sometimes thought and often wished for. Freud is surpassed in a way analogous to how Copernicus, Newton, or Darwin is. But the earth keeps traversing through the universe, the apple keeps falling from the tree, and man continues to be the result of biological evolution. All the while, the unconscious continues to be ignored, but affects our ways of thinking, feeling, and acting.

In summary, then, we could say that Freud is present and valid in the psychoanalytical movement and is recognised as its founder. At the same time, he is recognised as an instance of evolution and radicalism. Freud continues to be relevant in the sphere of contemporary psychology as the most important inspirer of the clinical–dynamic stream and as a challenge to the experimentalist suffocation that marginalises the subject. Also, Freud maintains a presence in our culture by nourishing currents of thought and, above all, as an example of truth, facing the unavoidable phantasies of the "animal of realities condemned to become ill through illusions" which is man.

Faith must pay attention and listen to this constant challenge coming from psychoanalysis and must also formulate, with humility but with courage, what faith is working out in response.

PART I

THE FREUDIAN INTERPRETATION OF RELIGION

CHAPTER TWO

Religion and neurosis

The process analogy

The Freudian interpretation of religion, as already mentioned in the introduction, is based on two hermeneutical models, those of neurosis and dreams. In this first chapter on Freudian texts about religion, we are going to focus on the diverse relationships Freud establishes between religion and neurosis and on a whole series of consequences and problems stemming from these associations.

Early on in Freudian texts, religion is associated with the study of hysteria. Here, the splitting of consciousness, or dissociation, the basic phenomenon that opened the doors to psychoanalysis, exposed the process which Freud called perversion of will (Freud, 1892–1893, p. 123). In other words, an unconscious wish from the repressed that prevails over the subject's conscious wishes and will. In this battle of wills, Freud views the religious experience as an element that clearly plays in favour of the conscious and repressive will. Religiousness is, thus, an important opponent to the subject's world of wishes and instincts. In consequence, it frequently plays a decisive part in neurosis generation.

Repression, undertaken with the help of the religious experience, continually requires that help to maintain control over the repressed wish, which retains, however, its penchant for free expression. Since this first Freudian proposal, certain religion-inspired ravings and some extreme forms of devotion were considered clear symptomatic expressions of repressed instincts.[1] Yet, still, many important theoretical consequences entailed by these phenomena remained unresolved.

After the initial research into the field of hysteria, obsessional neurosis provided Freud with another fundamental area of investigation of the unconscious. It is within this second type of neurosis that Freud finds the main interpretative key to his whole subsequent analysis of religious beliefs. Unlike hysteria, obsessional neurosis offered him a type of language very similar to that of cultural phenomena. It seemed as if we were looking at a kind of "dialect" of cultural language (Freud, 1909d, p. 155).

In that observed similarity between obsessional neurosis and cultural formation, religious practice came to occupy an exemplary place. Actually, in Freud's eyes, the rites of obsessional neurosis revealed a surprising analogy with those of religious practice.

Once this new relation between religion and obsessional neurosis is established, religious experience will no longer appear just to oppose unconscious drives, as in the *Studies on Hysteria* (1895d), but also serve as a disguised expression of the instinct itself and the guilt feelings associated with it. Indeed, in the obsessional symptom, religious behaviour presents a "compromise formation" trait, that is, a transaction or pact between the instinct on one hand and the prohibition of the instinct itself on the other; a pact, however, between instinct and prohibition that is hidden from the subject, making him unaware of its meaning.

In his essay "Obsessive actions and religious practices" (Freud, 1907b), his first important work on the subject of religion, Freud remarks on the parallels, not merely superficial, between obsessional and religious rites. Both seem to be motivated by intense guilt feelings, caused, in turn, by repressed unconscious wishes, against which both (the neurotic and the religious person) defend themselves by means of rites. The analogy in the expression is matched by an analogy in the origin of both behaviours: in both cases we find the repression of an instinct.

Later on, the threat that those repressed contents cause to the subject's neurotic consciousness lead him to develop a whole series of defensive measures that, unfortunately, precisely trace the desire he wished to avoid. It is the symptom as "compromise-formation" between prohibition and desire.

In religious practice, Freud also finds the same transaction between prohibition and wish, between the repressive and repressed tendencies; as he tells us, all those actions officially forbidden by religion are frequently undertaken precisely in the name of religion.

Many things still remain unknown regarding this ambivalent and double tendency in religious experience but, from what we can glean so far, Freud dares to propose an eventually well-known formulation: from a psychoanalytical point of view, obsessional neurosis must be considered as an individual's religion and religion as a universal obsessional neurosis (Freud, 1907b, pp. 126–127).

This is as far as the analogy between religion and neurosis is taken in the early writings. The difference established in those days (to disappear later) lies in the fact that the obsessional neurotic has repressed sexual contents, while, in religious behaviour, he guesses the repression of antisocial and selfish tendencies. The outline of the first theory on the instincts, with the ego opposing the sexual drives, can be seen through the differentiation Freud makes between obsessional neurotic repression and the religious man's repression. The former is afraid of sexuality and his neurosis is born out of this fear; the latter fears his selfish, antisocial tendencies and his religiousness comes out of this fear. This differentiation will fail when, from 1914 on, a new instinctual life theory asserts that ego instincts are libidinal, too (Freud, 1914c). Going beyond analogy, an identity is established on the originating conflict of both obsessional and religious behaviour.

The identity of origin

The establishment of an identity in their origin for both neurosis and religion is made when, in *Totem and Taboo* (Freud, 1912–1913, pp. 156–157), the oedipal conflict is identified as the common source for both the neurotic conflict and culture and its great institutions. (I have focused on the general characteristics of *Totem and Taboo,* on its long and hazardous composition, and on the problems involved in its reading in a full chapter of *El psicoanálisis freudiano de la religión*, Domínguez-Morano, 1991, pp. 99–144.)

Totem and Taboo represents an essential step in the development of Freudian thought in general and, no doubt, is a key work in relation to the subject of religion. In this work, the so-called Oedipus complex goes beyond the purely psychopathological and becomes a fundamental anthropological category. It is no longer just about seeing the Oedipus complex as the core of a neurotic complex, but of building the very foundations of human and cultural behaviour upon its structure and dynamics. In this way, the oedipal situation becomes a basic universal structure.

From this new understanding of the oedipal issues, Freud thinks he has the key to establish an identity for the origin of the behaviour of the neurotic and the religious man. Both will be, in their diverse activity, perpetuating that oedipal structure without managing to avoid the predicaments of that infantile situation: the neurotic person experiencing the suffering which any individual neurosis entails, the religious man seeing his anxiety mitigated by belonging to a generalised cultural formation. His conflict is not an open wound, because it is placed in another register, the social and collective one, from which he tries to ease his difficult contact and relation with the real world (Freud, 1924f). However, the dynamics to which it responds are essentially the same.

How, then, is the oedipal situation perpetuated in religion? In Freud's eyes, it immortalises a conflict with the father, elevated now to the status of God; a conflict in which emotional ambivalence, that is, simultaneous coexistence of love and hate, keeps playing a basic role.

According to the innovative *Totem and Taboo* hypothesis, the God of religion existed actually on earth as mortal flesh and was the object of a radical, we could even say deadly, conflict. The book's originality came from a dramatic, mythical presentation and not as the result of a theoretical formulation.

On the basis of certain ethnic and anthropological theories of his time (specifically, the primitive horde hypothesis, such as Darwin and Atkinson described, and the Robertson Smith theory on the totemic meal celebration), Freud imagined a primordial drama in which a jealous and omnipotent father was murdered and devoured by his sons, who saw this action as their only way to access the women that their father kept exclusively for himself. That primal murder, that kind of original and originating sin, would be the basis of the great social institutions: ethics, law, and religion.

But that murder was, in a sense, a great failure, since the children knew that nobody could take the father's place unless the crime be perpetually repeated. His place had to remain empty and it was precisely in this empty space left by the father where religion found its birthplace.

It was, indeed, from this hollow space that the dead father returned to existence, first as the clan's totemic animal, and then in his transformation, through heroes, gods, and demons, to finally reach his complete resurrection as the single Judeo-Christian God, expressing more clearly than any other religion the primal father's resurrection.

Better than any other religious manifestation, Christianity, with its original sin doctrine, would, indeed, bring to light that primal event, the father's death. In necessitating the son's death, it atones for the original sin against the father through dogmatic phantasy. But the eternal ambivalence which religious expression is known for results in the father being reborn and reasserting himself, by way of Christian dogma, in the resurrection and divine status of the dead son, who, in this way, impersonates anew the father (Freud, 1913c, p. 154, 1939a, pp. 87–90).

Judaism, however, saw the horde's primal father reborn in the single god Aten, brought from Egypt by Moses, but did not come to admit to the father's murder. The price of its refusal to confess to God's murder has been paid, on the one hand, by being reduced to the condition of a fossil, and on the other hand, by persecution all throughout history (Freud, 1939a, p. 90).

In his *Moses and Monotheism*, published one year before his death, Freud dares to hypothesise on the origin of Judaism. For him, Moses was an Egyptian, a proselyte of Aten, who, at seeing the old polytheism restored, brings together a group of Semites to whom he transmits his faith. That Moses, however, will be murdered by his followers, who are unable to endure a religion so highly spiritualised as that Egyptian monotheism. A new Moses succeeds him, but this time with a new God, Yahweh, the Volcano God, a much more anthropomorphic divinity generating a rougher and more superstitious religion. Judaism is then explained (and the neurosis model as well) as a compromise between two opposed tendencies that, finally, through the "return of the repressed" process, end up restoring the primal tribe's father back to life in the magnificent figure of the single God of the prophets.

In this way, *Totem and Taboo* illustrates a conflict in which the relationship with the father rests on a kind of "you or me", all-or-nothing ultimatum, with the father's death being the only solution to make possible the son's own existence. But the perpetual emotional ambivalence prevents the son's freedom, since the guilt feeling (due to the loving pole in the relationship) binds him longingly forever to the dead father. That father, admired and hated at the same time, is now reborn and regains an unimaginable power. Only in this way can the son believe he can fill the dreadful void left by that dead father.

However, if guilt brings the father back to life, if love and nostalgia for his presence cause his constant reappearance, then hate, expressed as radical incompatibility, forcefully reappears at the very heart of religion. Unable to express himself openly and directly in front of the father who is magnified by divinity, he does it in the masked ways that religion itself provides. So, time and time again, the great originating father dies, sacrificed in dogma and in religious rites and celebrations, repeating the original crime in an everlasting chain. In the end, we see that emotional ambivalence is always ready to flare up as this everlasting death–resurrection of the originating father.

Thus, the "return of the repressed" (*Wiederkehr des Verdrängten*), which is Freud's key explanation for the understanding of religions, enables a perennial repetition of the primary ambivalence, never resolved, towards the father.

The theoretical difficulties, which Freud had to confront as he assigned the value of a real event to the oedipal drama, are important and we shall have to address them in our critical evaluation. The psychic transmission of the consequences of that primal crime resulted in notable stumbling blocks (so much like those found by theologians in explaining the transmission of original sin . . .). Freud tried to circumvent them with the help of certain hypotheses with a biology bent, such as the "inheritance of acquired characteristics".

In any case, *Totem and Taboo* establishes a key piece in the Freudian interpretation of religious fact, in its essential relation with the Oedipus complex and in its analogy with neurosis. Religion, like neurosis, offers "solutions" to perpetuate in the phantasy dimension the fight between the son and the father. Paradoxically, on the other hand, this is a fight that satisfies the desire to live forever sheltered by the father's protection. This second dimension of religion is best analysed by the application of the dream model to the interpretation of religious fact.

The double father figure: God and the devil

In the oedipal structure that religion maintains, God and the devil appear as two disguised representations of the father. Their roots are hidden beneath two poles of emotional ambivalence, positive and negative.

In the essay about Leonardo da Vinci, we find the first clear association Freud establishes between the father figure and God's image, with its roots in the "father complex" (Freud, 1910c, p. 123). Soon after, the analysis of the paranoia delirium made in the "Schreber case" highlights again, through the psychotic break, the father's function and his extreme exaltation to divinity (Freud, 1911c).

The clinical cases dedicated to the analysis of obsessional neurosis, such as the "Rat Man" and the "Wolf Man" (Freud, 1909d, 1918b), highlighted the intensity of the emotional ambivalence towards the father, which, in both cases, provided in God's image a more bearable outlet for the subject.

Freud's research into neurosis led him to the unequivocal conclusion of the close association between the specific conflict with the father and its relation to the divine. This was demonstrated by case studies such as that of Christoph Heitzmann (Freud, 1923d), Dostoyevsky (Freud, 1928b), and of a young American physician in "A religious experience" (Freud, 1928a). God is a substitution for, and an exaltation of, the father (*ein Vatersatz ein erhöhter Vater*) that only the religious cultural formation has been able to generate. In contrast, to Freud, the philosophers' pompous theoretical constructions on God seem to be ridiculous surrogates or cheap pastiches (Freud, 1927c, p. 32). Only through the pressure of guilt, born of emotional ambivalence and from the nostalgia for the father it breeds, can this father's exaltation be acquired. It creates, in this way, especially in Judeo-Christianity, the whole dimension that the primal father figure had for the son.

As Freud evolves his ideas and integrates these thoughts on religion, the question is posed: how could a father acquire such grandiosity from a limited human being? Time and time again, Freud comes back to the subject, always revealing, however, a deep dissatisfaction with the results obtained. So it is with the "Schreber" case study in 1911 (Freud, 1911c, pp. 55–57), continues with *Totem and Taboo* (Freud, 1912–1913, pp. 149–151) in 1913, and culminates in *Moses and Monotheism* in 1939 (Freud, 1939a, pp. 83–84).

Freud never looked for the solution in proper psychoanalytical terms, but resorted to not always consistent material from the history of religions. He revealed once again the inadequate evolutionist background in which he formed the question, but we shall revisit this later on.

The oedipal emotional ambivalence shown in the analysis of neurosis also opens the door to the interpretation of another religious figure somehow parallel to God. Satan, who, in the first Freudian writings, appears as a symbol of repressed meanings, is progressively acquiring a distinctive profile by association with the father. In this way, he is going to be revealed as the other face of the paternal.

It is, perhaps, in the "Wolf Man" case study where we can best see the progress, via the love–hate ambivalence towards the father, to the transfiguration from God to demon (Freud, 1918b, pp. 69–70; Urtubey, 1983). But best of all is "A seventeenth-century demonological neurosis" (Freud, 1923d), where Freud, in a more precise way, analyses the association between the bad father model and Satan's figure through the case of the painter, Christoph Heitzmann. If love and nostalgia for the father build up God's figure, hate and fear of him give birth to the devil. Thus, the Oedipus complex, neurosis's fundamental node, also becomes the fundamental node of the greatest religious representations.

In this way, an intimate relationship is established between neurosis and religion. First, by positing the oedipal structure as the common dynamic source. Second, through its diverse manifestations: on the one hand psychopathological, and on the other hand cultural, they demonstrate an analogy in the dynamics they set in motion. So, we have identity in the origin, analogy in the formation process. For both we have a traumatic event (the Oedipus complex) at the origin, then a latency period, and, finally, a return of the repressed. This return of the repressed comes displaced by the symptom in one case and by dogma, ethics, and rites in the other (Freud, 1939a, pp. 72–92).

The dynamic relationship between religion and neurosis

Freud viewed neurosis, particularly in its obsessional form, as a caricature of religion, and religion, in turn, as a collective neurosis, as we saw in the well-known 1907 postulation. This was repeated time after time (Freud, 1907b, 1924f, 1927c). The same idea appears in a letter dated 8 October 1936 to Binswanger (Freud, E. L., 1961, p. 431). There, Freud says, ". . . I have already found a place for religion, by putting it in the category of the *neurosis of mankind*" (my italics). What this relationship between neurosis and religion means dynamically is worthy of closer analysis.

It bears pointing out that, in Freudian writings, religion appears as one of the basic forms of protection that culture offers from neurosis. As Freud expressed, by accepting a general neurosis, many subjects are spared the "task of forming a personal neurosis" (Freud, 1927c, p. 43).

There are several reasons for that. First, because religion, in offering a source of authority on which the subject depends, and a manual for life, releases him from the personal risk which always comes with one's freedom. So, religion provides both dependency and a source of support. For this reason also, Freud believes that the loss of religion brings with it an important increase in neurosis. We saw him express these ideas in texts such as, for instance, "The future prospects of psycho-analytic therapy" (Freud, 1910d). As we shall see, in Freud's view not everybody is equally capable of unbelief and atheism.

Religion, on the other hand, aids significantly as a defence against neurosis, because of the support it provides in the important and always difficult task of instinctual denial that life in the community entails. The religious illusion, attracting a substantial amount of libidinal energy (thus hindering the more specifically genital goal), helps to channel the remaining sexual drives. An important road to neurosis is avoided in this way. Those who take shelter under illusions which are specific to religion find "the most firm protection against neurosis" (Freud, 1921c, pp. 142–143).

Finally, perhaps in a still deeper sense, the protection that religion, as a collective neurosis, provides against individual neurosis is rooted in the support it offers in navigating the difficult conflict of the emotional ambivalence towards the father within a social framework. Religion, in this fight between fathers and sons, presents the widest range of solutions to prevent the fight from tearing the subject away in conflict (Freud, 1919g, p. 262).

Religion, then, from the perspective we are analysing, though characterised as a collective neurosis, also has positive potential in Freudian theory. It stands as an important step in the general development of humanity's growth. From this evolutionary perspective, religion should still be considered as a neurosis, but also as a necessary growth neurosis.

Indeed, in the evolutionary context in which *Totem and Taboo* (1912–1913) is framed, we can verify how religion represents a moment in human development which corresponds to the libidinal development time in which the child, overcoming the narcissistic position, turns towards a type of object-relationship marked by libidinal fixation on the parents. According to this model, if the animistic worldview amounts to a reproduction of early infantile narcissism in which the subject claims omnipotence for himself, the religious worldview, instead, amounts to a step forward on the road to maturity, in so far as it implies a denial of omnipotent feelings in favour of the gods. From this analytical perspective, the religious worldview represents a step forward in the process leading to the ultimate developmental stage, identified as total denial of feelings of infantile omnipotence, exactly in the exemplary way resulting from the scientific worldview, with its rational and complete adjustment to the external world (Freud, 1912–1913, pp. 87–90).

From this optimism regarding the power of reason, illustrated by Freud in *The Future of an Illusion* (1927c), this access to the scientific worldview and, hence, this surpassing of the religious neurosis, is seen as an inescapable step in civilisation's road to general maturity. Abandonment of religion "will be fulfilled with the inexorable fatality of a growth process", Freud predicts in the enthusiasm of that moment (Freud, 1927c, p. 43).

Meanwhile, he believes that a substantial effort is required to accelerate this general maturity process. The way to do this is to engage in action (there is a certain militant tone in this Freudian text) aimed at what we now call an "education for reality". Here, the ultimate goal would be to achieve a rational (non-religious) control of the instincts (Freud, 1927c, p. 44).

In time, this Freudian optimism waned. Convinced of the necessity to wage a relentless fight against religion, he recognised, years later, the enormous force he was trying to confront. The deep emotional roots of the religious experience forced him to reassess the challenge: "a really serious enemy" to the scientific worldview. As he would tell us in Lecture XXXV, "The question of a *Weltanschauung*", "religion is a tremendous force, which exerts its power over the strongest emotions of human beings" (Freud, 1933a, pp. 160–161).

Two clinical cases, placed between *The Future of an Illusion* (1927c) and that featured in a 1932 essay, appear to illustrate the complex difficulty inherent in the execution of that secularisation project Freud dreamed about. The first analyses the religious experience of a young American physician and the second is centred on the study of Dostoyevsky's biography and work (Freud, 1928a,b). Freud discovers in both subjects an incapacity for unbelief, which, in certain moments of their lives, they struggled to conquer. These two characters refer us to another topic related to the relationship between neurosis and religion, which we believe worth touching on for several reasons, not least because it is often overlooked.

Neurosis and atheism

In effect, Freudian texts provide the perfect cause to analyse the connections which Freud himself establishes between the denial of God and unsolved unconscious conflicts. Obviously, given Freud's personal position towards religion, one should not expect those relations between unbelief and neurosis to acquire the same degree of interest and analysis as those dedicated to religious life. There is, however, plenty of data that invite reflection.

It is remarkable that these examples share a nexus between the denial of God and, as in the case of faith, emotional ambivalence towards the father.

From the start, anti-religious behaviour, such as blasphemy, is invariably associated with emotional ambivalence, even when that concept has not yet appeared (the concept of ambivalence appears in the analysis of the obsessive neurosis of the "Rat Man" (Freud, 1909d)). Hysterical blasphemy, for instance, is associated with repressed unconscious representations converted into actions by a kind of "contrary will" (Freud, 1892–1893, p. 159–160, 1895d, p. 49, n. 2).

The blasphemous ideas in the case study of the "Wolf Man" (1918b) become intertwined with the intense emotional ambivalence towards this famous patient's father figure (Freud, 1918b, pp. 65–68).

The phenomenon of religious rebellion or irreverence is also associated from the start to the same ambivalence process. For instance, Freud sees the disrespectful joke about religion as a non-conflictive vehicle for venting repressed feelings contrary to the subject's conscious will (Freud, 1905c, p. 115). In a still deeper way, dramatic representation becomes an excellent excuse to act out, by substitution and, hence, without conflict, the rebellion against the gods led by the hero figure (Freud, 1942a, p. 306).

However, it is in the clinical writings that we can best appreciate the link Freud establishes between emotional ambivalence and unbelief. As in the case of religion, obsessional neurosis serves as the best guide to follow.

In the "Rat Man" case study, we see how, when an individual is around fourteen or fifteen years old, emotional ambivalence initiates a whole series of doubts and compulsive blasphemies and then determines the transition from faith to unbelief (Freud, 1909d, p. 169).

In the fascinating "Wolf Man" case study, we better appreciate this ambivalent relationship oscillating between love and hate towards the father and the affirmation or denial of God.

Indeed, in the study of this young subject, a pure sense of devotion, expressed through intense prayers and devout practices, became mixed with a stream of blasphemous and irreverent thoughts, caused by his unconscious hate for his father (Freud, 1918b, pp. 16–17). Doubts and ruminations about certain dogmatic and moral issues made clear, in this case too, the complex, intense, and barely elaborated emotional relationship with his father.

In the same work, we also find that Freud himself analyses in detail a full series of "resistances" which, from the patient's emotional dynamics, were mobilised against religion: they were related to a series of inner conflicts, unconscious to the subject, notably the repression of his homosexual leanings (Domínguez-Morano, 1991, pp. 172–186).

Beyond obsessional neurosis, we find still other cases in which a clear relationship is established between rejection of the father and denial of God. Notably, among them, we find the Leonardo da Vinci case. Here, Freud establishes a relation between the father's alleged absence during the artist's childhood and his supposed disbelief, using data he collected from the painter's biography. (I already took a critical look at the biographical basis used by Freud in his essay on Leonardo (Domínguez-Morano, 1991, pp. 75–85).) Freud seems to view Leonardo (in what appears to be a clear identification with his personal position) as a worthy example of man facing destiny without expecting heaven to mitigate life's difficulties. Leonardo, Freud tells us, went "well beyond both dogmatic and personal religion, moving on his search away from the Christian conception of the universe" (Freud, 1910c, pp. 123–126).

Just the opposite happens in the case study of the paranoiac President Schreber, considered, perhaps, to be the most famous patient in psychiatric history, who, as we know, Freud analysed on the basis of an autobiographical text (Freud, 1911c; Schreber, 2000).

It is precisely with this man that we witness a libidinous homosexual desire towards his father, not recognised at the conscious level, which provokes a formidable psychotic delirium with a religious expression. Schreber did feel persecuted by a God that was, in a morbid way, trying to turn him into a woman with whom to conceive a child, who would then become saviour of the universe. During the healthy part of his life, Schreber was sceptical towards religion, but "changes produced by his illness . . . after it he was a believer in God" (Freud, 1911c, pp. 24, 32). His God, erotised presence and persecutor at the same time, through the delirium ruse, satisfied old repressed wishes towards his father's person. Thus, a connection is established in Freudian theory between liberation from the father figure and unbelief, and submission to the father and religiousness.

The case of the young American physician analysed in "A religious experience" (1928a), and that of Dostoyevsky, as interpreted by Freud in "Dostoyevsky and parricide" (1928b), shed light on the unconscious motivations that can also lead the subject towards unbelief.

In the first of these cases, the young physician experiences a denial of God when he looks at the kind face of an old woman's corpse lying on a hospital dissection table. According to Freud's interpretation, the subject associated this experience with certain infantile oedipal phantasies in which the father seemed to exert sexual violence against the mother. From there, the young physician feels a drive to rebel against his father again. But his unconscious wish to finish off his father is displaced at the conscious level by a denial of God's existence (Freud, 1928a). Everything happens without the subject's awareness of the underlying mechanisms of his reaction, which, thus, appears in his consciousness as a feasible option of metaphysical character, instead of a question linked to his past infantile emotions. Motivations of the same infantile nature (guilt associated with the Oedipus complex) came later to favour the process of a new conversion to belief in God.

In Dostoyevsky's case, remorse over death wishes towards the father shields him from his unbelief in God, which those death wishes, through the displacement strategy, had created. From their unrecognised unconscious position, the feelings of guilt keep forcing the subject into a progressive loss of freedom in the areas of religion and politics, privileged areas where paternal authority is symbolised (Freud, 1928b). Unbelief, identified as freedom from the father, becomes impossible because of the unconscious guilt feelings in both cases.

In this regard, we have remarked elsewhere, it is possible to deduce an idea which is not stated formally in Freudian texts, but which can be clearly inferred from the available data. We refer to the repeated connection Freud makes between the passive–feminine position towards the father (not equivalent to what we usually call homosexuality) or an active–masculine position towards him, the first related to faith and the second to unbelief (Domínguez-Morano, 1991).

We can observe, in the case study of the "Wolf Man", and more so with the Shreber case, and also in the case studies of the painter Christoph Heitzmann and Dostoyevsky (although in this case less explicitly in Freud's text), that God's substitution for the father (or the devil's, in Christoph Heitzmann's case) is made on the basis of an emotional fixation with its passive, feminine side.

The "Wolf Man", in effect, was caught in the net of feminine oedipal identification. This drives his identification with the painful and patient Jesus of the Passion and the fight in the ambivalent submission to the Father. Schreber, with both an openly feminine fixation and homosexual leanings towards his father, turns his persecutor God into a lover who emasculates him and turns him into a woman from whose womb a messiah will come. Christoph Heitzmann is also a subject with an intense feminine position towards his father, feeding a series of hallucinations in which the devil appears with feminine breasts and a penis. Within the intense bisexuality which Freud highlights in Dostoyevsky's personality, and in his consequent passive–masochist position towards his father, important aspects of his religious experience seem to come into play (Domínguez-Morano, 1991, pp. 88–95, 172–186, 213–219, 254–260).

This fixation with the passive–feminine position should not, however, be simply identified with what we usually call homosexuality, but with one of the two poles in which emotional dynamics tend to be expressed, especially during the oedipal stage. This becomes evident, particularly if we take into account the case of Leonardo, of whose homosexuality Freud seems certain but where we find an openly active–masculine position towards his father and also in relation to all paternal, social, and religious symbols.

That said, we insist, particularly in the clinical cases analysed by Freud, on highlighting a relationship between the religious attitude and the passive–feminine position towards the father, displaced to God at the level of the religious experience. No doubt a complex but interesting issue, suggesting a psychology of religion that would require a deeper study than that undertaken here. Additionally, these questions are probably linked with some of the conclusions regarding the differences between masculine and feminine religiousness, based on the diverse oedipal structures to be found in man and woman. We refer to conclusions from experimental studies (Demoulin & Jarpard, 1965; Vergote, 1969).

It is true that Freud never fully explored this question in the works in which he analysed religion. A reason could be that femininity was generally, to him, in his own words, an "ignored continent". Perhaps for this same reason, the relationship we have tentatively proposed in the clinical cases, so clearly concerning femininity, did not find its proper place in his general reflections on religion.

Religion and madness

Although neurosis has always been the basic reference point for the analysis of religion within the psychopathology field, in Freudian writings we also find many references to psychosis that can be used for comparison.

From early on, in *The Psychopathology of Everyday Life,* Freud compares the "construction of supernatural reality with the projection mechanism as done in paranoiac psychosis" (Freud, 1901b, pp. 258–259). The Schreber case confirmed this idea years later, through the formidable delirium of being transformed by God into a woman. Freud interpreted this delirium as an attempt to soothe the conflict derived from an intense homosexual fixation the subject experienced towards his father. The figure of God permitted, at the delirious level, what the father, or the physicians who later replaced him, made impossible in reality: the fulfilment of homosexual desire. Religion was there, inside the psychotic conflict, at the very crossroads between ban and wish. On the other hand, the Schreber case highlighted something fundamental within the Freudian theory on religion: the role of the father and his symbolic replacement by God. The psychotic rupture made evident what neurosis disguises and "normality" hides (Freud, 1911c, pp. 32–33, 55–56).

Without doubt, however, it is the 1914 work on narcissism where Freud makes the most decisive exploration in the field of psychosis (a field which, as we know, he treated in only a theoretical way). For Freud, the narcissistic framework becomes the basic model for the interpretation of the psychotic phenomenon. It is the madman who, through radical narcissism, denies the reality that does not fit into his world of desires. Therefore, he creates his own extreme subjective reality to operate within.

In this work, within the framework of his discussion with Jung over the process of insanity, Freud makes a distinction between what occurs with the psychotic subject and what happens in certain types of religious experiences. The madman succumbs under the introversion of his libido in his own phantasies or within his ego, while, for instance, in the case of the hermit (who, in his separation from the world, might resemble the psychotic who breaks away from reality), what takes place is a "sublimation" through which he converts his sexual interest towards an intense interest in the divine (Freud, 1914c, p. 80). The hermit is, thus, saved while the madman succumbs.

Thus, it seems possible to infer that religion cannot be compared to psychosis although, within a psychotic context, the religious experience can obviously perform important functions, as can be seen in the Schreber case or in that of the young American physician, whose renewed conversion to belief in God takes place also in the form of a "hallucinatory psychosis" (Freud, 1928a, p. 171).

Even if, in Freudian texts, it is not possible to establish an identity between the psychotic and religious structure, it is quite possible to signal a partial analogy in the dynamics both entail. This analogy, however, is most vivid within the context of "illusion", using the model of dream interpretation, as we shall analyse later.

It is not surprising, on the other hand, that this approximation between psychosis and religious illusion is made through the model of dreams. Indeed, the dream takes the shape of a small-scale everyday psychosis, in which the subject locks himself up in his own subjective world, breaking away from reality. Only then is wish fulfilment possible (in some delirious and hallucinatory way), which, in essence, is the purpose of dreams. Along with this wish fulfilment, which imprints narcissism in both dreams and, more radically, psychosis, we should also contextualise the illusions within religious experience. We shall analyse this in a deeper way later on.

So, taken to the extreme, the religious experience also draws parallels with psychotic processes in so far as, departing from reality and denying its limitations, it becomes a delirious distortion of that reality. That is how it is seen, mainly in *The Future of an Illusion* (1927c). The beliefs, to the extent they assume "wishful illusions with a disavowal of reality", are comparable to "amentia, in a state of blissful hallucinatory confusion" (Freud, 1927c, p. 43).

There are collective deliria that, like those of psychotic cases, are inaccessible to logical criticism and that contradict reality. The reason for their power lies in the fact that they also possess, as in the case of madness, a core of "historic truth" that returns from the repressed (Freud, 1937d, pp. 266–268). That "historic truth", which, for Freud, goes back to the proto-father's murder, imposes itself with an enigmatic and characteristic force. That irrational force is shown, for instance, in the religious "*Credo quia absurdum*". A position that can be understood, declares Freud in *Moses and Monotheism*, only by comparison with the psychotic delirium, since ". . . the articles of religious creeds have the character of psychotic symptoms that have avoided the isolation of anathema by being presented as collective phenomena" (Freud, 1939a, p. 35).

Note

1. Translator: In the present translation of *Belief after Freud*, we have followed in general the "instinct" option taken by Nicholson-Smith

when translating Laplanche and Pontalis's book *The Language of Psychoanalysis* (1973). As Nicholson-Smith explains,

> The authors . . . argue for the use of the term "pulsion" as the French equivalent of "trieb" rather than the common rendering "instinct". Mutatis mutandi, their arguments would support the replacement of the English "instinct", wherever it stands for "trieb", by one or other of the much less popular alternatives "drive" or "urge". Given the almost general adoption of "instinct", however, it has been retained throughout this book. The question is discussed in the General Introduction to the Standard Edition, where the editors give their reasons for choosing "instinct".

CHAPTER THREE

Religion, dream, and delirium

The dream model

Dream analysis served as a starting point, a bridge between psychoanalysis and the sciences of the spirit. Dream analysis opened a doorway to the unconscious inner processes. It also revealed that the mechanisms underlying pathological symptoms are also active in our normal psychic processes.

Dream hermeneutics gave Freud an explanation for multiple cultural formations, with mythic and legendary structures standing out among them. As early as *The Interpretation of Dreams* (1900a), there are frequent references to the most diverse legends and myths.

This conviction of finding in dream interpretation the fundamental keys of mythology is maintained throughout Freud's life and is expressed without interruption every time that the subject of dreams comes up in his reflections (Freud, 1933a, p. 25). Even in a text left unfinished on his deathbed, he saw no less than a significant source for the understanding of human prehistory, since he believed the dream contained elements that came neither from the subject's adult life nor his forgotten childhood (Freud, 1940a, p. 167). So, for Freud, the dream becomes a privileged key to reveal the essential modes of unconscious psychic activity.

We will not go into the full Freudian theory on the meaning of dreams; suffice to say that the fundamental assertion, "dreams are the fulfilment of wishes" (*Wunscherfüllung*) (Freud, 1900a, pp. 122–133, 555–578), was considered as the opening sign of psychoanalysis itself. Freud always viewed this proposition as a demonstration object, even in cases in which it could be called into question, such as with anxiety dreams or punishment dreams. In *Beyond the Pleasure Principle,* at the time of Freud's radical revision of his conception of human instincts (pointing to a set of "death instincts" opposing "life instincts"), the theory of dreams as wish fulfilment flickered, but did not cast any additional light. This idea of dreams as wish fulfilment appeared early on in a letter to Fliess, dated 19 February 1899 (Freud, 1950a, p. 278; Masson, 1985, p. 345).

Freud quotes Isaiah (29: 8), "As when a hungry man dreams he is eating, and awakes with his hunger not satisfied, or as when a thirsty man dreams he is drinking and awakes faint, with his thirst not quenched" (Freud, 1900a, p. 124, n.). Wish fulfilment it surely is, though seldom shown as transparently as in the prophet's words. Instead, dreams go through a series of distortions that make up the dream-work (*Traumarbeit*) (Freud, 1900a, pp. 277–508).

This type of work, so important to the Freudian dream process, is what also must be used to decipher popular myths and legends. "There is", Freud says,

> an obvious distortion between historic facts and its mythical representation . . . distortions which are of the same nature, and not more violent, than those we daily admit when we rebuild our patients' dreams and their repressed infantile feelings. (Freud, 1932a, p. 187)

In this way, the text, be it cultural, mythic, religious, artistic, or philosophic, will be approached as if it were the text of a dream. The "manifest content" (what we see) must be explored in order to find its "latent content", that is, a set of meanings related to hidden, repressed, and unsatisfied wishes. Between both contents, latent and manifest, takes place all that work which, as in dream-work, through multiple distortions, disguises the true individual or collective desires. As Freud asserts, for instance, in the biblical interpretation in *Moses and Monotheism* the reader of the cultural text will need to detect and give an interpretation to the distortions produced by certain, sometimes conflicting, tendencies; constructions disguised by other secret tendencies, mutilations and extensions which can even reverse their meaning, etc.

In the end, the language of culture, like that of dreams, simultaneously reveals and disguises the voice of unconscious desires. The formation of God's image involves the intervention of a dream production mechanism.

We should keep in mind that the God originating from the father's image in the oedipal context is impregnated, like the father himself, with the love–hate polarity of emotional ambivalence. That ambivalence, however, is not apparent in the unlimited father exaltation manifested in the God of monotheism. Thus, the loved and hated father has been transformed into a God who embodies only the positive side of the emotional spectrum. Something has happened along the way to remove the dangerous, distressing side of the relationship. Only in a latent, hidden manner, by way of displaced actions, might that negative side become apparent. In the realm of the manifested, we see the father only in a positive light, as a provident, wise, and mighty God. Nothing at all like the feared and dangerous father in the infantile oedipal phantasy (Freud, 1927c, pp. 16–18).

As in dreams, desires have intervened to transform the latent meanings into something more manifest and bearable. In this way, beliefs are born, which, based on the model of dreams, should be diagnosed as "illusions". We shall delve further into this idea in short order.

Belief as illusion

In Freudian writings, the relationship between neurosis and religion surfaces early on. The relationship between religion and dreams, however, takes some time to appear and is never explored with the same explicit clarity. Freud considered the question of dreams more in relation with the generation of myths and legends, seen as the people's collective dreams.

Only as Freud's view of reality acquired more dramatic undertones did religion appear as a means for wish fulfilment. This is similar to the way in which dreams create a subjective reality separate from the objective external world. This is how the concept of "illusion" was born. In earlier Freudian texts, this term does not yet have the precise meaning of wish fulfilment detached from reality, which becomes more apparent in the work I refer to here. Formerly, the term "illusion", as understood in the psychiatry circles of the times, referred only to the malfunction of sensorial organs or in relation to aesthetic pleasure.

In his work, "Thoughts for the times on war and death" (1915b, p. 280), Freud brought the concept of illusion into bloom and explored it more deeply in the coming years. This work was the first to display a pessimism that Freud would not depart from.

Here, illusion appears closely linked to the concept of disappointment (*die Enttäuschung*). It is a disappointment that emerges particularly in view of human reality, a reality that has been tainted by the force of desire. Situations such as war force us to remove our rose-coloured glasses, revealing a reality with all the dark undertones that we were determined not to see.

Illusion alludes to the hypocritical idea of man as an animal in whom rationality prevails and takes control of his instinctual world. But, in reality, that control was merely irrational. Situations such as war topple this idea, dismantling the illusion we had created about the moral and civilising nature of society. The only honest response possible, then, is to do away with any type of illusion.

"Illusions are pleasant", Freud tells us in this text, "because they save us from disdainful feelings and permit us instead to enjoy gratifications. But then we will have to accept without lament that sometimes they crash against a piece of reality and fall to pieces" (Freud, 1915b, p. 280).

At this point, the most important elements, which will later characterise the concept of illusion, are defined as a search for pleasure that does not take reality into account. Illusion avoids displeasure and gives satisfaction. The drawback is that the enjoyment of the illusion comes at the expense of sincerity with oneself, and once the illusion falls apart, the price is disappointment. In this context, religion is also presented as the supreme guarantor of illusions, particularly the grand illusion of immortality, which is produced by human narcissism (Freud, 1915b, pp. 292–294).

Later on, when Freudian thought reaches the highest levels of pessimism, particularly in *Beyond the Pleasure Principle* (1920g), the suspicion of illusion falls on thought itself and on Freud's own theory in relation to the death instinct. Freud tells us that perhaps this theory, presenting death as ruled by sovereign Ananké, is nothing more than another comforting illusion created to endure the idea of a gratuitous death.

Religion does not have a monopoly on the concept of illusion in Freudian work. As an example, the romantic idea of an instinctive human evolution towards perfection, which would culminate in the appearance of a superman, must also be diagnosed as another benevolent illusion (ethical in this case), which Freud does not seem to be ready to support at all (Freud, 1920g, p. 42).

Freud, unable to overlook any cultural element that raises any suspicion, looks with a critical eye at government institutions themselves, as well as the relationship between the sexes, or even scientific work (so essentially attached to the outer world reality). He also analyses certain political theories, such as those of Marxism and anarchy (Freud, 1927c, p. 34).

While religion does not monopolise the world of illusions, it can surely claim to be its best representative and ally.

Even before *The Future of an Illusion* (1927c), we find a text in which the concept of illusion is inextricably linked to religion: *Group Psychology and the Analysis of the Ego* (1921c). In this work, Freud notices the "loving illusion" at the very heart of Christian belief and, more particularly, in the Roman Catholic denomination.

That illusion starts from the belief that the religious leader, Jesus in the case of the Church, as an elder brother (a father), loves all the believers equally and forges among them the bonds of brotherhood. The illusion of a harmonious family is, thus, supported by the faith. Furthermore, Christ is not only an object of love for the believers but, in the height of the loving illusion, becomes also an identification model from which every believer must reach for a love as total as his (Freud, 1921c, pp. 93–95, 134). This loving illusion, not religious in itself, but supported by the Christian position of belief, brings with it consequences of great magnitude.

The first consequence, in effect, arising from this type of illusion, is that love, ignoring in bad faith the conflictive dimensions of personal reality, unleashes precisely what it tried to ignore: aggressiveness, intolerance, and the exclusion of all those outside the illusory circle. That is why, Freud tells us, any religion is a religion of love for its faithful, and, conversely, a cruel and intolerant religion for those that do not recognise it (Freud, 1921c, p. 98). The loving illusion nested in the believer's position, he tells us in another text, might even sometimes turn into a mere pretext to justify destructive zeal (Freud, 1933b, p. 210).

It is in 1927, with *The Future of an Illusion*, that Freud fully undertakes his critical analysis of the religious illusion. An especially spirited and militant tone marks this work, one of the least psychoanalytical, and even least essentially Freudian, texts written by Freud. At its core is the analysis of religious belief as the creation of desire.

Freud considers religious beliefs in general, from the dream model interpretation, as illusions, that is, wish fulfilments, in so far as they are not based on positive knowledge of reality (in fact, the only foundation they allege is tradition and the ancestors' authority) and, in so far as their only purpose is giving protection and life support, they are neither generated by personal experience nor reasoning, but are, rather, spin-offs from humanity's most archaic, intense, and pressing wishes (Freud, 1927c, pp. 28–29). The secret of their power, like that of dreams, rests exclusively on the force of the originating desire.

An illusion in this sense is not equivalent to a mistake, as neither the dream's content nor the young shepherdess's expectation of winning the prince's love is a mistake. What characterises religious belief is its ability to manifest outside the realm of reality and to cling to the wish itself. Its only assurance is given by the satisfaction it brings, while its contempt of reality entails the grave risk of approaching a state of delirium.

Illusion and delirium

Following the path of the dream model, Freud's work on religion once more brushes up against the subject of madness, since delirium, as a symptom of the break from the desire-negating reality, generates dynamics which approach the category of madness rather than a mere neurotic disorder.

Schreber's religious system illustrates the attempt to solve anxiety by means of a delirious creation. Indeed, Judge Schreber set in motion a full feminine phantasy, related to his unconscious erotic link with his father, and found in religion the vehicle to fulfil wishes which otherwise produced an unbearable anxiety. God would turn him into a woman in order to engender a son who would become the world's messiah. The dynamics of desire seem limitless once they are placed in the register of a religious context.

Delirium and hallucination have enjoyed wide space in religion, in spite of the limits which religious institutions have tended to impose (in a telling example of external restraint, Freud says that ever since the Church modified its attitude towards apparitions and allowed police and doctors to examine the visionaries and mystics, "the Virgin makes only rare appearances") (Freud, 1910d, p. 149). Here, Freud refers to the countless cases of saints, nuns, chaste women (Freud, 1893a, pp. 10–11), children and adolescents with a strict upbringing (Freud, 1900a, p. 406), or persons such as Katharina Emmerich (Freud, 1911f, p. 343), who demonstrate an uncontrolled wish that breaks through the constraints of the outer world and imposes itself as a subject without any type of restraint. Religion provides such an opportunity.

But there is no need, Freud thinks, to visit such surprising and somewhat shocking territory as that of religious psychopathology in order to notice how close religious belief and delirium are to each other. The religious dogma maintained by almost all the believers sometimes bears the traits of wish phantasies which appear as something so far-fetched and out of reality that Freud does not hesitate in comparing them to delirious ideas (*Wahnideen*) (Freud, 1927c, p. 31).

However, from this perspective, a troublesome problem arises: what criterion to use to differentiate between a delirious idea and a healthy human expectation? A full range of problems related to the idea of utopia immediately comes up, and Freud was very conscious of the difficulty.

If the criterion is measured relative to how much a belief is removed from the present reality, as Freud does, it would be hard to tell, for instance, how much an expectation on the future of mankind can be considered utopia, illusion, or delirium. Only a personal and subjective criterion (*nach der persönlicher Einstellung*, as Freud tells us honestly) will solve the question. There is no objective criterion, as Freud is forced to recognise.

However, Freud thinks that the bigger the noticeable presence of old infantile wishes, and the bigger the distance between expectation and the conditions of reality, the greater is the measure of suspicion that should be applied (Freud, 1927c, p. 30).

His attention fell on these reality conditions in a sharp and disturbing work in 1930. We are referring to *Civilization and its Discontents* (1930a). Here, following up on threads initiated in *The Future of an Illusion*, Freud returns to the analysis of cultural gestation. From this analysis, in which instinctual repression is presented as the very engine of civilising genesis, he infers that happiness is a yearning condemned to failure. The only option is to search for palliatives (*Linderungsmittel*) to mitigate the hardness of existence: some will look for powerful distractions, such as scientific work itself; others will go for alternative satisfactions, such as art; others finally will resort to more expedient methods, such as drugs.

Religion, in its turn, with more pretences than any of the others, will try to provide a meaning to existence. That search for meaning, which Freud already sees as an expression of anthropocentric vanity, is, however, not made unless a "delirious deformation of reality" is carried out before (Freud, 1930a, pp. 76–81).

The purpose of that is to deny the most wounding elements of reality and to replace them with others that are more in accordance with the subject's desire. Naturally, the attempt is condemned to failure: reality will not bend by the mere force of a wish. Freud recognises that, by means of those dynamics, some subjects will avoid the fall into an individual neurosis, but nothing else; happiness will continue to elude them, too.

Approaching the end of his life, in *Moses and Monotheism* (1939a), Freud described the whole Judeo-Christian dogmatic aggregate as delirious also. Applying his *Totem and Taboo* hypothesis on the primal father's murder, he considers the ensemble of Christian dogma as a delirium (mainly the fruit of Paul's mind) born to cover that "criminal and memorable" fact. It will be called (as, in effect, it was) original sin and a joyous salvation message will be phantasised (Freud, 1939a, p. 135). The wish, once more, as in the dream or in the delirium, eliminates the conflict, recreating reality to its own taste.

Following up on the dream model as wish fulfilment, religion, depending on how much it insists upon denying the hard and frustrating conditions of reality, will become more or less close to an infantilising illusion or, more dangerously, to a delirious transformation of reality in accordance with the psychotic delirium model.

The illusory God

The dynamics of illusion, like those of dream and delirium, work by eliminating our representations of those elements that become unbearable for consciousness. God's representation does not escape from these dynamics.

We find, then, that the original emotional ambivalence that marks the relation with the father, hence with God, is removed through the "isolation" mechanism, so that only the positive, non-conflicting, side of the relationship is apparent. If God's image was born indissolubly bound to the oedipal ambivalence conflict, where love and hate intertwine, its last image will have to be modified in order to make conscious feeling tolerable.

Nothing is so disturbing, Freud tells us in *Inhibitions, Symptoms and Anxiety* (Freud, 1926d, p. 121), as what was first united and later separated in the course of development. For this reason, the aggressive component has to be isolated from the relationship with God, in the same way as the urges of the secretory organs have to be kept separate from the loving emotions, Freud tells us in a second example. Only by isolating conflict do we have access to God the protector, whom we can this way call the illusory God. Let us see now what he is like.

The illusory God is fed exclusively on the conflicting traits that were conferred on the father during childhood. He is a creative, good, fair, powerful, and wise father. Of these traits, Freud posits the last three as the most important. We shall come back to them in Chapter Six, when dealing with the God of the child and the God of Jesus.

God the creator is, for Freud, an exalted alteration of the engendering father (Freud, 1920d, p. 266). (In "The question of a *Weltanschauung*", Freud tells us that a religious man pictures the creation of the universe just as he pictures his own origin (Freud, 1933a, p. 163).) But, above all, the God of illusion, once his dangerous violent rival traits are eliminated (projected on Satan's figure), becomes a father of supreme goodness. He loves all his children equally, is close by to understand their needs, is ready to forgive, and, in Judeo-Christian terms, even lowers himself to make a pact, an alliance, with them (Freud, 1921c, pp. 93–95, 1930a, p. 74, 1939a, pp. 109–111).

Like the family father who has protected the weak and defenceless child against all the perils of the outer world, the God of illusion provides all the security the adult needs to survive in a world so often hostile (Freud, 1930a, p. 74, 1914f, pp. 242–243). However, like the father from our childhood, who magically knows everything, the God of illusion will also possess the attribute of omniscience (Freud, 1933a, pp. 55–56). From that unlimited knowledge, the adult subject will also receive a powerful explanation for all the mysteries and unknowns that life brings. Finally, the God of illusion, created on the model of the educator father model, appears as the guarantor of final justice and as benefactor, through the gift of immortality, for all the renunciations and sacrifices which man has to endure with difficulty throughout his earthly life (Freud, 1927c, pp. 17–19).

During this life, man suffers from strong feelings of neglect and helplessness. Such feelings bring him back to that early experience when, as an infant, he was so well protected and cared for. Then nostalgia for the father returns (*Vatersehnsucht*) and becomes the engine for the genesis of the divinity: a strong, good, and protective deity that, for Freud, as we shall see next, has only a masculine, fatherly face.

The ignored maternal protection

When considering the Freudian interpretation of the illusion of the protection of the gods, this question, unavoidably, comes up: what role is given in this context to feminine and maternal representations?

On this analysis of the religious illusion according to the dream model, Freud does not try to reach the most arcane level in the origin of faith, but remains at the more superficial and manifest level of the most common beliefs of religious persons. Taking into account that these feminine representations are plentiful throughout the history of religion and particularly in the environment in which Freud did his research, the question can, in effect, be posed about the role assigned to the mother figure in the development and success of religiosity, which (it could not be missed by Freud) represents the first and most important protection during childhood.

However, maternal references are strikingly absent in the whole field of Freudian interpretation of religion, an absence which, in certain contexts, points to the existence of a "blind spot" in the observation of the founder of psychoanalysis. Let us look closer.

In the 1910 text on Leonardo, the maternal dimension appears as an important datum both in the painter's biography and in the mythological expressions that Freud uses for his analysis. From there, a clear relation is established in the text between the maternal component and nature. "The almighty and just God, and kindly Nature, appear to us grand father and mother sublimations . . ." (Freud, 1910c, p. 123). But that relationship all but disappears in Freudian text, without any insight into its connection with the religious experience.

More striking is the fact that in other texts apparently focused on feminine religious figures, such as "Great is Diana of the Ephesians!" (1911f), the maternal function of religion is set aside in favour of other theoretical interests (in this specific case, the eternal preservation of psychic elements).

It is also particularly surprising that in a writing as impregnated with maternal dimensions as "The theme of the three caskets", the ambivalence which Freud observes in feminine deities, fertile or destructive, is not evaluated in relation to a possible primal ambivalence towards the mother (Freud, 1913f, pp. 298–299).

Any emotional ambivalence is exclusively focused on the father; this can be seen in the case history of the "Wolf Man" (1918b). In this text, the role of the mother and the other women in the subject's past seems to be limited to that of mere transmitters of the religious experience, while everything concerning the origin of the religious feeling is assigned to the paternal function.

In *The Ego and the Id* (1923b), Freud refers to the separation from the mother and the loss of her protection in the traumatic birth experience (p. 58). For Schur, this implies a first acknowledgement of the protecting maternal function and of the mother's prevailing role during life's earliest stages (Schur, 1972). However, such predominance of the mother does not appear, as could be expected, in later works; at least where the analysis of religion is concerned.

Thus, we have, as an example, the analysis of the painter Christoph Heitzmann, with plenty of references to the figure of Mary, which are not associated to the painter's religious feeling, not even when Freud insists on his trait being "eternal suckling" and on his need to be orally supported. Even in this context, it is the father, not the mother, as would be expected, who is the provider of subsistence and support (Freud, 1923d, pp. 104–105).

Neither is Freud able to put forward a maternal origin for the so-called "oceanic feeling", in spite of the fact that, in its analysis, he associates it to the primal fusion condition of the ego, so clearly marked by the early relationship with the mother. (The "oceanic feeling" concept came from Hindu culture and was offered by Freud's friend, the orientalist Rolland, who saw in it the ultimate and most decisive kernel of the religious experience (Vermorel & Vermorel, 1993).) Faced with an exceptional opportunity to penetrate into the psychology of the early relationship with the mother and its connections with the mystic side of the religious experience, Freud once more refers to infantile helplessness and the nostalgia for the father that comes with it (Freud, 1930a, pp. 64–72; Domínguez-Morano, 1991, pp. 261–266, 2016, pp. 29–34; Masson, 1980).

This monopoly by the father on religious functions seems to become more nuanced in the later works. That happens, for instance, in "The question of a *Weltanschauung*" (Lecture XXXV, 1933a). In that work, when referring to the father as the ultimate source of security, Freud explicitly corrects himself and uses the more precise expression of a parental instance (*Elterninstanz*), literally integrated, he tells us, by father and mother. However, the pleasant initial surprise of such a keen observation fades instantly as we see that just the father's mnemonic image (*Erinnerungsbild des Vaters*) comes back to play a role in the creation of divinity (Freud, 1933a, p. 163).

In that same work, Freud avoids discussion of the maternal deities from diverse worldviews, reserving all creational activity for the male gods built according to the infantile model of the engendering father (Freud, 1933a, pp. 162–163).

Finally, in this review of Freudian oversight on the relationship between motherly functions and religion, we should point out the fact that Mary (a central religious figure in Roman Catholic Austria) is barely taken into account in his various religious analyses. She is no more than one aspect of the regression to the great Mother Deity that, in Freud's view, was just a further distortion of the magnificent achievement which is Jewish monotheism (Freud, 1939a, pp. 87–88, 1911f, pp. 343–344). Not much else is said of her except when she appears in order to frustrate sexual activity in his patients' dreams (Freud, 1900a, pp. 319, 652, 1905e, p. 104) in hallucinatory visions (Freud, 1910d, p. 149, 1911c, pp. 32–33, 1923d, pp. 73–75, 77–78, 101–102) or in hoaxes, which Freud believed the Lourdes events to be

(Freud, 1893, *GW, XIX*, pp. 167,169 (this does not appear in the *Standard Edition*), 1911f, p. 342, 1933a, p. 152). Besides this, there is only a brief mention of the Christian belief in the Immaculate Conception, mistakenly seen, as usual, as virginal conception (Freud, 1913c). There is also a reference to Mary explaining her idealisation as a juxtaposition to culture's misogyny in a letter to Abraham dated 18 February 1909 (Abraham & Freud, E. L., 1965), and as a subject's dream figure who questions the concept of the Immaculate Conception, we find another mention in a letter to Pfister dated 18 March 1909 (Meng & Freud, E. L., 1961).

So, even if Freudian text is, in effect, gradually giving increasing relevance to the primal relation to the mother, it never attains any importance in connection with the origin of religion or in the development of belief, not even as a protection and comfort against the harshness of life, so apparent in the dream interpretation model and so obviously linked to early protection and comfort by the mother. Women remained for Freud, in the religiousness analysis also, an "ignored continent", his own expression when referring to the subject of the feminine. The father monopolises the realm of protective illusion, which, from a position of helplessness, is assigned to divinity. It is also his voice, and not the mother's, that calms our anxiety by singing his "heavenly nursery rhyme" (*Eiapoeia von Himmel!*) (Freud, 1930a, p. 122). This will force us to pay particular attention to the motherly element when we reflect on the genesis of the image of God and its relation with the God made known as Jesus of Nazareth.

Science and religion

Coming back to the subject of religious illusion, it is necessary to observe Freudian thoughts on its social effects and on the unavoidable confrontation between religion and science.

These matters have obviously lost a good part of the bitterness they had during Freud's life, when reason still exerted the imperialism that the Enlightenment willingly gave it. The so-called postmodern mentality seems, in effect, to unseat reason from the privileged position it was granted at that time. I shall come back to that in the next chapter, but I believe it worthwhile to look at a summary of

Freudian approaches to this matter, which also resonate within certain social strata.

Religion is expected to perform a series of social functions, which are analysed in *The Future of an Illusion* (1927c), and in "The question of a *Weltanschauung*" (1933a). Religion has several functions. First, it tries to drive away the terrors of the natural world. Moreover, calling for a state of resignation, it hopes to reconcile man with the cruelty of his fate (especially as it becomes evident with death). It also offers compensation from the pain and hardship that civilised life imposes. It aspires to satisfy his yearning for knowledge and, finally, it insists on establishing itself as the fundamental framework for moral behaviour (Freud, 1927c, pp. 17–18, 1933a, pp. 161–162).

All of these attempts, however, are condemned to failure one way or another. Scientific reason amounts to a mortal blow to these religious aims; in addition, psychoanalysis has revealed the hidden motivations that caused religion to make these pretentious proclamations.

Religion, from this psychoanalytical perspective, must be considered as a frustrated attempt to dominate the sensorial world by means of desires developed from a series of biological or psychological needs. Experience tells us that the world is not a nursery and the requirements of life within a society demand an ethical foundation that remains independent from religious beliefs (Freud, 1933a, p. 168).

Man will not manage to attain a sufficient degree of wellbeing and rational command of his instincts by forsaking reality by means of illusions or by distorting it in a state of delirium. On the contrary, it is a matter of adjustment to reality in all its conditions and, from there, honestly and industriously aiming at a transformation of that reality to achieve a higher degree of happiness. This mission should be trusted to science, never to religion. To this idea, psychoanalysis tries to contribute its part by means of uncovering reality within its own field. Only through the discovery of reality will it be possible to advance, slowly but surely, towards sociocultural development.

From the very beginning, Freud tried hard to present psychoanalysis as a branch of that scientific knowledge. And, as indicated in the introductory chapter, in spite of the important withdrawals from the positivist creed that he was forced to take on in order to comprehend some of his findings, he always maintained his unbroken faith in scientific reason.

From the first approach to the subject of dreams, Freud did, indeed, establish clearly his scientistic purpose, distancing itself from any other interpretation of the subject that hinted of a spiritual and supernatural world because of the insolubility of the dream enigma (Freud, 1900a, pp. 4–5). The same purpose presides in his investigations in the new paths forged by him within psychotherapy (1905a, p. 257), leaving, at the same time, an explicit record of his refusal to frame psychoanalysis inside any particular worldview (*Weltanschauung*) which could vainly pretend to give a unitarian solution to all our existential problems.

For this same reason, he always showed his determination to prevent psychoanalysis from being impregnated by the mystical halo which Jung's theory, obscure, "opaque and confused", was beginning to present in 1914, suggesting a "revelation or a new worldview (*Weltanschauung*)" (Freud, 1914d, pp. 59–60).

That was not what Freud wished for psychoanalysis, so he always vigorously undertook its defence from not only its enemies, but also from certain well-intended friends who, like Putnam (a psychoanalysis apologist in the USA), hoped to use it in support of certain philosophic world conceptions with the goal of imposing a certain "spiritual nobility" on the patients. "The intention is noble", Freud says, "but nevertheless it amounts to violence against psychoanalytic theory" (Freud, 1919a, p. 165). (See also the letter to J. Putnam dated 8 July 1915) (Freud, E. L., 1961).)

The Freudian purpose of inscribing psychoanalysis as a branch of scientific knowledge did not ignore the fact that some psychoanalytic concepts hugely facilitated mystic or philosophic type extrapolations. The field of the irrational revealed behind the concepts, first, of the unconscious and, later, of the id, lent itself to belief in a "psychoanalytical conception of the universe". But nothing could be more opposed to its founder's wish than to let psychoanalysis be caught up in the confused tangle of a somewhat romantic worldview. Knowledge of how repression works, Freud says along these lines, is perfecty adequate at holding the analyst back from these types of conceptions. "You", he tells Groddeck, the father of the id term and one of the representatives of the mystical tendency, "disregarded reason and science too early" (12 February 1922) (Groddeck & Freud, 1970). And, in a letter to Pfister dated 14 February 1924, he comments on a work by Sandór Ferenczi and Otto Rank: "That psychoanalysis is leading to a new outlook on life I cannot and will not admit. All analysis can do is make valuable contributions to building up such an outlook" (Meng & Freud, E. L., 1961).

But it is, no doubt, in "The question of a *Weltanschauung*" where, in the most categorical way, he expresses his refusal to consider psychoanalysis as a worldview, reasserting his clear scientific purpose. "Psychoanalysis", he says, "is unable to create a worldview of its own. It does not need it; it is a piece of science and can be integrated in the scientific conception of the Universe" (Freud, 1933a, p. 181).

So, Freud is also conscious—and here we can highlight one of his contradictions—that psychoanalysis will have to renounce any type of militancy. In 1923, he tells us, "It is absolutely unscientific to ask whether psychoanalysis can come to pull apart religion, authority or morals, since, as any science, it has no bias and its only purpose is to apprehend exactly one piece of reality" (Freud, 1923a, p. 252).

In that openly polemic work, *The Future of an Illusion*, he asserts that psychoanalysis tries to be a research tool, "an impartial instrument, like the infinitesimal calculus" (Freud, 1927c, p. 36). Or, as he writes to Pfister on 9 February1909, in one of his most quoted texts about the relations between faith and psychoanalysis, "in itself psychoanalysis is neither religious nor non-religious, but an impartial tool which both priest and layman can use in the service to the sufferer" (Meng & Freud, E. L., 1961). (He expresses himself in a similar way in the letter dated 26 November 1927.)

However, it is evident that, deep down, Freud is convinced of reason's supremacy in judging and condemning, if deemed necessary, that other type of "inferior" discourse that is the religious one. In texts such as "The question of a *Weltanschauung*", religion is clearly condemned: it is presented as the worst enemy for the progress of scientific reason, the only true benefactor of mankind.

Science should not fear the arts or philosophy, the other two cultural sectors, which, together with religion, appear to be plausible candidates for satisfying the great human aspirations. Only religion should be distrusted, since it commands the most intense human emotions and competes with science for fulfilling aspirations in which scientific work is clearly at a disadvantage. Even though, in matters of knowledge, science seized the power and dominion that religion had held since time immemorial, the latter maintained its sway on the protective function, mitigating the men's fear with its comfort in misfortune and its promises of future life. Even more conclusively, religion was relevant in the area of morality, where science, on principle, refuses to intervene (Freud, 1933a, pp. 161–162).

As could be expected, Freud is even more explicit on this point in his correspondence. So we see that, having generally shown a certain tolerance with Pastor Pfister, a moment comes when he reveals his most authentic belief and his highest expectation. "You are quite right", he tells him in February 1929, "to point out that analysis leads to no new philosophy of life, but it has no need to, since it rests on the general scientific outlook, with which the religious outlook is incompatible" (Meng & Freud, E. L., 1961, p. 129).

Because of that, in the far future, it will become impossible to merge religious faith and psychoanalysis. Meanwhile, a series of unavoidable contradictions will have to be tolerated with a certain elegance. "That you should be such a convinced analyst and at the same time a clerical gentleman is one of the contradictions that make life so interesting" (Meng & Freud, E. L., 1961, p. 142), he comments years later to Pfister himself.

Freud is firmly convinced that in the essence of religion there is something that dynamically opposes, in the manner of a resistance, a complete psychoanalytical investigation and practice. This is the foundation for his denial of the possibility of Jung, the Christian, and his followers accepting the most important postulates of psychoanalytical theory (Freud, 1914d, pp. 60–61). And the same conviction over the psychodynamic impossibility lying between psychoanalysis and religion is, no doubt, hidden behind the ironic question he poses to Pfister in 1918: "Incidentally, why was it that none of all the pious ever discovered psychoanalysis? Why did it have to wait for a completely godless Jew?" (Meng & Freud, E. L., 1961, p. 63).

Freud's faith in scientific reason as the only valid way of approaching truth, as well as the ingenuous positivism of his time, were determinants of his scientific stance. To these should be added a vision born out of the social evolutionism in which Freud always participated with enthusiasm.

According to Freud's outline, as proposed in *Totem and Taboo* (behind which Comte's three states doctrine can be hinted at), there is an evolutionary connection between the animist, religious, and scientific outlooks on life. These, in turn, correspond analogically with the three libidinal development stages: animism would be similar to the infantile narcissistic position, the religious stage would correspond with the oedipal stage of libidinal fixation on the parents, and, finally, an adult stage, renouncing the pleasure principle and submitting to reality, would correspond with the scientific outlook on life (Freud, 1912–1913, pp. 77–78, 81–82, 89–90). Humanity, in parallel with the individual's development, would progress and climb towards that final stage of maturity in which there is no place for the religious worldview.

We know that in *The Future of an Illusion* (1927c), Freud showed his optimism for the advent of full scientific reason: the god Logos, with whom full maturity would be reached. This optimism, we also know, lessened considerably later on in his writings. Religion, thanks to the emotional forces within its power, resists strongly in order to retain its field of influence, in spite of the weakness of its rational basis.

The damage entailed in this resistance is substantial. Religion hurts thought, generates conflict, does not bring the happiness it promises, nor achieves a morality worth its name (Freud, 1908d, pp. 199–200). It is, we know, an illusion, which ignores reality and sometimes even insists on a delirious deformation of reality. However, in spite of unavoidable retreat, it has succeeded in entrenching itself in every sector of the cultural landscape, expressing its firm refusal to loosen the grip it once held. Illusion huddles under the pounding reality represented by science.

This can happen, for example, even if illusion is in pathetic retreat, when it resorts to a kind of philosophic reflection impregnated by animist thinking, which tries to replace the grand God of the religions by a deplorable, impersonal, and abstract image of the divine (Freud, 1933a, pp. 164–166). "I believe for myself, these things cannot be said aloud, that some day metaphysics will be discarded as useless, as an abuse of thought, a remnant of the religious Weltanschauung". It was in such a whisper-like way that Freud expressed himself in *The Future of an Illusion*, in a letter to Achelis dated 30 January 1927 (Freud, E. L., 1961).

Even political ideology itself, and, paradoxically, those that represent a militant fight against religion, such as Marxism and anarchism, seem unable to avoid the religious impregnation from an earlier worldview and fall within the clutches of an illusion which responds with a defence mechanism in the face of reality (Freud, 1921c, pp. 98–99).

In the ethical sphere, the interweaving with religion is even more intense than with other aspects of culture, partly because science, on principle, renounces intervention. The moral sphere, which finds its rational justification in "a kind of highway code for traffic among mankind" (Meng & Freud, E. L., 1961, p. 123), is permeated, however, with a grandiose, enigmatic, and overtly mystical flavour because of its links with infantile oedipal realities transmitted by religion (Freud, 1939a, p. 230, 1927c, pp. 40–41).

Perhaps, though, where illusion most clearly demonstrates its resistance is exactly in the religious impregnation which science itself seems to present. In effect, scientific work, called to reveal the real against the illusory, does not manage to completely shed its old ties with the religious worldview. Some, precisely from the most positivist positions, demand from science a type of security that, paradoxically, leads scientific thinking to become a kind of substitute for old religious catechisms (Freud, 1920g, p. 64).

From there, society's relationship with science and technology is also contaminated with a halo of religiosity, which is evident, for example, in medical practice. There we see that credulity, and the craving for omnipotence typical of magical thought, provide elements of clearly pseudo-religious character, which can be observed in some practitioners performing trendy treatments, giving the image of "secular miracle-makers" (Freud, 1905a, p. 257). Therefore, the suspicion cannot be avoided: like religion, scientific theories and activities are also powerful illusions (Freud, 1927c, p. 34).

Thus, we see that the religious experience seems to prowl shadow-like through all sectors of cultural activity, impregnating them, in more or less explicit ways, with an illusory character, reluctant to disappear and let full reality be seen. Only by fully assuming this reality could we truly grow up. In Freud's opinion, there are only a small number of brave men who have achieved a full victory over illusion.

A secularist project

Nobody, not even the analyst, can alleviate the nostalgia for the father, who, like an empty void, is the basis for God's emergence. Because of it, the analyst needs to be conscious in his practice of the inappropriateness of "calling anyone to overcome a piece of infantilism which only a few are capable of overcoming".

Freud writes in the above terms in a 1927 letter to Pfister, in relation to the recently published *The Future of an Illusion* (Meng & Freud, E. L., 1961, pp. 117–118). Few, in effect, are capable of that sober and mature submission to the "divine couple of Logos and Ananké" without feeling the need to transfer to God or to nature the libidinal links that attached them as children to their parents. "It seems very hard", Freud insists elsewhere, "to free oneself from a parental view of fate" (Freud, 1924c, p. 168).

His fundamental purpose, however, was that concrete goal, to reduce to a minimum the illusory dimensions of culture, "to leave God out altogether and honestly admit the purely human origin of all the regulations and precepts of civilization" (Freud, 1927c, p. 41). A secularist project which, leaving heaven to the angels and the sparrows, would have the capacity to annul the neurotic relics of religious doctrines which, though having played an important role in other stages of collective development, at present can only delay the advent of reason and full maturity (Freud, 1927c, pp. 42–45, 50)

However, beyond all these Freudian proposals, it would be unfair to forget about his thoughts on another attempt, in the field of the "spiritual and supernatural", to avoid reality and seek refuge in illusion. We refer to the problems concerning the so-called occult phenomena.

The personal ambiguity shown by Freud in relation with this type of phenomena is well known, pointing, no doubt, to his own difficulty in facing unvarnished reality according to his own submission model. But if, at the personal level, a significant ambivalence prevailed in his attitude towards occult phenomena, in the public eye he was especially careful to avoid any type of confusion on the subject.

In his last writings on the matter, especially in "Dreams and occultism", his position left no room for doubt. Occultism is another way to avoid the frustration that the rational mind faces in life and so falls prey to the "seduction of the insane" (Freud, 1933a, p. 33). But also, and Freud saw this is as a great danger, if we consent to the enticements of the occult phenomena we will be enabling all those who wish to regain the basis which religious doctrines have gradually lost. In parallel, the fight against occultism's pretentions represents a fight against the very foundations on which religious faith has depended for support (Freud, 1933a, pp. 33–36). This last motive heightened Freud's disdain for what we now call parapsychological phenomena.

But the difficulty seems to come through relinquishing all the comforts that might shield one from the realities of life. This naturally generates a fear of feeling unprotected and defenceless, devoid of any parental provision or comfort. Compared with the desirable security provided by religious doctrines, total and complete, the partial and fragmented explanations provided by scientific reason can appear quite poor.

However, Freud is fully convinced that in the humble and stoic resignation to "Ananké", once having abandoned "the house of the father and the mother", man will find his development and all the happiness that this world is ready to give. There is, then, nothing to fear. "When Saint Boniface cut down the tree that was venerated as sacred by the Saxons," Freud reminds us in this respect, "the bystanders expected some fearful event to follow upon the sacrilege" (Freud, 1927c, p. 40). But nothing terrifying happened during that demolition of the sacred. There is nothing to fear, then, in undertaking parallel work with an education for reality in which the denial of infantile wishes and fears becomes the basic paradigm of the project.

It is within this same context of reflections on religious illusions where we should also account for Freud's position towards the religious ecclesiastical organisation.

It is obvious that, having the unconscious as the main focus of his research, Freud's interest set aside the properly sociological and institutional issues. A proper psychoanalytical approach to the problem is possible only in so far as the intervention of the unconscious can be expected also in the organisation. In effect, we also find in Freudian writings some, not many, references to the ecclesiastical institution.

The Church appears in Freud's writings mainly as tantamount to repression and illusory incitement. Sexual repression, which Freud considered to be such an important cause of neurotic disorders, has been encouraged by the ecclesiastical institution and its learning centres.

Furthermore, Freud is not very optimistic about the real possibilities of transforming these institutions, since he considers that mechanisms of denial and rejection of sexuality are at work in their very foundations. So, if it is desirable effectively to change this situation at the educational stage, these ecclesiastical institutions should be sidestepped. "Once again," Freud says, applying the evangelical motto, "we see the unwisdom of sewing a single silk patch on to a tattered coat, the impossibility of carrying out an isolated reform without altering the foundations of the whole system" (Freud, 1927c, p. 139).

Freud believes that it is only by the denial of things genital that the Church can have at its disposal that wealth of energy required to maintain its institutional structure and the loving illusion aforementioned. Thus, the ecclesiastical institution is forced by its own dynamics to annul sexual activity. Here, Freud also seems to find one of the most important reasons for its justifications for celibacy by the Roman Catholic Church (Freud, 1921c, pp. 93–95, 141).

The price paid for it, as previously mentioned, is excessively high. The Church, in fact, cannot avoid tangentially developing feelings in opposition to those lying outside those loving links. So, intolerance, dogmatism, and aggression arise.

Observing the poor handling of sexuality on the one hand, and badly contained aggressive behaviour on the other, Freud views the Church as the epitome of a harmful cultural management of the world of human desire. This also implies its inadequacy as defender of moral values. Bad management of instincts brings, in effect, all the conflicts of neurosis; prohibition and desire do not have proper articulation. Therefore, it is precisely why, in the name of the most high, every outrage which the ecclesiastical institution forbids is committed in its midst (Freud, 1907b, pp. 36–39). In *The Future of an Illusion*, he additionally accuses priests of trafficking in commandments and sins in the midst of sacramental confession (Freud, 1927c, pp. 36–39).

With this view of the ecclesiastical institution, it is not surprising that Freud distrusted the idea of possible relations between psychoanalysis and representatives of that institution.

A problem of possible competition arose very early when comparing the behaviour of the analysand with that of the penitent in sacramental confession. The question comes up more than once in Freudian writings. The analogy, doubtless annoying for him, is therefore clarified, carefully limited, and also minimised. In psychoanalytic treatment, unlike in confession, there is more than a cathartic function. Confession has never achieved the suppression of neurotic symptoms; furthermore, the sacrament has constituted a fundamen-tal instrument of control and ecclesial command of the conscience (Freud, 1926e, pp. 187–190; 1930e, pp. 210–211; Meng & Freud, E. L., 1961, p. 22).

On the other hand, the more important problem of a possible use of psychoanalysis by the clerics caused him concern more than once, although in that respect he kept a rather ambiguous position.

It was evident that, for tactical reasons, Freud was not interested in inflaming a controversy with the ecclesiastical institution. The possible prohibition of carrying out psychoanalysis because of the Roman Catholic Church's influence, in particular that of the famous and influential Father Schmidt, weighed on Freud as a threat not to be underestimated. (Father Schmidt (1868–1954) was director of the Vatican Ethnological Missionary Museum and, after the publication of *Totem and Taboo,* declared himself an enemy of psychoanalysis. His influence was also strong in the political circles of the Austro-Hungarian Empire, and in those of the Vatican as well.)

It also was not desirable to close the doors of analytical practice to the members of the clergy who might desire it. "If these spiritual gentlemen wished to use analysis, that is no affair of ours, they just should apply for permission to their bishop", he writes to Pfister (Meng & Freud, E. L., 1961, p. 105), whom he took in, as we know, among his faithful followers, presenting him on several occasions as a pioneer and a driving force in the application of psychoanalysis to the pedagogical and pastoral fields (Freud, 1923a, p. 253). But, besides strategy and political convenience, it also seems evident that Freud always maintained the expectation that a moment would come when the perceived contradiction between the analytical and religious perspectives would eventually favour the first, although for practical reasons he would not declare it openly (Domínguez-Morano, 1991, pp. 229–233; Meng & Freud, E. L., 1961).

With these reflections on the role of the ecclesial institution in Freud's secularist project, we close the present chapter on religious illusion. Belief, analysed like dreams and deliria through the lens of wish fulfilment, is viewed by Freud as a way to evade the conditions of reality and to reinforce, therefore, the resistances against an adult position, in which the submission to "Ananké" would signal the beginning of collective progress and freedom.

Dreams and neurosis are, thus, the basic pillars on which the full Freudian interpretation of religion rests. Upon these foundations, and on others of a complementary nature from other disciplines, we shall deal in the next chapter in order to carry out our critical review and assessment.

CHAPTER FOUR

Faith challenged

Confusion and Freudian slips

From early on, Freud's interpretation of religion caused one of the most acrid intellectual controversies of his time. We know how easily being "for" or "against" religion can trigger discord. It is no surprise, when we consider what psychoanalysis itself has shown: how many and how deep are the social and psychic functions linked to the religious experience.

We must add that the particular interpretation of religion offered by Freud also provokes conflict because of the perspective from which the analysis is made: the unconscious and its contents are essentially what need to be rejected as the very possibility of our being and of our conscious discourse. Linking it with religion cannot fail to result in the activation of all kinds of resistances.

But, in order to understand how the controversy became so bitter, we should note the especially provocative tone that Freud employs on so many occasions, as faithful follower of a scientistic mentality quite common at a naïvely positivist time. As we know, it was particularly in *The Future of an Illusion* that he adopted more resolutely that openly militant and provocative attitude.

It is, then, not surprising that, from the start, a deluge of protests, condemnations, and criticisms fell upon Freud's theories, in defence of religion.

Freud, it has to be conceded, made that task extremely easy. Guided by his psychoanalytic sixth sense, he frequently rushed to propose as well-founded general theses what were just intuitions, using unfamiliar disciplines which he handled sometimes quite arbitrarily. Many of his adversaries had plenty of fodder with which to exercise criticism.

His own analytical instrument, psychoanalytic interpretation, also offered his enemies a priceless weapon. They rushed in to interpret the hidden threads that seemed to have helped Freud's unconscious and his personal biography to drive him into those anti-religious positions. He could not, for instance, admit to God's existence because that would activate within him a threat of punishment stemming from the guilt he felt about his brother Julius' death when he himself was eighteen months old (Zilboorg, 1962). With that, Freudian criticism of religion was, for many, stripped of its value. As so frequently expressed, it was, in the end, just "Freud's personal matter".

Saying "yes" or "no" to Freud will always be a highly delicate and difficult matter. Our own personal positions (as psychoanalysis forces us to acknowledge) are inevitably going to come into play one way or another (obviously, ours too). The true problem will then be to keep those personal positions from hindering all analysis and nullifying its results. It would have to be recognised, also, that Freud himself tried more than once, in an exemplary way, to ensure that his own personal options would remain separate from his interpretative effort.

It should be possible to place the response to Freud on the religious theme at different levels, from lower to higher difficulty. We have, on a lower level, the criticism that can be made in all legitimacy (some psychoanalysts try to prevent it) of the elements from non-psychoanalytical fields that Freud used in his arguments. Being able to differentiate what, in Freud's analysis, is properly psychoanalytical from what is taken from anthropological, biological, Biblo-exegetical, or philosophical positions will be an essential and relatively easy task.

In parallel, but with more difficulty, a distinction could and should be established between what within Freudian texts regarding religion is properly psychoanalytical and what comes from Freud's biography and personal options. Obviously, not everything Freudian has to be psychoanalytic.

On a second, higher difficulty level, the dialogue with the Freudian interpretation of religion can dwell also (and psychoanalysis should appreciate it) upon the very psychoanalytical foundations that Freud used and which present a series of difficulties from its own internal logic. There are, in effect, a series of contradictions, oversights, and unsolved problems, which can and should be approached from psychoanalysis's own internal logic.

The dialogue between psychoanalysis and faith, however, will reach its right position only at a more difficult third level: that of confrontation of the experience, the psychoanalytical experience and the experience of faith, because, as we shall see later on, the most salient questions are played out at that level.

Let us approach now, even if very briefly, the first two response levels which can be taken in the face of the Freudian positions. All the rest of the present work (particularly the latter half) is nothing but an attempt to respond on that third level, which is the binary experience of psychoanalysis and faith.

In Freudian analysis of religion, there are, in effect, a series of sometimes important limitations and oversights, of which I have tried to offer a detailed summary in my earlier work, *El psicoanálisis freudiano de la religion* (Domínguez-Morano, 1991, pp. 421–464; Meissner, 1984, pp. 21–133). Because of this, we shall limit ourselves to a simple enumeration of the most important of them. As believers, we are more interested in what Freud got right in his analysis on religion than in what he missed.

If we look first to the non-psychoanalytical basis which Freud used in his reasoning on religion, it is possible to assert strongly enough that the sociological, ethnological, and biological grounds used in his key work on religion, *Totem and Taboo*, lack sufficient foundations.

On the one hand, the Darwinian hypothesis regarding the existence of the "primal horde", in which, according to Freud, the primal father's assassination took place and became religion's genesis, seems clearly untenable today (Muensterberger, 1976). In the same way, the hypothesis of a "totemic meal" as the founding ceremony, with the religious meanings conferred by Robertson Smith, is still harder to prove. The very idea of totemism as a primal and necessary stage of human evolution is now also indefensible (Lévi-Strauss, 1962, pp. 307–337, 1969) and the hypothesis of the "inheritance of acquired traits", which Freud needed when he granted the primal father's assassination the character of a real event, was rejected from the beginning by the psychoanalysts themselves. Even Roheim, the first anthropologist to become a psychoanalyst and a staunch follower of Freud, called the existence of such biological process into question. Other distinguished psychoanalysts, such as Jones and Kris, regretted Freud's stubbornness in holding to a theory that nobody in the sphere of biology believed in (Jones, 1953–1957, *Volume 3*, pp. 309–314; Roheim, 1962, p. 158) and is, of course, unanimously rejected by all current biology (Pichot, 1993; Simpson, 1953, p. 133).

So, the primal father assassination drama, the cornerstone of the Freudian construction on religion, is left essentially questioned. There is only one argument to back it: infantile zoophobia, clearly not sufficient to support so risky a thesis as making the proto-father's primal assassination the founding event of civilisation. If *Totem and Taboo* is to remain of interest, it will be through a new reading on elements different from those Freud explored.

If we look at the basis of the work that tries to apply *Totem and Taboo* to the Judeo-Christian tradition, the verdict will have to be still more severe. Really, *Moses and Monotheism*, from an exegetical and historic point of view (which is the one which Freud himself insisted on taking), has to be considered practically untenable. Presented in the manner of fiction (a "historic novel" was Freud's original designation) it would have deserved a prize for fiery imagination. With the pretention of a historical explanation, Freud did an injustice to his reputation as a demanding intellectual.

The idea of a Moses of Egyptian origin is far from being proved; that his monotheism would originate from Aten's Egyptian monotheism has all of confirmed history to disprove it (Meissner, 1984, pp. 107–109). On the Exodus' chronology, Freud himself is conscious of the huge difficulty posed in placing it almost a century later (the only way to support his idea of Jewish monotheism's Egyptian origin) in view of what all documented evidence demands. The Moses assassination thesis had, at its time, scant support, which at present has to be considered non-existent (Assmann, 1997; Bernstein, 1998; Certeau, 1988; Domínguez-Morano, 1991, pp. 429–436; Faesler, 1978, pp. 143–156; Grubrich-Simitis, 1991; Lust, 1989, pp. 81–93; 312–358; Paul, 1996; Yeruschalmi, 1991). The errors regarding New Testament data (such as, for instance, ascribing to Paul the authorship of the original sin concept, or interpreting the Apocalypse as a work aimed against Paul himself, etc.) are, if anything, still more striking and surprising (Domínguez-Morano, 1991, pp. 435–436; Pfrimmer, 1982, pp. 295–296).

If we turn our attention to differentiating what, in Freudian text, is properly psychoanalytical from what is specifically Freudian, that is, what comes from a series of personal, psychosocial, and epistemological variables of Freud the man, we find then another series of important observations that need to be made.

The personal or biographical variables are, no doubt, the most broadly highlighted (Rizzuto, 1998), sometimes even with the precise faults that Freud is blamed for: a radical reductionism and a truly extreme psychologism. Overall conclusions that try to disqualify the whole Freudian theory on religion have been drawn merely from some loose biographical elements.

We are, no doubt, standing on shaky ground in which it becomes difficult to be objective. It seems clear that incidents in Freud's life had a clear impact on him. These included events such as his brother Julius's death at sixteen months of age, or the incidents with the thieving Catholic servant who took care of him during his first years. There was also his mostly secular upbringing, an undisputed sense of Jewish belonging, his ambivalent identification with great figures of Jewish history, in particular with Moses. All these elements came together to influence his turn to atheism and in the positions he took towards religion in general and towards Christianity and the Roman Catholic belief in particular (Domínguez-Morano, 1991, pp. 438–447).

On the other hand, certain incidents in his adult life brought back a good measure of his unsolved oedipal problems and this played a determinant role in his most important writings on religion. As we have proved elsewhere, *Totem and Taboo* (Domínguez-Morano, 1991, pp. 91–110) was particularly affected by the complex situation that resulted from his falling out with Jung. Also, during the time Freud was writing *Moses and Monotheism* (Domínguez-Morano, 1991, pp. 295–306), the Jewish question had a direct impact on very deep unconscious problems.

Additionally, in order to understand Freud's atheist and anti-religious positions, a series of frequently forgotten social and cultural determinants should be considered. Standing out among them, we find the religious atmosphere marked by a Roman Catholic Church in a totally defensive position against everything that modernity had brought (Domínguez-Morano, 1991, pp. 447–450; Nédoncelle et al., 1960, pp. 107–114; Pottmeyer, 1975, pp. 21–36). An example of this is shown in Issue 80 of the 1864 Syllabus, which condemns those who were trying to reconcile the Church with progress, liberalism, and modern culture. The condemned proposition read like this: "Romanus Pontifex potest ac debet cum progressu, cum liberalism et cum recent civilitate sese reconciliare et componere" (Denzinger & Hünermann, 2012).

We should consider even further the philosophic terms that conditioned Freud's thought and the birth of psychoanalytical theory. Positivism with materialist connotations, which permeates all scientific and medical thought of the time, is the background frame of reference which has strongly conditioned Freud's thought since the time of his youth (Jones, 1953–1957, Volume 1; Meissner, 1984, pp. 68–72; Pfister, 1928).

The philosophy of suspicion in which Freudian thought is framed bears the legacy, as Trías (1991) asserts, of the inquisitorial Voltairian gestures, even if with subtler and more sophisticated manners. Freud's critical view on religion is indirect and inquisitive: rather than condemnatory, it tries to question it and open up an enquiry which would reveal to the scientist or the analyst the "truth" or the "sense" it contains, even without knowing that it does. The key to that truth and sense is reserved to the enquirer who knows it before the enquiry. Again, in terms of Trías, "reason" and "logos" are, in this way, merged together; however, this "reason" is just one of the ways in which the "logos" is expressed (one of many "linguistic plays" of Wittgenstein, with their own immanent logic). That reason then, unless it turns into the "superstition" it hates, cannot exercise dominion by imposing a sole method to approach and understand reality (Trías, 1991).

Evolutionism, which prevailed after Darwin's theory as a frame of thought, also left its imprint on the whole Freudian interpretation of the origin and development of religious forms (Roazen, 1968).

Finally, the influence of Schopenhauer's pessimism (Assoun, 2009) also had an impact on Freudian thought with a series of permeations that later psychoanalysis has been rightly obliged to question. Many of the theoretical approaches in Freud's work are, in effect, previous and marginal to psychoanalysis, and condition in great measure the anti-religious position taken by Freud in his writings. So, for instance, the theme of illusion, undoubtedly less psychoanalytical than the relationship between religion and neurosis, had already been posed before Freud. In effect, Feuerbach was already able to observe the analogy between dream and religion and the role of human desire in the birth of belief when he said that "religion is the dream of the human mind" (Feuerbach, 1960, VI, p. 169).

If we move on now to the second level of criticism we established, that of the internal logic of Freudian text, we have to point out a series of difficulties of proper psychoanalytical character. This criticism can be summarised in the assertion that Freudian interpretation of religion clearly overlooks the feminine element, a contradiction in the appraisal of the role assigned to reality or phantasy and a great unsolved problem as to what role sublimation can play in the religious experience.

As we read the Freudian text, the overlooking of the feminine aspects is so remarkable that we have dedicated a full section to it in the previous chapter ("The ignored maternal protection", p. 48). As we can confirm, it constitutes a true blind spot for Freud when interpreting the data available to him. This makes his obvious discomfort with religious systems such as the Eastern ones, so clearly infused with feminine and maternal elements, more understandable.

As for the role assigned to material reality, that is, the external event as opposed to psychic reality, we can see a clear contradiction with regard to the subject of religion. If we take into account that, in the clinical analysis (particularly in the "Wolf Man" case study, 1918b), he was forced to recognise the dominant role of phantasy over external reality to explain certain behavioural phenomena, it is hard to understand why he maintained, in the analysis of religion, that which he discarded in clinical analysis. For religion, he felt obliged to postulate a real event (the proto-father's, or Moses's, murder) as the basis of, and last resort in, the explanation of religious endeavours (Domínguez-Morano, 1991, pp. 458–462).

A more complex subject is that of sublimation. Understood as a change in the aim and object of the instinct, sublimation opens up the possibility of channelling psychic energy to the subject's advantage by means of the interest in certain cultural values. Religious experience could, then, become an opportunity, a healthy opportunity, to carry a series of instinctual contents through the changes that sublimation sets in motion.

However, in sublimation we find a highly difficult concept for metapsychological and clinical definition. It has been rightly named the most obscure term in all Freud's work and one of the nuclear points of controversy and for diversity of approaches in psychoanalytical theory through all times (Freud, A., 2011; Hartmann, 1955, pp. 9–29; Lagache, 1984; Laplanche, 1980; Loewald, 1988; Ricoeur, 1965; Vergote, 1997).

Adding to this difficulty in the theoretical concept, Freud is hugely ambiguous, even contradictory at times, when assigning a sublimation status to religious experience. In a way, we find that, in as much as he views religion as being interlinked with neurosis, it is considered as a formation in which the pathogenic mechanisms specific to the neurotic conflict intervene: trauma which leads to repression, a latency period, and, finally, a return of the repressed (Freud, 1939a, pp. 80–92). Nevertheless, the other texts that I have analysed in *El psicoanálisis freudiano de la religion* (Freudian Psychoanalysis of Religion) present the religious experience as a clear way to carry out the sublimation of certain instinctual drives (Domínguez-Morano, 1991, pp. 359–364).

We have to believe that Freud's difficulty in granting the possibility of sublimation in religious experience, as he did with artistic experience or with scientific work (Freud, 1910c), is the result in large measure of his anti-religious prejudice. His personal positions and his epistemological options caused, to a great extent, religion generally being set aside when deciding which cultural values could make sublimation possible.

Such are the most important voids, the contradictions, and the unsolved problems that can be detected when reviewing the internal logic of Freudian writings on religion. If, on top of these difficulties, we add those that come from his non-psychoanalytical arguments, it becomes necessary to re-examine how we value his complete hermeneutical work on religion. In other words, whether it is worth it for a believer to pay heed to Freudian psychoanalysis of religion in order to obtain something significant for his life of faith. Our answer, obviously, is affirmative. Let us see how.

Faith and omnipotence

We think that in the Freudian interpretation of religion we can and should find something more than merely Freudian material. In other words, we should not dismiss it as something merely pertaining to Freud's personal problems with, and views about, the religious experience. Something must be said there about religion, in addition to what it says about Freud the man. However, this "something" needs to be examined beyond the writings directly dedicated to the analysis of religion. In the end, the great challenge to faith presented by Freudian psychoanalysis is not so much in its direct application to religion, but on what psychoanalysis itself reveals about human nature: that the unconscious is something which cannot be within reach of the subject who speaks.

From this point of view, the most important question is not what Freud has said about religion but what psychoanalysis, as a tool for unearthing all things human, brings up in general on the "false conscience" problem. In other words, what Freud has written about psychoanalysis regarding religion does not matter as much as what he has written on psychoanalysis, full stop. This should be the starting point for approaching the relationship between psychoanalysis and faith.

Having established the properly psychoanalytical question, penetrating the mists Freud creates around his texts on religion, we can undertake a new reading of those same texts, which would then reveal what, in the first reading, remained hidden.

This re-reading of Freudian references to religion requires the removal of a series of elements foreign to what we must consider specifically psychoanalytical. If we look at the critical work previously done, it becomes obvious that Freud's texts on religion can no longer be read as anthropological, ethnological, or Biblical exegesis texts. From these points of view, we must conclude that those texts have a scant or null value.

These are texts that only find their place and their full significance in the overall architecture of psychoanalysis as steps in the general construction of a theory of the unconscious; only when understood in this way can they be relevant and of interest. That relevance and interest are also related to the knowledge of the birth of Freudian thought in general. We are convinced that the topic of religion offers some of the most interesting insights into the understanding of that thought in its entirety. It was in *Totem and Taboo,* his key work on religion, that Freud takes the decisive step of considering the oedipal complex as a universal structure, a foundation for things human, going beyond a purely individual and psychopathological phenomenon.

All this brings a change in many of the references proposed by Freud himself in his basic works on religion. Furthermore, it is necessary to do a specific reading in which a structural key takes the place of the evolutionary and historicist lens imposed by Freud and the intellectual trends of his time. (I have dealt with this whole issue in Domínguez-Morano (1992).) This is something quite similar to what present theological and Biblical exegesists had to do in their reading of the Adam in paradise and original sin myths, seeing in them, rather than an event which took place sometime in history, an allegory which reveals a general structure of the human in relation with the Creation and with God.

In parallel, *Totem and Taboo*'s central thesis of the primal father's murder should be considered (Freud himself used these terms) as a "scientific myth"; a myth that shows human existence in its individual oedipal structure and its access to symbolic and cultural registers. The *Totem and Taboo* myth (in analogy, surprising, too, in its content, with the Adam and Eve allegory in Genesis) represents the drama of desired omnipotence and the son's defiance in his aspiration to take the father's place, and (as in Genesis, too) the forced renunciation that is established as the unavoidable requirement to access the human condition itself.

With this key for the reading, all the rest of Freudian interpretation on religion will unravel and many of its elements will appear (contrary to what happened when the reading was done with the key proposed by Freud himself) as a rich contribution to the knowledge of religious behaviour and experience. Other elements, however, will have to be discarded eventually as expressions of Freud's own biographic and environmental conditioning.

We believe this way the subject of infantile omnipotence is placed at the very heart of the range of problems involved in Freudian psychoanalysis of religion.

In effect, we believe we have already established elsewhere (Domínguez-Morano, 1991, pp. 380–417) that the two great themes Freud applies to religion, analysed in the two preceding chapters, find a common root in the area of feelings of infantile omnipotence. These two themes are the intent to dissipate the guilt derived from emotional ambivalence towards the father, on the one hand, and the search for protection and comfort, on the other.

Following this route, the Oedipus complex is primarily understood as the refusal to lose the omnipotence in the narcissistic claim to no limits: that of dying, having origin in another being, and also (not necessarily the first or the most important) possessing or not possessing the mother, the symbolic representation of the total object. As N. O. Brown put it so cleverly, becoming God is the idea, "causa sui", in Spinoza's formulation, or "être-en-soi-pour-soi", in Sartre's. It is, again in Brown's words, the attempt to trump death by becoming one's own father (Brown, N. O., 1959, p. 118).

Through overvaluing the subject's own feelings and ideas, feelings of omnipotence help, too, in generating illusions in obvious contempt of the external conditions of reality.

Those feelings of omnipotence play into man's refusal to abandon the primacy of his own subjectivity and his own desires when confronted with the reality of an inescapable limitation related first to his origin (the contingency of being or not being), second, to his development (the continuous restrictions that arise from physical and, above all, interpersonal reality), and, last, to his inevitable end in death, inherent to the human condition.

Obviously, the problem posed is that, from this position, religion can offer a formidable and shrewd alibi to maintain, on another level, feelings of infantile omnipotence that, in spite of the pounding from external reality, refuse to be vanquished. Theology will have to take those feelings into account when undertaking its elaborations on the life of faith.

Theological echoes and resonances

In our introductory chapter, we upheld Freud's validity, not only in the psychoanalytical field, which he created, and in the rest of psychology as a science of behaviour, but also in the wider field of cultural debate. Man's image has been deeply transformed since the psychoanalytical discoveries, and the world of values has undergone a series of important re-examinations. Ethics, pedagogy, and art have accepted psychoanalysis's decisive influence. The "false conscience" problem, as we said, has had a strong impact on the way man thinks in general and thinks about himself in particular.

Theology, we also mentioned, has not exactly excelled in listening to the anthropologic revolution that psychoanalysis implies (Vande Kemp, 1984).

Theology, in Spain in particular, seems to have neglected paying attention to psychoanalytical discoveries. Diverse and numerous reasons have led, no doubt, to this kind of indifference with regard to facing the challenges which unconscious contents have posed for theological work.

On the one hand, the whole culture of Spain was deprived of psychoanalytical contributions both generally and at the level of psychology and psychiatry research. Angel Garma, the most relevant figure in the emerging world of Spanish psychoanalysis, was forced into exile in 1936 to Argentina, where he played a leading role in the flourishing psychoanalytical school in Buenos Aires.

As could be expected, during Franco's years other, less critical, and almost "phobically" anti-psychoanalytical, schools of thought were openly encouraged against Freudian theory. The subject of sexuality, treated as a taboo because of its wide and close connections with the subject of power, played an important part in the proscription of all Freudian psychology. The faith of the Spaniards did not feel especially challenged (as that of the French did, as a clear example) by the new vision of man that psychoanalysis set in motion. Because of this, theologians did not pay any special attention.

On the other hand, the particular socio-political situation in Spain under the dictatorship and the attacks it led to against basic human ideals, such as justice and freedom, became the main source of concern for theological thought (especially after the 1960s, and here we refer, of course, to the best Spanish theology; that is, the one really concerned by what in those years we called "signs of the times"). The social, economic, and political themes crowded out others of a more anthropological nature, among which psychoanalysis could have been heard. The Latin-American theological impact, too, marked by its socio-political urgencies, further strengthened that situation.

However, there are many important theological questions which can be illuminated by psychoanalytical approaches: the image of God, man's relation with God, and, hence, everything related to spirituality, the themes of guilt, sin, and salvation, the belief in the afterlife and immortality, the conceptual and practical aspects of the sacraments, important aspects of Mariology, biblical exegesis, and pastoral relations between individuals and groups. These are some of the theological themes and dimensions that can be particularly enriched by a thoughtful approach to psychoanalytical matters.

Among believers in Spain, only those directly concerned with anthropological matters chose to take on the psychoanalytical challenge: Tornos, Freijo, Font, Rof Carballo, Vázquez, Uriarte, and Villamarzo are among them. Their voices, however, did not succeed in being heard in the field of theological thought, drowned out, as they were, by other voices and concerns.

Others in psychology, philosophy, and in theology also, perceived psychoanalysis as a threat from which they had to actively, even aggressively, defend themselves (Ancona, 1973; Homans, 1970). They grasped only what psychoanalysis meant as a challenge to moral order. This excused them from paying attention to other more important questions concerning dogma, exegesis, or pastoral areas. This attitude, of course, was not exclusive to Spanish believers. Also, in the few statements from Rome on psychoanalysis, everything seems to revolve around levels of moral behaviour (Domínguez-Morano, 1991, pp. 476–479; Torri, 2014, pp. 75–150).

If we briefly review the diverse positions taken by believers in regard to the psychoanalysis–faith issue, the following ones stand out.

Some authors had enough with the first confrontation level we mentioned, that of criticism of the non-psychoanalytical instruments used by Freud in his reasoning. Whether it was because of the insufficient anthropological, biblical, or philosophic foundation of Freud's propositions or because of the obvious interweaving of his personal problems in religious analysis, they thought they had found sufficient reason to shrug off Freudian suspicion of religion. We think they should at least have shown some gratitude to Freud for making that task so easy for them.

Others have paid more attention to his hermeneutics on religion and dug a little deeper. They have taken the time to understand the psychoanalytical and not exclusively Freudian content of his writings. From that viewpoint, the responses have been quite diverse (Domínguez-Morano, 2000, pp. 143–181).

One of the more characteristic responses consisted in delineating acceptable from non-acceptable theories presented by Freud. The acceptable was limited to Freud's interpretation of "stray" types of religious behaviour. Freud was right in describing many kinds of religious behaviour as neurotic, but, obviously, those kinds of behaviour do not correspond to authentic religious experience and practice (Dalbiez, 1941; Dempsey, 1956).

Using a different approach, there have been those who have seen in psychoanalysis a kind of "gospel" of faith purified. In various ways, the most unsettling aspects of psychoanalytical criticism of religion were removed, stripped of any threatening element, in order to integrate them into their own system of beliefs. Psychoanalysis, then, becomes a road to inner purification from which faith can then be authenticated. This clearly concordist position believes the ultimate truth of psychoanalysis must coincide with the ultimate truth of the believer, which is obviously an *a priori* which should always be verified.

I have defended the idea of an impossible synthesis between psychoanalysis and religious experience (Domínguez-Morano, 2000, pp. 170–181); an impossible synthesis which accepts the partiality of the two experiences and of their respective corresponding discourses and where all the dialogue is situated in a permanent, mutual questioning which never reaches a unitary and final response.

Psychoanalysis does not question faith, but our relation to faith, whatever the manner in which it was reasoned. A faith which is rooted in the deepest emotional structures and is expressed in terms which, being similarly rooted, can be felt on many levels, that is, at purely imaginary levels or just at symbolic levels: Father, Son, Spirit, Mother, etc., are, effectively, terms which can mean very different things depending on where those imaginary or symbolic levels are placed.

Psychoanalysis does not have a previous understanding of what those terms mean in religious experience, it merely manifests as a suspicion about what those terms can be in our relation to them. It is not, therefore, a question on the formulations of faith, but on the subject of that formulation, a believing subject who proclaims his faith in a God called Father.

Psychoanalysis, then, should not be considered as "a knowledge that knows what is going on" in religion; it is not an inquisitor who, from a position of superiority, searches out the hidden meanings within our own experience. It does not posses our inner truths. It offers the opportunity for us to open ourselves to a dimension of that truth. Psychoanalysis does not have, should not have, messages or intentions.

Neither should faith, in turn, presume to know "what goes on" in psychoanalysis. It should not consider itself to be above the process of searching out the unconscious to establish meaning. Neither does it have the right to repeat (paraphrasing the reductionist discourse which Freud sometimes adopted on religion) the assertion that "psychoanalysis is nothing but . . .".

In the end, the dialogue between psychoanalysis and faith finds an even ground in the realm of confrontation, in spite of the difficulties and risks: confrontation of the double experience of hosting both faith-based and unconscious discourse. As we shall see in the next chapter, the pew and the couch could very well express symbolically the optimal setting in which the confrontation should begin and the basic starting point on which to build all the consequent theoretical constructions.

PART II
THE RESPONSE OF FAITH

CHAPTER FIVE

Prayer after Freud

The pew and the couch

Praying has always been a risky business. Long before Freud and psychoanalysis, the great masters of spiritual life spent much time warning about the numerous ways one could become entrapped. Texts dealing with the discernment between prayers that lead to God and those that are the fruit of evil spirits have always been prominent in the great treatises of spirituality.

An awareness of the frequency of self-deception and mistakes within prayer has seemingly always been present. Hence, the constant need for spiritual training, consisting, *inter alia*, in constant self-analysis and a progressive detachment from externally focused prayers in favour of meditations in which the subject becomes less self-centred. The path of prayer has never been easy and spiritual history has recounted myriad ways of going astray.

The introduction of psychoanalytical views might seem to complicate matters and cause discouragement. But the truth is that suspicion and distrust during prayer are normal for many persons of good will who question themselves regarding the ultimate meaning of their own prayer. If there was always doubt in that connection, it is obvious that the birth and development of the new psychology has visibly extended it.

It seems evident also that suspicion and distrust have spread. It is not just strange phenomena of extravagant revelations or exacerbated mysticism that prompt questioning. It is known that the most straightforward prayer and the simplest praying manner can entail many childish and deceptive attitudes. The question of what we are really doing when we pray comes up. The fear that praying might lead to a dive into a delirious phantasy world easily arises. And, in the end, we begin to question to whom we are really speaking when we attempt to speak to God in prayer.

All those questions seem to consolidate and express at the same time a suspicion that, mainly after Freud and Marx, spread throughout the field of religion. To modern man, religion looks loaded with dark motives, foreign to his conscious themes, and is seen as a phenomenon that can easily generate alienation from human reality. Prayer, at the very core of religious experience, would strongly accentuate all those suspicions.

Going back to our psychoanalytical perspective, as we have seen through Freud's interpretation, religion seems like a very fertile land for the rise and development of all sorts of infantile phantasies as well as the sly perpetuations of neurotic structures. Prayer, the quintessential religious experience, might, therefore, appear to be the greenhouse nurturing major ghostly flowerings. Any type of phantasy is possible for one who prays.

Returning to our present interest, we should say, therefore, that prayer becomes the ideal vehicle to approach problems in the relationship between psychoanalysis and religion mentioned in the previous chapter.

In effect, it is here, in the place of prayer, where we have to try to respond to the problems posed by Freud and psychoanalysis. Confronting, as is frequently done, psychoanalytic theory on religion with religion's theory on itself amounts in great measure to a cover-up of the core of the problem, because religion, just as much as psychoanalysis, primarily and essentially involves an experience that will, inevitably, always be betrayed by their respective theoretical interpretations.

Therefore, confronting psychoanalytic theory with theology's rational formulations will inevitably lead to a confrontation between two distortions of the original experiences. These will mutate into an infinite number of distortions, as can happen when two irregular mirrors are set face to face.

Thus, only from the very place where the theories originate, that is, the psychoanalytical experience and the religious experience, will a valid and fruitful reflection be possible. It is on the couch where the patient lies that we find the ideal place to elucidate, from a psychoanalytic point of view, what might constitute a religious experience. And from this encounter between the couch and the pew (and not from Freud's complete writings and from treatises on dogma and ethics) might emerge the reflection which will rightly approach the problems in the relationship between psychoanalysis and faith.

As we have signalled in the previous chapter, we should not make global assumptions about these problems, or attempt formulaic solutions. It would be in the experiential process of both psychoanalysis and faith where progress could be generated, fragmentary and provisional responses that psychoanalysis and faith could offer each other. Of course, it is neither necessary nor convenient to submit every dialogue with Freud and with psychoanalysis to a previous experience on the couch. But it does require that any reflection on the psychoanalysis–faith equation must be sensitive to what happens when the two experiences confront each other in the same personal subject.

In addition, no psychoanalytical experience can be precisely classified or defined. It is always a particular and unique process, as particular and unique as the history of each analysand. Therefore, all theoretical knowledge about that process is necessarily inadequate and deceptive to some degree. Equally, prayer constitutes a pure experience with all the ineffable character that all masters of spirituality have always emphasised. However, even if at the cost of inevitable distortion, we are going to try to detect the basic steps in the praying experience of a person submitting to the psychoanalytic experience. We shall, therefore, identify exclusively those steps which might posses a certain paradigmatic character and can hardly be missed by the experience of the believer when submitting to a more or less classical psychoanalysis. For the sake of consistency with what we wish to express, the present chapter will not provide any critical element or bibliographic references on the subject.

Suspicions and defences

The path of psychoanalytical experience takes a direction that looks just the opposite to the one taken by the path of spiritual life. The latter seems to be a matter of effort, of building up and climbing, of taking progressive steps on the way to perfection in search of an ideal. Psychoanalysis, in contrast, is a matter of letting oneself go, following the fundamental rule of expressing whatever comes to mind, regardless of how incoherent, ridiculous, or indecent it might sound.

In spite of first appearances, it is a hard (ascetic, we could say) effort in spontaneity, generally full of intense resistances. Loosening the controls built up during his life, a person finds things of a quite different order, which gradually gain weight and presence. At the same time, the world of his ideal objects seems, in contrast, to languish and fade.

In this way, the God of prayer also seems to become progressively blurred and less real. From this, the suspicion arises that the *you* to whom prayer is addressed is just a narcissistic extension of the self, or a mirrored image of the bruised infantile omnipotence, or a great breast for a demanding mouth, or a father who relieves the weight of guilt, or . . .

The result is that the religious experience is, thus, very seriously compromised. In the same way that prayer performs important functions in the subject's life, analysis will be viewed as something quite disturbing and dangerous. This is the moment at which, inevitably, the resistance to proceeding along a road that could lead to a serious breakdown will surge. There will be attempts to brake and stop. With great sincerity, the defenders of prayer and religious experience will appear from within.

The prototypical defence mechanism in those predicaments is usually that of rationalisation. The greater the subject's theoretical and theological framework, the greater is the rationalisation. A thousand "reasons" appear to relieve the virulence of the experience: "After all," it will be said, "all that is at risk is a pseudo-prayer to an 'idol', which will be properly purified by acquiring a new and authentic image of God". In this way, or in other similar ways, the subject seems ready to keep "analysing" as long as some untouchable points remain preserved. In the end, God is *necessary* for life. The possibility of unbelief is a theory applicable only to others.

Crisis and breakdown

However, the analysis goes on and does not care much for distinctions between idols and gods, religion or faith, natural or supernatural (such distinctions would only amount to false barriers, which perhaps make methodological sense in theoretical debates, but on the couch are only defence mechanisms). Everything is being questioned relative to the unconscious.

It is quite possible that the theme of prayer and religious experience in general does not explicitly come up very often. None the less, it is a matter of fact that work is being done on other areas that are intrinsically linked to it, even if they do not appear to be. An example is the whole world of early infantile relations, in which the so-called "religion of the parents" is rooted: the primary feelings of love, hate, guilt, and unconscious reparation that shape the subject's whole personality. The reference points for his own truth change, and certitudes are dissolved in the face of another certitude which, in those moments, is becoming immovable: that of his desires, his fears, his defences, and his controls.

Praying is no longer possible. Prayer is perceived now as full of lies and pathologies: the need of a father or a mother or the search for a salvation quite different from the one consciously chosen because the subject, and this is very important, now suffers the dreadful chasm between his "ideas" of prayer and the deeper "lived experiences" (*Erlebnis*) hidden behind those ideas. A full theoretical construction on what prayer is and should be falls apart as we scrape to see what lies just beneath the surface: an anguished cry looking in despair, magically, for salvation. It is possible that the subject might have sincerely embraced the possibility of living without prayer, without faith, and without God, but could discover instead that his heart was always on its knees, made into a child before divinity's great father or great mother.

The subject is progressively becoming conscious of the deeply unconscious, irrational, roots of his religious experience. Behind God the Father he might now find the tormentor; behind secularism, magic; behind rationality, superstition and totems. After all, he faces something that has no thought and no words, so it is safe from any attack. May the soldiers die on the battlefield: practices and rituals, dogma, thought, and theory. But, in the end, he finds a kind of ever-protected "totem". The army can die. It does not matter. He is hidden, unassailable, sure in his omnipotence, with its roots in force itself, in the irrationality that nobody reaches. His temple is there, a temple of self-adorations, of massacres and sacrifices, of reassuring slaveries. As if his unconscious could not abandon religion. As if, once all commandments are suppressed, the law would remain unscathed in the end. As if, once all dogma has fallen, the father's protection or punishment remained forever. In the end, it is in that unconscious where the subject has now found the "great beyond" of religion that protects him from the hardships of life. And he has discovered that it has an unexpected face. With a very different meaning from the one expressed by Moses (Exodus 33:20; Judges 13:22), he has also felt that it can be terrible to see God's face.

After that, the person finds he does not know how, or if he wants, to pray. The whole religious language sounds like illusion's ally. So, praying turns him an accomplice of deceit and superstition. He prefers to suffer for a time in pain (because it is really hard), choosing to go through without God.

Generally, hidden ambivalence manifests as aggression. The world of religion is identified as the instrument of repression and falsehood. Old spiritual consolations might give out a stench of corrupted, disguised, and feared sexuality. Prayer could be just an escape from radical solitude, from man's helplessness. Past moral imperatives might now have the taste of the most irrational taboos. Old dogmas that coloured spirituality might now reveal the traces of perverse infantile relations.

Now, if the subject inadvertently sighs "My God!", the call will feel like a bad thought, like a real temptation, the temptation of sinning against himself, against his liberation and his growth.

Helplessness assumed

Psychoanalysis supposes a ruthless departure from the focus on oneself, a merciless ascetic exercise that drives the subject from the phantasy of a lost paradise to the reality of helplessness in the world. He sees himself as a son of the earth and feels able to live as such; he knows that really now he could be (not as a pure theological "Death of God" ideology) an atheist. He does not need God. He does not need prayer to go on living. He does not need it from the depths of his being.

At this time, nothingness, unbelief, seems real and possible. Nothingness, on the other hand, that does not lead necessarily (as is usually thought) to the absurd or to discouragement from facing life. On the contrary, it can, by itself, present the possibility of an encounter with oneself, with others, and with the world; a real encounter, arisen not from need but from the desire that recognises its absence. From that, the other appears, man or woman; the others as comrades-in-being; the world opens up as a potential for creation, as a sense and as a project to accomplish.

Perhaps God can also come up again, but it will be in another way. The "totem's" place remains empty. The place of dreams and illusion, the sum of total objects, is deserted. In that empty space, obtains only a desire that refers to one's history and to one's future. If God is present, it will be in a different way. The subject knows very well which path he can no longer follow, even if the analysis does not indicate where (it never should) he should redirect his steps.

"Leave the home of your father and your mother . . ."

Something is now unavoidably broken in the religious experience and in its expression through prayer: that certainty, that unquestionable security of a God who listens. God is no longer always there, so handy and so reliable, so evident and so obvious. The analysand can still *believe* that God hears him in his prayer, but he no longer *knows it* and that is quite a risk . . .

It is not only a matter of having opted for belief. He does know that this option contains the risk of becoming a deluded dreamer. It is exactly this awareness of risk that frees him from everything becoming just a dream.

From this point on, prayer is quite different from what it might have been before. He knows that this God he faces, as real as He can possibly be, cannot stop being, for him, a "phantasy". Something that escapes any verification or any immediate experience, and, in addition, entails the acting presence of his desire: in effect, quite a risk. He knows that, in reality, he can never, with any kind of prayer, come into direct contact with God, but only with His mediations. In other words, through representations, symbols, myths, or rites which are human creations. Therefore, in prayer, even if addressing a Thou, he is alone with his "I", in a closed discourse in which those symbolic representations play a part.

The analysand knows we are alone, that a void and an ultimate helplessness are necessarily hidden in desire, and that it can be an extremely perilous journey towards the dream and the hope of an evident, obvious, and secure God who comes to satisfy his deprivation. In the end, he knows that when he prays he is behaving like the poet: taking on the risk of transcending reality and, at the same time, like the poet, signing off with only his own signature.

Is this not precisely the fundamental intuition that all the great mystics had? It is exactly because they went fully on the path of prayer that it dawned on them that the reality of God could not be confused or identified with human mediations; that in the end, as they progressively did away with those mediations, they were left with an absolute silence, a cloud of darkness, a non-knowledge, nothing.

The suspicion of nihilism that has frequently fallen on the mystics is significant in this respect. Because, on the road of prayer, if that prayer is true, all representation falls until, finally, it reaches a loneliness, a kind of death, the confession of a Presence which is unavoidably Absent.

The glory of God, we have been told, lies in His not needing man, and the glory of man lies in his not needing God to exist, precisely because he has been created "in God's own image". When God is made necessary, He is then turned into an object of consumption and, hence, an object of destruction. The necessary God, the obvious and evident God, is a God confused with His mediations, like the baby that confuses the mother with the breast that feeds him.

Instead, the God that comes not from necessity but from desire does not allow Himself to become trapped in a time, a temple, or a type of knowledge. That God is a gift that commands respect and which cannot be owned or manipulated according to one's whims. That God also keeps a necessary distance as a condition for existence. Because desire accepts a void at its centre, it assumes a radical loneliness and accepts that nobody, nothing, not even God, can fulfil that desire or calm that loneliness.

Religion as a barrier against anxiety, as a magical key to solve any unknown, as a warrant of immunity against the contingencies of being, is just a dream, an illusion, or even delirium. It is, in any case, in the margins of a certain gradation, pure wish fulfilment. The prayer that arises from it would be the stratagem to remain forever under the shelter of the family home.

". . . and go to an unknown land"

In effect, it is not enough to abandon your father and your mother's home. That is only the irrefutable condition for setting out on the road, venturing towards an unknown land; in other words, towards the freedom under which one becomes the agent of one's own history. This entails the risk of walking alone without knowing where to go. Through this engagement with life itself and in the encounter with others and with historic reality, one finds the only ground on which it is possible to maintain belief. On the other hand, this existential engagement will be also the only criterion to test the worthiness of one's own religious experience and one's own praying experience.

Going to an unknown land means projecting one's faith as a practice for liberation that goes beyond the world of one's own symbolisations and even knows how to set them in perspective. This makes it possible to refocus the suspicion that, during the psychoanalytical exercise, fell on one's own religious experience on the modes of prayer. The engagement with history has, in effect, the virtue of playing down the importance of the magic, animist, or childish elements that might still remain unscathed in our relationship with God.

The question of whether or not there are still magic elements in our religious experience is no longer the main question. What matters is where that experience is taking us. The suspicion, which might have been absolute during psychoanalysis, can afterwards find its fair place. After having left the parents' home, what matters is living rather than analysing, going out into the world, avoiding the danger of remaining trapped in permanent efforts of inner purification, taking on the harshness of reality and, still more importantly, engaging in its transformation.

If the God of Jesus cannot be seen except in history and in the encounter with the other, the psychoanalysed subject cannot and will not look for Him elsewhere. Any dialogue in prayer which does not lead, one way or another, towards reality (his own or that of others) leaves him perplexed, as in a dream or a delirium. Therefore, prayer acquires the character of a fundamental principle in the engagement with the wide and multi-dimensional reality he has to face.

With whom are we speaking when we pray? What for?

Prayer, in a strict sense, is a dialogue. Somebody speaks with someone else and expects a reply in return. From a psychological point of view, the question lies in finding out what a person is doing when he speaks with somebody he does not see, somebody who does not say a word. We do not know if he is listening, or even whether he exists. Obviously, it is a psychologically risky matter, because the line separating prayer from purely delirious phantasy could be quite blurry.

This simple example might help to better understand the core of the matter. If we were to find a person on the street speaking to himself, gesticulating wildly, and expressing intense emotion, we would think he is mad, experiencing delirium and hallucination, lost to reality. However, if we see the same person in a temple, we would assume he is praying. But we can see that they are doing, at least on the surface, the same thing. What is the difference? Who is speaking to whom? And, above all, where is the dialogue leading? Or perhaps it becomes acceptable if we can write it off as a cultural *a priori*.

From that point on, we could, however, point out some ideal differences. The mad man on the street is, in effect, absolutely convinced he is speaking with somebody. He is certain he is being heard. It is even possible that he hears the voice of his imagined companion. The person in prayer cannot be so sure. He *believes* he is listened to, but he does not *know*.

It could also be said that the man on the street, if he is really mad and not just putting on a show, lives outside reality, neither confronting it nor trying to improve it. He has created his own reality, because he does not like the alternative. The man in the temple, though, is assumed to speak only in the belief that God hears him and with the *intention* that reality, his reality or that of others, changes and becomes the kingdom of God.

However, we shall have to agree that these differences are just theoretical. We think that things should be that way, but we have no secure way of verifying that, in effect, one and the other do not have the same conviction of being heard. Above all, that one and the other are not doing something that not only is not leading to reality, but can even be moving them away from it.

The core of the problem is to know whom we are praying to and what for. For this purpose, it is possible to establish, from certain elements of psychoanalytical interpretation, some kind of typology on the modes of prayer. The next chapter, "The God of the child and the God of Jesus" will explore this subject. It is, however, possible to present some insights for reflection.

The first type of prayer reads like a particular case of narcissistic dialogue with a mirror. God in this case would be nothing but a mirror image, being merely a reflection of what it receives. Imaginary identification, we will say later on.

Such a model of relation would tend to reproduce a primitive infantile relationship (that we will describe later on) in which the baby experiences himself as a good or bad object depending on the alternating presence or absence of the mother. We would be in a situation in which the subject wishes to merge into a good object, a "Mum-God", in order to surmount the abandonment anxiety that threatens his very existence. The "you" of prayer becomes, for the subject, an instrument with which to build a foundation for himself. Everything is, however, placed on the level of a purely imaginary play, in which there is no possibility of encounter or link with reality. "Otherness" does not exist yet; neither does God, since He has been reduced to a mirror image, an inflated projection of the "I" that searches anxiously to constitute himself. A prayer in which the "consolations" and "desolations" would stray far from the meaning given to them by Saint Ignatius of Loyola (Ignatius de Loyola, 1914). Instead, they would rather respond to the alternating presence–absence of an "imaginary mother" who ensures existence.

It is possible that prayer is established also as a kind of oedipal dialogue with the subject's superego. We would then have the paternal imperative prayer, in which the subject takes God as a "model father and lawmaker" who sets an ideal and forbids transgression. In this case, the dialogue is forever revolving around the themes of guilt, of rebellion–dependence, of purposes and "conversions", as expressions of an anxiety to conform to the wishes of that introjected father, the superego. Narcissism is also present in a function of ego-ideal, as a model that demands and rewards depending on how one walks the path of "virtue". We remain at the level of the imaginary.

Sometimes, this type of superego prayer is such an unbearable torture that the time devoted to it becomes an inescapable burden: the superego hounds him and brings him to his knees.

In these dynamics, this type of prayer usually hides deep ambivalence: that God who conceals the superego is loved because he protects, but is deeply hated, too, because he controls and punishes constantly. In any case, we are still dealing with a type of prayer which closes the subject within himself, as pure confrontation with the law and his ideals, and in which God and reality cannot come up as opportunities for encounter and engagement. We shall have to return to this in Chapter Seven, dedicated to the theme of guilt and salvation.

Praying to the God of history

However, praying can also be a dialogue in faith with the God of Jesus, who is the God of reality and of men.

Only when one leaves the parents' home, that is to say, only when God is no longer the mirror that confirms existence, or confirms the law that creates submission, does it become possible to reach the reality that exceeds us. Also, to find in that reality the possibility of a not needed but desired "you", who, in turn, leads us back to that reality as a project of the kingdom of God. Only when one leaves the parents' home is it possible to walk towards an unknown land, towards one's own future and one's own history, with the resolve of transformation, in which God can emerge as an encounter in faith. Here, prayer is carried out "with the feet on the ground", that is, in loyalty to that ground, that earth, and not in its more or less disguised denial, since the God one finds in this type of prayer transcends, of course, that earth, but leads unmistakably to it.

It is important to take into account that this God of reality and history can be felt symbolically as father and mother, with all the connotations that those symbols can stir within us. In effect, it is not a matter of stepping into prayer without affection or without intervention of any parental element to ensure an adult and "psychoanalytically valid" prayer.

It is a matter of living that relation on a *symbolic* level rather than a purely *imaginary* one. In other words, a matter of a relationship that is rooted in the deepest levels of our affective world, but, at the same time, does not ignore the conditions and limitations that reality or intersubjectivity imposes.

This prayer has no reason to be afraid of praise, gratitude, or petition. From love comes praise, from having received comes gratitude, and from pain comes request. But this prayer must be made in such a way that one's desire does not try to prevail and uproot one's impotence, loneliness, or autonomy. It is, therefore, a relationship which maintains a "reverence" to God, that is, which respects the distance from Him, which assumes the lack of control of His signs of presence or absence, which does not try to force His liberty, because conscious that only by respecting freedom can we be faithful to our own liberty.

Prayer, placed at this symbolic level, would offer us the possibility of making flesh of our flesh all the world of evangelic values that we wish should inform our life, in addition to our reason. Because the final justification of our faith will never be the refined and elaborate discourses that we may produce, but the deep experience we may obtain from it.

Prayer, then, should be a privileged way of opening up to the experience of all those realities of faith in which we profess to believe: the experience of God, the experience of evil and sin in the world, the experience of the crucified and resurrected, the experience of the Spirit, of fraternity, of hope . . .

This implies, let us emphasise, all of our psychic system and, perhaps even more, our deepest emotional and symbolic structures, since only by means of their active participation will it be possible to modify and "Christianise" our most hidden sensibilities, in order thus to ensure the spontaneity and wholeness of our response in faith. Otherwise our Christian experience will be reduced to the level of pure ideology, of obsessive ritualism, or mere moral support. As we shall later elaborate, the mystical dimension of the religious experience constitutes a basic pillar of the life of faith, without which the level of engagement will hardly be sustainable.

Therefore, a prayer that does not know how to delve into the deepest levels of our psychic world, which does not succeed in connecting with the most potent longings, will be a prayer that moves nothing and transforms nothing, and also a prayer which only requires a dive into an imaginary affective world to stir up infantile nostalgia, becoming, thus, a defence against the limitations, frustrations, and conflicts of reality; that prayer, in addition to being quite distant from the Gospel, will also be putting us in danger of reinforcing whatever dreams and delusions might exist in us.

"You will know them by their fruits": in other words, according to the relationship that will be established, after the encounter with the symbolic world of the sacred, with ourselves, with others, and with the world. We will then have the only valid criterion to trust or not trust the kind of poetic creation that prayer is.

Epilogue on praying and power

Prayer, we have always heard, is an instrument full of power and effectiveness. Everything can be achieved with it, and everything is at risk without it. It is, however, necessary to acknowledge the phenomenon that occurs with some people: that, just as they are becoming more spiritual and giving more time to prayer, they are also becoming less engaged, more elusive in the face of conflict, more intolerant and intransigent with others, and, in short, more selfish.

Paraphrasing Gabriel Celaya, a well known Spanish poet, we could say that "prayer is a weapon charged with the future" but also that, if the future, that is, history, is denied, prayer is simply a "charged weapon", presenting a very serious threat of self-destruction and destruction of others. In other words, prayer can be a most powerful instrument of oppression or liberation.

The reason is simple: prayer, as any religious experience, is rooted in the deepest and most determinant layers of behaviour. Thus, the religious power structures have never been indifferent to prayer and have so frequently manipulated it to their advantage. In many situations, it is understandable that power insists so vehemently on prayer and warns of many perils invited by those who neglect or abandon prayer. Power finds in prayer a perfect ally and associate to help pursue certain goals, not always clear in their evangelical motivations.

Prayer, as a narcissistic dialogue with the mirror, makes us "good" and harmless, "spiritual" and easy to handle. Prayer as oedipal dialogue with the superego makes us incredibly obedient. A very powerful weapon: God as the father image in whose face the only option is submission to the law.

On these occasions, when the subject finds himself in conflict and in disagreement with certain approaches from authority, it is frightening to hear that old "pray on it" advice. Frightening because we are left doubting whether what is really wanted is that the matter is taken up with the God of Jesus of Nazareth or with the god of that figure in the unconscious, the superego. Who dares to say no in the face of a superego made sacred as God?

However, if prayer is a dialogue in the faith with the God of the Gospel, then prayer will become a most valuable instrument for the deep and effective introjection of the values of the Kingdom. Prayer then becomes, as for Jesus, a source of freedom that can often turn into an authentic means of subversion. We shall have to agree, then, that prayer can introject as much courageous patience as rebelliousness and fearless opposition. Praying is, then, a "weapon charged with the future", a risky weapon certainly, but in the same way in which Jesus' message was risky in front of a system of oppression that used God as a safeguard of the negative values of prestige, power, and money.

Praying to the God of the Gospel must necessarily lead to the Gospel; to give birth to a liberty that surpasses the ideals of the "spiritual" and the canons of the "moralist"; that goes beyond "virtues" and "sins" and, in the end, inspires a fidelity to the land in which God does not die, but resurrects.

CHAPTER SIX

The God of the child and the God of Jesus

The God of our prayer is also in debt to history. A history which is precisely our own, in so far as God, as a mental object, takes shape all along our life, closely related to successive changes in relations with ourselves and with the world. God has been accompanying our most determinant biopsychic needs and taking the shape and colour of our deepest vital experiences.

God does not rise up in us as a direct and spontaneous fruit, as certain theological and/or psychological positions have presented, or as faith, anxious for evidence, would like.

The faith that looks for evidence and certainties would desire a God that, almost as a natural instinct, would progressively and spontaneously manifest as a child grows up. In this way, religion would have an inescapable psychic dimension, without which it would not be possible to speak of a psychologically healthy or complete person (this has been the view of certain authors in the history of the psychology of religion, such as the well-known Gemelli (1952, p. 256), and Arago-Mitjans (1965, p. 42)). Such a view, besides raising a good number of theological problems, tempts us to make God "a natural need". (The well-known educational psychologist, Montessori, often expressed herself in similar terms. However, as Vergote affirms, no research has proved the existence of a specific religious need (Vergote, 1966, pp. 145–153; Milanesi & Aletti, 1973, pp. 85–88).)

Thus the facts, at least in psychology, do not point in this direction, as we shall see. So it will be necessary to assert here, too, that *man is not born religious, but makes himself religious* in the same way that he makes himself an ethical, social, or political man.

However, at the same time, it is necessary to state that the religious dimension enjoys better opportunities than any other to take root at the deepest personality levels of man. His emotional world contains fertile ground to give birth to gods, demons and spirits. For this reason, the religious experience has better possibilities than any other cultural formation. Hence, the highly powerful force it has been in human history, for or against man's own good, as we will analyse in due time at the individual level, in much the same way that the history of religions has shown us at the collective level. Therefore, many other cultural formations, particularly politics, have recognised in religion a powerful ally for their own goals and objectives. The other institutions have also had to learn, sometimes dramatically, how dangerous it can be to have religion as foe. The functions it fulfils and the frustrations it prevents can unleash the worst violence when a power confronts religion.

No other dimension of human life is able more precisely to fit the *other's* vital need to become *"I"* and achieve the aspiration of totality that marks this search.

In this need of the other to be himself and in the aspiration of totality it entails, the mother and father figures, as we shall analyse, constitute the two primary and fundamental poles. Hence, the religious experience, which can never ignore human development, has always tended to articulate symbolically around those two great human references. The maternal and the paternal are, thus, presented as the two hallmarks, the two privileged references through which all the great religious streams, Judeo-Christian included, have expressed the fundamental contents of their beliefs. According to psychoanalytical investigation, symbols with deep religious echoes, such as the earth, nature, the centre, water, the sea, the house, home, and cave, refer to the maternal pole of the human experience. In contrast, the sky, force, tree, and thunder present indisputable connections with the experience of the paternal.

This progressive forging of God from the main experiences of human development offers great possibilities, but also significant risks. The religious experience can take root within the depths of our emotions and become the authentic flesh of our flesh, a strong, vitally coloured vision of life, deeply rooted in our most basic trusts and certainties.

Yet, it is evident that it also entails high risk. On the one hand, the risk of God's image becoming subject to the distortions, mistakes, traumas, and turbulences that can occur in the complex relationship between the maternal and the paternal. On the other hand, there is the risk of eventually reducing the religious experience to purely psychic needs without ever really listening to a God that might say words different from those they know and expect. That is why the God that was born in us from our most basic life experiences needs to be ever ready to be changed by a word that comes from another origin, but never reduces the mediation of our image. Once again we will be forbidden from confusing God with His representation.

The maternal totality as grounding for divinity

The analysis of Freud's interpretation of religion has revealed his great oversight concerning the feminine and maternal element in the origin of religious feeling (see the section titled "The ignored maternal protection", Chapter Three, p. 49). That remarkable and surprising omission was quickly addressed after Freud by depth psychology, beginning with Jung himself, with a different structure from that of the founder, and by other psychoanalysts who, using the same Freudian references, delved into the feminine and maternal dimensions of the main religious streams. (Among the texts with a Jungian approach, we can highlight Neumanns, 1956. In the Freudian line, those of Jones, 1974; Roheim, 1955, 1962; Vergote, 1966, 1978).

The primary relationship between the baby and the mother has rightly been called pre-religious. It is a fusion experience in a pleasant and enveloping wholeness, although not without the presence of certain threatening elements, which also will leave their mark in the religious beliefs related to evil symbols.

From the early stages of life, the mother is the polarising object of the child's desire. Somehow, the newborn tries to recreate the total symbiosis situation he enjoyed during his intrauterine existence. During the first months of his life, his psyche denies the separation that took place during birth. Through hallucinatory means, the baby feels himself as part of the totality of the world he lives in: he does not have yet an ego to give him the feelings of independence and autonomy. Essentially dependent on others, in that radically immature biological state, the infant does not manage to feel himself as different from the world around him. Somehow, he is everything, and everything is he. Breastfeeding defines his bio-affective life and the baby cannot recognise if he is that sucking mouth or the breast that feeds him. So much is fused and confused with the world he lives in.

This is a complex experience, marked by diverse and even opposing feelings. As Melanie Klein and her school have posited, love, hate, guilt, and atonement spring up necessarily in the face of a maternal reality that cannot and should not provide a total and immediate presence in the fusion the baby yearns for (Klein & Riviere, 1964). Loving acceptance of the mother's alternating presence and absence and loving acceptance of his own limits is achieved only with the birth of an ego, distinct from the surrounding world, after a process which must be accomplished for his life to have a solid foundation.

Later, the capacity to symbolise will be born in order to cope with the necessary distance for the relationship and encounter with the other as another being, beyond his own world of needs and desires.

But all will result from the underlying total fusion situation that, as an aim, will never abandon us. According to Lacan, the longing for the "all" supposes a "perfect assimilation of totality to being", and we have to recognise it in "the metaphysical mirage of universal harmony, the mystical abyss of affective fusion, the social utopia of totalitarian dependency—all derived from the longings for a paradise lost before birth and from the most obscure aspirations for death" (Lacan, 1978, p. 43, translated for this edition).

That longing for totality remains as a basic structure of human desire, and will, therefore, nourish each and every future encounter. Naturally, religious desire does not escape this and becomes a desire for a transcendent All.

In effect, the religious experience seems to find the basis for its mystic expression in that open aspiration for totality in the human psyche. The mystic desire to lose oneself in totality and be dissolved in the divinity (in what has been called an "oceanic feeling") has its basis in that primal experience of fusion with the mother and its very possibility. (I have already closely analysed Freud's resistance to identifying the maternal pole as creating the "oceanic feeling" elsewhere: Domínguez-Morano (1991, pp. 455–458, 2016, pp. 29–35).)

Psychological research has proved that religious experiences could hardly reach maturity, especially in that mystical version, if the first experience of happiness enjoyed in the primal fusion with the mother had not taken place. As Vergote affirms, clinical psychology discovers, in that primal feeling of integration, of insertion in the totality of being, the indispensable condition for the awakening of the religious attitude (Vergote, 1966, pp. 174–178). Without that early trust and the protection afforded by the mother, fundamental attitudes for the experience of faith, a hopeful confidence, or the feeling of protection and support in life could hardly be possible.

Our image of God will take shape, as we shall see, from the symbol of the father. But that image will always present elements, reminders, and hues that are clearly determined by the experience of the maternal relationship. There are many diverse studies that show this integration of parental images in our representation of God. Without the maternal, in effect, our representation of God would never be as it is. (The most significant studies in this respect are those made by Vergote and Tamayo, 1980. A good, commented upon presentation of it can be found in Vergote, 1983, pp. 197–212. Also available are those of Deconchy, 1967; Font, 1999, pp. 46–97; Godin, 1986; Godin & Hallez, 1964, pp. 81–114; Nelson, 1971, pp. 46–49; Rizzuto, 1979, pp. 87–173; Strunk, 1959).

In this same respect, it is significant that the impact of the maternal image seems to be especially marked in those persons for whom the religious component has a particular preponderance in their life, such as monks and priests,. This has been shown by a good number of diverse studies (Castilho Pereira, 2004; Rey, 1974; Vergote & Tamayo, 1980, pp. 136–142, and also the questionable work by Drewermann, 1989, which I have already criticised (Domínguez-Morano, 1996, pp. 61–128)). The desire of a life especially close to God seems to be activated precisely from these maternal dimensions of the psychic structure.

The relationship established between the desire for God and the search for a maternal wholeness casts doubt on the value of mystical experiences, because it hints at an infantile desire and of possible pathological dimensions. Even if these problems cannot be tackled in all their complexity using our present frame of reference, we can at least determine their basic direction. That, however, will be possible only once we have properly transformed the wish for maternal totality through psychic maturation in order to prevent the desire's dynamics causing the downfall of the subject himself. Liberation from the fascination for melting with the mother will be achieved by the intervention of the paternal symbols.

Paternal image and God's configuration

The divine representation born out of the desire for fusion has not yet any shape or form, name, or image. Only by the advent of the father, breaking the maternal fusion, can God acquire a name, a figure, and an image. If the maternal is the prime mover in the desire for God, the paternal is what gives it an image and a configuration (Rizzuto, 2003).

The child is forced to relinquish the fusion he has tried to keep and enter into a new situation, generally known as a "dual relationship". It is there that the reality of the world and "the other" as different and autonomous begins to appear, but still in a mostly subjective way, accepting the other as a mere opportunity for the child to satisfy his own needs and desires. Really, the other does not exist as such, yet. Therefore, neither does the ego, that is, as a different and autonomous phenomenon.

From this position, the child must progress towards a "triangular relation", which begins with the oedipal conflict. Only in this new context can the child accept the difference, the distance, the limitation, and, from there, accept the other as other, beyond his own wishes and interests. It is the father who frees him from the fascination of the imaginary dual relation. He appears as an "other" who prevents total and exclusive access to the loved object. All this, we know, unleashes difficult and complex problems, interweaving love and hate, guilt and phantasmatic threats, which finally trigger identification processes with the same sex parental figure. At this point, introjection of the law occurs, symbolically, as limitation of the devastating omnipotence of desire, which is the vital condition for achieving an autonomous existence and for the true attainment of freedom.

The father, as we have seen in Freud's analysis, constitutes an image on which the child projects omnipotence, an omnipotence that he initially felt as his own until his own experience forced him to give up that belief. The father then appears as the full accomplishment of omniscience, omnipotence, and omni-benevolence.

The parents constitute, as Bovet so accurately described, the first "object of adoration", since they are, in a way, the object of a kind of divinisation by the child. All of this could indicate that religious feeling is primarily a filial feeling (Bovet, 1925). But the child, if he does not change his religion, has at least to change his gods, as Bovet again affirms. This is what happens during that conflictive oedipal situation (Bovet did not succeed in detecting the incidence of oedipal conflict in this transference he refers to, when relating the change from the omnipotence of the parents to that of God (Bovet, 1925, pp. 37–49)).

These developments mainly take place in the field of omnipotence feelings. As I have maintained in another work, Oedipus, beyond mere rivalry for the maternal object, is the refusal to give up omnipotence (Domínguez-Morano, 1991, pp. 407–417). If the father is a rival, it is not so much as the possessor of the mother but as the possessor of omnipotence and, hence, of the mother *as well*.

But, at the oedipal phase, the child has to confront the law, that is, the limitation of unlimited and omnipotent desire. Omnipotence must be irretrievably forsaken. That father, who was imagined to be its possessor, must die in order to leave his place to a father, subject to the laws of birth and death, who does not know everything, is not able to do everything, and is, furthermore, unforgivably deficient in the area of love.

The god of the child, the new god of the child, if we accept Bovet's interpretation of parents as initial gods, is now shaped by the figure of a father that knows everything and can do anything. From that all-powerful and all-knowing position, he will become an object of veneration but also an object of fear and mistrust.

Through the father, God has taken name, shape, and an image. It is a decisive matter, which cannot be confused with a diffuse totality in which to dilute and lose ourselves. Through the paternal dimension, we come to understand that God confronts us with ourselves as free and autonomous beings, and with reality as limitation against the exorbitance of our emotional demands. Through the father, we shall also shape an image of God called to grow along moral and religious parameters.

However, an important question, which we believe crucial for the life of faith, remains open still on the Freudian position towards religion. We refer to the question of whether this faith is used as a way to maintain an infantile attitude, within the aforementioned oedipal context, by means of a clever displacement, which can never be properly resolved; in other words, if that faith was not there as the attraction to keep alive infantile omnipotence feelings that refuse to give way. In the end, what matters is whether that name, shape, and image acquired by the infantile god taken from the father symbol are just the name, shape, and image of the God who reveals Himself in Jesus of Nazareth. Before approaching this matter, it would be fitting to make some observations about the maternal and paternal dimensions of the religious experience.

The difficult articulation of mysticism and engagement

We have already seen how the primal fused relationship with the maternal totality constitutes in some way a necessary basis for the desire of God, the mystic side of religious experience, which, to a greater or lesser degree, is absolutely necessary for a religious attitude to take root and live within us. Without a desire for God, without an aspiration to be near and in contact with Him, without longing for his His presence, we could hardly understand an authentically religious experience.

Yet, it is also obvious that the mystical dimension does not, by itself, lay the foundation for, and give validity to, a life of faith, at least to a Christian life of faith. The Gospel proposal cannot be understood as a mere invitation to immerse ourselves in a mystical inner world or a simple search for peace and harmony with a universal totality. Without confrontation with reality, without a project in human history (in the many varied ways in which this can be understood), there is no possibility of accessing a religious experience that we could rightly call Christian.

The great mystics of the Church are the best witnesses of what we want to say. St John of the Cross, St Teresa, and St Ignatius of Loyola provide the best evidence of what the desire for God can passionately mean, without, however, embodying a regressive and narcissistic hideaway that ignores the conditions of reality. On the contrary, for these great mystics, the desire for God was always a basic driving element in their tenacious commitment to the transformation of the historic reality each of them had to face in their lives.

With regard to the temptation to create a hideaway, in the end the mystic surge takes away that reality we are called to face lucidly and to change with energy. The fall into that temptation of limitless union ends, in effect, in a purely imaginary space, built as a lost maternal paradise, but, obviously, we will never have the right to identify that imaginary space with the loving God of Jesus of Nazareth. Such "mystical" experiences take away not only reality, but God himself, too, since He cannot be confused with an enveloping mother who induces an immense infantile regression.

The analysis of the traits of today's religious experience seems to point to a clear increase in its affective and emotional dimensions (Champion & Hervieu Léger, 1990). After the rise of the political engagement of Christians in the 1960s, the world of contained feelings and emotions, set aside in those times, emerges now with renewed momentum. The preponderance of the emotional in present Western culture seems to be a general phenomenon, which, at the level of the religious experience, would explain the success of the mystical and esoteric practices inspired by Eastern religions. The charismatic movement seems to correlate with this rise of the emotional trait we are witnessing in the experience of faith. Obviously, this new phenomenon offers a whole range of possibilities, and significant risks, too.

In effect, the best and the worst of what religion has to offer can appear in the mystical dimension of the religious experience, its clearest meanings and also the worst of its pathologies. The search for what is conceived as the secret of existence, source of life, and object of desire can result in a liberating and fulfilling human experience or a trap that maintains and encourage conflicts left at the unconscious level. Vergote refers to this in his excellent reflections on the mystic's desire: the nostalgia for a heavenly Jerusalem on earth can bring oblivion or denial of life's troublesome dimension. Polarisation to appease a desire can make us forget a fundamental fact of faith: the prophetic inspiration of a God who calls us to build a different world (Vergote, 1978, pp. 165–184). In that case, mysticism has lost its Christian link.

Only the intervention of the paternal symbol can free us from the fascination of religion conceived as nostalgia for the lost maternal fusion. The intervention of the law, which sets limits to, and imposes structure on, human desire, saves us from the natural confusion we are partly inclined to fall upon and confronts us with the conditions of reality we must live with. The God who takes up name and image from the paternal symbol invites us to restrain our desire and understand that communion does not mean that distances and differences must dissolve, since these constitute the pillars of our personal autonomy and the basic condition for our freedom.

However, that paternal symbol, so necessary for our human and religious maturity, can also set very powerful traps in the configuration of God's image. The fact that the fatherly symbol is indissolubly joined in human development with a situation such as the oedipal conflict can, indeed, favour the resulting configuration of God's image being impregnated by ambivalence and guilt. Thus, from the paternal symbol could come God's representations marked by the traits of intransigence, over-moralising, mistrust of any satisfaction or pleasure, and permanent discontent with ourselves. Despite its limitations, Freud's analysis of religion had the effect of highlighting those sides of the religious experience that are stigmatised by the conflicts with the father image.

Our Judeo-Christian religious culture, revealing the patriarchal structure of the Jewish society at its origin, has found special relevance in the paternal vectors of faith. Unlike other types of religious cultures, such as the Eastern ones, it has kept its distance from the more specifically maternal or feminine elements. Also unlike those in the East, it does not appear as an invitation to conduct a deep inner search in order to overcome outer limitations and conflicts, but, rather, to step into outer reality to make it different and better. The West, in its historical progress and development, owes much to this faith. However, the price paid for an excess of the paternal in our religious culture is that of maintaining unsolved emotional ambivalences in our relationship with God and the consequent aggravation of guilt.

Thus, if the maternal vector in God's image can lead us to nostalgia for an infantile fusion, the paternal vector can intensify in us the worst guilt feelings. In the next chapter, we shall address the traps and effects of unconscious guilt in the representations of faith and in religious practices.

The troublesome maturing of religiosity

The lack of maturity observed in some people, via certain religious behavioural patterns, attitudes, or approaches, is surprising, even shocking (in spite of how frequently, unfortunately, we see it). We get the impression that very infantile attitudes can remain in the religious area while in other areas of the personality there is progress towards adulthood. Qualified professionals, social leaders, and intellectually cultivated persons can surprise us at any moment with very infantile, dependent, magical, or illusory approaches in contrast with the mature, engaged, critical, and open-minded capacities they show in other areas of their lives, such as professional, economic, political, or family matters.

It is, indeed, baffling that a person can show such a high degree of critical capacity towards certain theoretical postulations, or healthy independence from some of the pressures in their environment, and yet, in the sphere of their religious beliefs, they can uncritically accept any dogmatic formulation. Or in their religious relationships with, for example, their spiritual counsellor or their religious groups, they might assume the most submissive and dependent attitudes.

Sometimes, we have to face the similarly scandalous fact of certain persons being more or less forced to abandon their religious beliefs and practices in order to see through a general maturation process. The religious baggage seems to be a burden that is incompatible with certain ethical steps that they honestly feel compelled to take.

All of this shows, on the one hand, that religious life rests on a basic foundation with very archaic emotional roots (linked to the maternal and paternal vectors we have analysed) and, on the other, that those emotional foundations suffer very special difficulties in maturing and developing when they articulate around religious contents.

In this respect, it is worth recalling the reflections made by Pohier in an important work on religious thinking in relation to infantile thought (Pohier, 1967, pp. 71–144: Godin, 1961). Basing his study on Piaget's work, Pohier reminds us how infantile thought evolves and matures through the intervention of three fundamental factors. One, the experience of the child's interactions with others, enabling him to correct the errors in his perspective that are excessively linked to an egocentric view. Two, the contact with material reality will force him to abandon an excessively magical, moralistic, and finalist view of the world, in order to realise that things happen according to very specific laws and that physical causality works without regard to man's will and wishes. Three, the painful experience of coming to terms with human limitations, particularly those of his most loved ones, will lead him to question the omniscience, omnipotence, and omni-benevolence he had granted them. All that will cause positive changes in his mental structure that will ease its adjustment into the world and will give him a deeper sense of his autonomy and his liberty.

The problem comes, as Pohier remarks, from the fact that the nature of religious thought significantly complicates the coming into play of the usual factors of mental maturity. The believer, for example, risks using his prayer to God to ask Him to reorganise things in his favour in the same way that the child asks the adult to arrange things just for him. Neither the socialisation processes, nor contact with reality, nor human limitation have an impact on religious thought as much as they do, fortunately, in the rest of our thought processes.

God does not know of any limits to His power, knowledge, or goodness. In our communication with Him, as said before in an earlier chapter, there is none of the usual interaction of human communication. We do not see or hear Him. We just believe, but do not know if He listens, and less so whether He replies. On the other hand, we have to recognise that it is in the religious domain where confrontation with reality, so inescapable but so fruitful in other areas of our mental life, is less commanding. Somehow, everything is possible in the religious realm, where, by its essence, we open ourselves to a world in which the usual parameters of our reality do not matter at all. The concept of God describes a psychological space beyond the world, the persons, and the societies, hence appearing as "an interval open to desire in the semantic reality", as Godin (1984, p. 13) so accurately states. On this point, see also Vasse (1991).

We see, then, that there are specific difficulties in the maturation process of religious thought and, still worse, it can seem like a way of evading or lessening the necessary frustrations and conflicts a person encounters in the general maturing of his mental structure. In this way, religion becomes a kind of shelter where he can find refuge and protection from the assaults of an almost unbearable reality. As a side note, we would like to recollect that extraordinary, although overlooked, film by Buñuel entitled *Él* (México, 1953) in which a person, unable to assume the frustrations he endures in matters of love, falls into a really psychotic (paranoiac) state and ends up taking refuge in a monastery where his psychotic condition continues, but where that psychosis no longer stands out or is identified as such. Religion gave him a space where his madness would no longer be called madness.

A whole series of questions on pedagogy and catechism follow. *The God of the child has to be catechised by the God of Jesus.* If the maternal and the paternal symbols have offered a deep emotional opportunity to listen to God in our lives, they also need to be open to Jesus' word, so that we do not confuse God with the mother who became unavailable or the father from whom we tried to reacquire omnipotence.

Pedagogy on Christian faith must then give up religious egocentrism, which turns God into a simple vehicle of our own desire. Particularly, catechism should also insist on the essential historic dimension of our faith, because only in history is the encounter with the God who entered history possible.

Catechism work, on the other hand, should not forget that, in historic reality, the believer is not in a privileged situation, as if his faith provided a kind of safe pass to truth, to the explanation of evil and human failure, and to the solution of any type of difficulty. Catechism should not, by any means, be used to hide the difficulties, the complexity, and the mystery, so often baffling, of human existence. On many occasions, perhaps the most honest, and the most pedagogically advisable, would be to tell the child that we do not have an answer to many of the problems he poses from his egocentric position; that God cannot solve so many things, but prefers to stimulate us in search of a solution ourselves and to keep us company when we do not find a solution or, simply, there is no solution.

Christian catechism should also not forget, as has been done many times in the past, that we discover God only in Jesus and that we should abstain from saying anything about Him that would not be backed by the Christological testimony. Because what we find there is a very radical questioning of the idea that, starting with our infantile experience, we tend to build ourselves on and around God. In a certain sense, we could, with good reason, assert that the God that became manifest in Jesus is certainly not the one we would expect.

The new conversion to the God of Jesus

The God of Jesus is a "different God", a fitting expression used by Duquoc in the title of one of his books (Duquoc, 1978). This God radically questions the ideas that, in a "spontaneous and natural" way, we tend to build up about him. Psychology in general, and psychoanalysis in particular, have given us clues about this "spontaneous and natural" way to that common idea of God, that is, the God of the child, the God of the narcissistic hideaway, or the God of omniscience and omnipotence. A God, we could say, built to fit the desires and fears of our childhood. But that is not the God of Jesus. To reach the God of the Gospel, a radical and deep "new conversion" is needed. If it does not take place, we would be in a situation which perhaps can perfectly be called religious, but by no means could be called Christian, since, as Duquoc says, "it is impossible to be Jesus' disciple and simply share at the same time the more common ideas on God and the Absolute" (Duquoc, 1978, p. 19, translated for this edition).

The task of distinguishing the God who emerges from the deepest and most primitive needs of our emotional world from the God who becomes present in the words, and, even more, in the actions of Jesus of Nazareth, makes for an interesting work because of its key consequences in our personal and collective life of faith. So, for the rest of this chapter, our attention will focus on the differentiating traits between the God of the child and the God of Jesus.

The God of the child is a "magical-providence" God who is primarily available to gratify and to make the harshness of life bearable. He is an ally of the ego. The God of Jesus, though, turns us towards reality, with all the hardness it might involve at many times of our life. Instead of solving our problems, He prefers to invigorate us so that we work towards a solution. The God of Jesus is not, in Klein's terminology, an omnipotent and omnipresent "good breast" that responds magically to our wish. The God of Jesus is the God whom we ask, in trust, to "Give us this day our daily bread", but having previously said "your will be done, on earth, as it is in heaven" and "not my will, but yours, be done". Also, perhaps at certain times, He will have to hear our most radical helplessness in "My God, My God, why hast Thou forsaken Me?" The God of Jesus is, then, a God who demands us to respect His liberty, since only that way can we be faithful to our own liberty and so be His adult and free children.

The God of the child is an "explain-worlds" God. He knows everything and has an answer for every problem and every unknown that might come up in life. Infantile narcissism demands that everything has a "why–because" and is unable to think that something might be due to random coincidence or chance. Many grown-ups, too, anchored in these infantile positions, suffer a substantial degree of anxiety in the face of ignored or still unknown things. They need, in their faith, a totality that leaves no dimension of life without a response. They have an explanation from alpha to omega for anything that happens. Furthermore, they do not seem to realise how irritating, or even how insulting, their arrogant omniscience can be for those who, without faith, honestly struggle eagerly to solve so many vital questions. Complete synthesis holds a huge, fascinating power.

However, the God of Jesus did not come to give us thorough explanations for each and every problem and unknown presented by life. Life in general, evil, the pain of innocents, the troubling future of humanity, etc., are all there as rough unknowns, for which the believer cannot give answers based on his belief. In that regard, he has no privilege over those who do not believe. The only difference lies in his hope of knowing that God is with him, but that knowledge, that certainty, on which he takes such a risk, does not stand as a global explanation of total reality.

The God of the child is an especially jealous God in the area of sexuality, which, as we know, is experienced throughout infancy as a difficult and complex unconscious situation. The father-law separating from the mother, the father-ban forbidding the intense infantile sexual desires, is too frequently displaced to God's image. This results in one of the most terrible deformations of the God of Jesus. This God, from what we are told in the Gospel, seemed to be more concerned by other kinds of realities, such as injustice, hypocrisy, greed, deception, or oppressive and legalistic religion. We will analyse this in more detail in Chapter Eight.

The God of the child, to continue listing the differences, is a God of prohibitions, threats, punishments, and perpetual watch on our actions and intentions. He is the God of the taboo, about whom an intense emotional ambivalence develops, because, with Him, desire is sin. The fear of the sacred is salient in the research work done on the concept of God during childhood. (To the question, "Would you fear to find yourself in the situation of Moses in front of the burning bush?", the affirmative answers increase clearly from the age of 5–6 years (just 8%) to eleven years (70%) (Goldman, 1964; Van Bunnen, 1964, pp. 341–354).) Deep inside, the child fears God because he considers Him able to bewitch, to perform miracles, and, above all, to punish what he considers evil. If the magic God is made according to desire, the taboo God is made according to fear.

The God of Jesus, however, reduces all kinds of ambivalence since He just wants the best for men. He is not a good God, but an *exclusively* good God: "God is light and in Him there is no darkness" (1 John 1: 5). He is not ambiguous like the infantile God, so He does not try to inspire fear in us: "perfect love casts out fear" (1 John 4: 18). He comes to offer a message of life and salvation, and, in a certain way, to free us from the anxious search for personal redemption, inviting us, rather, to a common project for our world to change into a Kingdom worthy of God and worthy of man.

The God of the child ignores death, since the child denies death because of the wound it inflicts on narcissism. The child, as we know quite well, resists understanding the reality of death, otherwise so undeniable. And when this fact gradually prevails in his perception of reality, the child still asks himself, and asks the grown-ups, if "the parents also die". Since he projects on them his feeling of omnipotence, he finds it especially difficult to accept such an essential limitation.

The God of Jesus, however, gives a place to death as a constituent part of human existence. Attributing the cause of death to sin can very well be seen as a stratagem of omnipotence. In the end, it would be something that had to happen, not because human nature is considered as essentially limited, but as the fruit of will, of a bad will, but, after all, in relation to power itself. The phantasy of an immortal human nature would be guaranteed in this interpretation of sin. The God of Jesus did not set His Son free from the conditions of human existence, and neither did he set him free from death as an essential moment of that same condition.

From this perspective, for the God of the child, resurrection becomes a prodigious way to eliminate death's narcissistic wound. Certain theological and pastoral positions rely excessively on such a concept. The afterlife, as such, is a disguised way of projecting the child's desire for immortality. Furthermore, this perspective overlooks that Jesus' resurrection does not try to reveal a God overpowering death, but a God that affirms Jesus' life and what Jesus revealed about Him.

Psychoanalysis, in effect, has shown us that our unconscious does not know about death and betrays us by inspiring belief in immortality. From this basic knowledge it is an unavoidable suspicion that certain theologies of resurrection, in their effort to blur what hurts so much to see, serve as allies of this unconscious denial of death. Resurrection is, thus, a way to disguise the undesirable and to project frustrated wishes of immortality: a world *à l'envers*, as Pohier so accurately has said. In other words, a world made precisely as the inverse opposite of the present world in all of its frustration of desire. This "other world" truly diverts us from God, from ourselves, and from others (Pohier, 1977, pp. 191–202; 1985, pp. 105–180).

Resurrection is not equivalent to immortality, but, rather, to overcoming an existence which is mortal, not through injury, but through nature. Immortality would mean perpetual permanence in what we are, and we know it has not been granted to the human condition. In the New Testament, Jesus himself does not perpetuate his earlier existence by a miraculous recovering of it. The condition of the Risen One is different: a condition which the New Testament texts tend in general, but not exclusively, to consider as derived from God's action rather than from Jesus' own being (Cullmann, 1956). Resurrection, then, as a new creation in Jesus, helps us to face the human experience of death in a different way, but it should never be used as a means to obscure what that experience means as limitation (Kessler, 1985; Moore, 1989).

In sum, all the traits we have indicated in the God of the child point in a precise direction; the God of the child is a God essentially characterised by the omnipotence attribute. He is, essentially, the God of "all-power".

The traps of the omnipotent God

The Freudian analysis of religion has shown that it is precisely within the feelings of infantile omnipotence where we can identify, at a psychological level, the ultimate and most decisive engine of religious motivation (Domínguez-Morano, 1991, pp. 380–417). There is a search for totality that, first in a maternal fusion key, then in a paternal power one, may find later in God's representation the ideal aim for projection. The problem then comes when faith serves as a privileged space to safeguard those feelings of infantile omnipotence from the attacks received along his necessary and beneficial contact with reality. Perhaps there is no other representation but God's so fit for the projection of those dreams of totality. God, as the imaginary father, has no beginning and no end, contains His own origin, does not know death, knows everything, owns everything; He is the origin of all law and all prohibition.

But it is precisely here that we have to ask if this image of God as omnipotent is the one we have received from Jesus of Nazareth.

We should decidedly answer that it is not. We have received that image from elsewhere, and it is in psychoanalysis, which has revealed those feelings of infantile omnipotence, where we have to search for one of the most important origins. It is there where we can find the collusion between a catechism, which distorts the image of the God of Jesus by emphasising the power themes, and an audience that eagerly accepts the message as it is presented. Strong unconscious motivations help to hook them in.

Never in the Gospel is God called omnipotent or almighty. As recent biblical theology has shown, the behaviour and the words of Jesus speak rather of a weak God, because God appears essentially as love and love is weak when its offer is rejected. In consequence, Jesus' gift of Himself even unto death constitutes the supreme manifestation of God as love without limits and, therefore, of a weak God, impotent in the face of the rejection of His offer (Mateos & Camacho, 1988, p. 109. According to these authors, the term "pantokrator", which appears in 2 Corinthians once (in an Old Testament quotation) and in the Apocalypse nine times, does not mean exactly "Almighty" but, rather, "Ruler of all").

Power is the capacity to influence others according to one's own will. Hence, Kessler (1985, p. 289) affirms, "the crucified, resurrected and elevated has no power or lordship. It is possible to escape his influence and reject it" (translated for this edition). Love always leaves the other free in the search for, and in the waiting for, the response. His power acts only when its liberating offer is accepted. That is the great scandal and apparent nonsense of the idea of God that Jesus offers us: "the Jews ask for signs and the Greeks search for wisdom". Power and wisdom, these are two emblematic representations of the imaginary father's omnipotence.

It is not about God Almighty that Jesus speaks to us. Even the acts of miracles, which could be understood so easily as the expression of a power beyond natural laws, always appear in the Gospel as signs of God's rescuing intervention in favour of men, never as a means to overpower them with the intention of obtaining their reverence or admiration (González Faus, 1982).

But that is not all. Going further, the fact is that the representation of power is always associated in the Gospel with Satan. He is the best representation of the God-power dynamic: "tell this stone to become bread"; "I will give you all their authority and splendour, for it has been given to me, and I can give it to anyone I want to. So if you worship me, it will all be yours"; "throw yourself down from here. For it is written: 'He will command his angels concerning you to guard you carefully'" (Luke 4: 1–13). Temptation. Like the temptation which turns up again in Gethsemane to ask for a God-power ("Everything is possible for you . . .") who imposes himself by force to amend the course of history in his own favour. A God who imposes himself instead of a God who exposes himself to remain at the mercy of man's fancy when he rejects his love. Jesus triumphs in Gethsemane in understanding that he must go to the end because only in this way can the reality of his God manifest. The love that is offered without restraint, without the possibility of taking it back, and avoids the risk of resorting to power. Gethsemane expresses Jesus' supreme fidelity to the God-love who gives himself and the exemplary victory over the God-power.

The reality of God as love requires, however, significant additional clarification. This vision of God that theology insists on these days from various sources (Hoffman, 2002; Pohier, 1985, pp. 337–387; Rowe, 2008; Wainwright, 2011) can run into considerable risks if certain aspects of the love from the God of Jesus are forgotten. The good, communicative, tender, weak God, in sum, the God-love, cannot be conceived as a mere representation activating infantile phantasies.

The name of love, which we rightly assign to the God of Jesus to best define Him, can also lead to a lot of confusion. This clearly can be seen by looking at the various definitions of love given by a dictionary. See for instance the first four of nine different meanings given by the *Merriam-Webster Dictionary*:

> 1) strong affection for another arising out of kinship or personal ties ("maternal *love* for a child"); attraction based on sexual

> desire: affection and tenderness felt by lovers; affection based on admiration, benevolence, or common interests ("*love* for his old schoolmates"); an assurance of affection ("give her my *love*"). 2) warm attachment, enthusiasm, or devotion ("*love* of the sea"). 3) the object of attachment, devotion, or admiration ("baseball was his first *love*"). 4) a) unselfish loyal and benevolent concern for the good of another. b) a person's adoration of God, etc).

Perhaps love is a very misleading word. In its name, terrible atrocities have been committed because, as popular wisdom says and clinical psychology confirms, there are loves that kill. Or loves that infantilise, or loves that are used as cover-ups to avoid conflicts, and so on.

The God of Jesus is the God-love, but in a very definite way that must be correctly grasped, understood, and differentiated through the words and behaviour of Jesus. The love shown there is not a love that mystifies or blurs differences. It is not an indiscriminating love, or a dreamy escape from the unavoidable conflicts with reality. The love we see in Jesus is a love that discriminates. It is a love that opts for caring for the weak, the marginal, and oppressed. It is a love that does not evade conflict and, precisely out of love, confronts, denounces, accuses, and attacks those who are sources of oppression, hypocrisy, hate, and exclusion. The love of God is not simply the plenitude for our nothingness or a clever excuse to bypass the unavoidable tensions of interpersonal, social, or political reality. The mystical dimension, as we saw earlier, if deprived of demands and engagement, dangerously adulterates the religious experience (Domínguez-Morano, 2016, pp. 39–46).

What is certain is that God, conceived as a love that opts for, and engages itself in, a role as saviour, does not present Himself in Jesus as the Absolute which, as such, imposes itself on human reality. He is primarily relational. His life, as Duquoc so accurately affirms on his analysis of the Trinitary symbolism, is not relating to Himself, and neither, hence, can it be understood within a narcissistic context (Duquoc, 1978, p. 97). Or, as the psychoanalyst Saussure has expressed, theology must qualify as sin (original sin) the unchanging human tendency to place God as absolute in order to religiously take shelter there ("and you will be like gods") in the illusion of the omnipotence of desire (Saussure, 2009).

That God, conceived as omnipotent and absolute and, moreover, an accomplice to our ego, easily generates dangerous attitudes in the interpersonal and social context. That power-God appears, in effect, as an accomplice that legitimises power and all its possible abuses. Since the absolute is the one that defends and legitimises, relative positions are not to be tolerated. Since the absolute is the totality, the fragmentary cannot be tolerated; there is no place for the different and dissidence is not admissible. Hence, the omnipotent God is a God of boots and war, inquisition and fire, orthodoxy and excommunication. The perfect substitute and ally for our own wish for dominion.

However, for the same reason also, the omnipotent God generates a somewhat disguised ambivalence and rebellion. He is the God adored for his power, but also the hated God because the longed-for power belongs only to him. Therefore, he becomes man's rival. Prometheus emerges then as a tempting alternative when perpetual immolation is not bearable (cf. on this point the section titled "Dios como afirmación plena del hombre" in Torres Queiruga, 1986, pp. 73–107). Nietzsche's assertion is well known: "If there were gods, how could I bear not to be a god? Consequently, there are no gods" (Nietzsche, 1968, pp. VI, 1, 324).

Within the context of omnipotence, God is no longer the basic element that embraces and provides confidence and security for life, and becomes instead a threat: necessarily, the more the other is, the less I am. The conflict would remain permanently unsolved. Either rebellion will emerge to fully conquer omnipotence (what someone has called "the Jehovah complex" (Jones, 1974, *Volume 2*, pp. 244–265)), or extreme submission will arise as a disguised way to recover it.

The great psychoanalyst Fenichel has been one of those who best expressed the dynamics of the omnipotence that paradoxically hides extremely submissive attitudes. Through them, the subject is pursuing fusion with the powerful and, in the end, making him dependent on himself. Poets have been most accurate on this, daring through the aesthetic play to express such a stratagem: "I am as great as God, He is as small as I / No higher than I is He, nor I than He less high / I know God cannot live one instant without Me / If I should come to naught, needs must He cease to be". This was the expression of Angelus Silesius (*The Cherubinic Wanderer*, quoted by Fenichel, 1973, p. 453).

Furthermore, with the omnipotent God, the conflict of emotional ambivalence will be constantly activated and refreshed. From that ambivalence, it will be unavoidable that guilt themes come up to take centre stage in the faith experience. An obsession with sin and guilt, a permanent threat of condemnation, an anguished search for salvation, a narcissistic enclosure, a ritualistic belief, and the like will invade the very core of the faith experience. We shall, in the following pages, focus on these themes of guilt and salvation.

CHAPTER SEVEN

Guilt and salvation

Guilt at the forefront

It seems all too common that in order to approach God it becomes necessary to confess one's own guilt as a prerequisite. As if God, in order to be present in our lives, requires the confession of our littleness and our indignity as a condition. Only once that requirement is fulfilled can things be "right" and communication possible.

It all happens without our having to be fully conscious of it. It is possible that our words do not ask explicitly for pardon or formulate a clear confession of our littleness. Sometimes, however, a deep attitude of self-depreciation and discontent feels as if it is an inner precondition for placing ourselves in the presence of God. Moreover, it happens not because of a justified consciousness of our littleness and our limitations in the face of God's greatness and sanctity, but, rather, because of an inner compulsion that propels us to abasement and to confession of our guilt. It seems that what is asked is that we kneel: symbolically, that we stoop inwardly. That is the problem.

On the other hand, we can be so accustomed to this that perhaps we miss the immature and un-Christian implications that are masked by that conception of God. As in many other instances, perhaps only by comparing this attitude towards God with our relationships with other people can we identify the odd dynamics in play.

Let us imagine the encounter of two lovers, two friends, or a son with his father. All of them figures that have been frequently chosen by God himself to help us capture the way He places himself in relation to us. All right then, what would we think if, under obligation, those two people, lovers, friends, or father–son, began their encounter with a confession of guilt and a petition for pardon, even before a first greeting? No doubt we would think that something odd is happening there.

It seems evident that in any deep interpersonal relationship it would be necessary to confess guilt and ask for forgiveness at certain times of life; assuming the pain we cause to another and acknowledging it explicitly before him is, in effect, a sign of maturity in an interpersonal relationship. But it is even more evident that offering the confession of guilt, as a preamble to any encounter, would indicate an authentic perversion of meaning in the relationship thus established.

Sometimes, we relate to God in such a way. Our reply to the greeting becomes a petition of forgiveness. The liturgical rite invites us daily, at the Eucharist, barely after hearing God's salute, to confess that we are sinners, without recourse, time and time again. Many of the prayers that are used during Lent or Advent seem to display a similar image of God forever waiting for our confession of guilt.

A pressing question surfaces: is God really the interested party in our permanent acknowledgement of misconduct as a prerequisite for an encounter? Or is it, rather, our conscience, or, better said, our unconsciousness of guilt?

Jesus to the fore

An elementary reading of the Gospel will tell us clearly that Jesus' pedagogy did not include a forced confession of guilt as a condition of entering into a relationship with him. The Gospel's stories lead us to think exactly the opposite. Jesus tried to improve the terms on which the religious man encountered God.

It is as if Jesus endeavoured to bring down the wall that separates the sinner from others and which, when internalised, also becomes a barrier that separates him from God. As if Jesus' resolve was to break the knot with which the sinner often tries to suffocate himself on the rope of his guilt. It is not pardon that Jesus first invites us to ask for in the model of the Lord's Prayer, but for "Your Kingdom come" (Matthew 6: 9–13; Luke 11: 1–4). It is not the confession of sin that the father demands from the lost son as the first condition for celebrating his return (Luke 15: 11–32). It is not acknowledgement of his unfair conduct that Jesus first requests in the encounter with Zacchaeus (Luke 19: 1–10). It is a joyous and caring relationship. It is the possibility of entering into the other's world, of receiving him as a host. In short, the possibility of an encounter. Only from that encounter, which does not request or require pardon, can the conscienceness of his sin emerge: "Behold, Lord, the half of my goods I give to the poor . . .". The others, the religious professionals, were scandalised at Jesus staying at the sinner's home. For them, guilt is at the forefront. Hence, they come primarily with accusation, judgement, and condemnation. However, the way Jesus proceeds, requesting encounter before confession, brings about a positive change within Zacchaeus. This is the result of a joyous encounter without foregoing humiliation.

We should not think, however, that Jesus' conduct implies an accommodating attitude or an ill-understood "tolerance" in the face of sin. We know very well that his ethical and religious demands are head and shoulders above those of the scribes and Pharisees. We have clear proof of how radical his approaches are, and how great his demands upon those who wish to walk with him. It is necessary to be ready to give up many things and reach further: to take on the cross in a total off-centring from oneself in order to fully align oneself to God's Kingdom (Mark 8: 35–38).

All this stems from the deep conviction of having been forgiven and that all the energy that was formerly squandered in a desperate attempt to search for our own salvation should now be directed towards the effort to transform our currently unfair and perverse society into God's Kingdom. Jesus was by no means complaisant in the face of sin, and neither was he an accomplice to the sinner. However, by not placing guilt at the forefront of the relation between man and God, he created an authentic theological revolution, which, apparently, we have not yet been able to discern (Pohier, 1985).

If things are effectively so, we should then ask a critical question: before whom do we kneel when, upon hearing God's salutation, we feel compelled to confess our indignity and our guilt? Psychoanalysis, particularly after Freud and Klein, can help us understand many of the elements at play in this serious, enigmatic question (Grinberg, 1992; Klein, 1937, 1975; Siebenthal, 1956).

The forgotten times of guilt

Nobody remembers when it all began. The feeling of guilt is, indeed, one of the oldest, most archaic, and primitive human experiences. It emerges as the offspring of emotional ambivalence, as a fruit of the love–hate polarity that presides over our life from its inception, even before the slightest hint of morality or religion appears.

Before prohibition and law, before any knowledge of good or evil, the feeling of guilt was there. Hence, a sense of guilt that is not the result of any transgression, born without even knowing which good was not obtained or which evil was committed. A sense of guilt tinted with the hue of self-destruction and death; a sense of guilt that belongs to us from the day we were born.

From that very day, hate and aggression threaten us, and phantasies of destruction and annihilation surround us. The mother's breast, transformed into an all-pervasive goodness, moves closer and then moves away, protects us and then leaves us. Thus, as a result of a situation that cannot be controlled or understood, that breast changes from good to bad, from friend to foe, or from protector to assailant.

From the lack of distinction between our own self and the outer world, love considers that breast as its own. But hate, in its most primitive phantasies, will devour it, will soil it, and tear it apart, because it is an evil, aggressive, and harmful object. The reason for that lies in the impossibility of understanding and accepting why that good mother's breast is not continuously present, satisfying as much as our infantile omnipotence would demand. If it is gone, that is not an absence, but an evil deed.

From this intersection of life and death instincts, the sense of guilt emerges as if to protect us from so much hate, avoiding and repressing so much aggressiveness and destruction. However, the bad breast, the harmful and destructive object, will remain as an introjected and internalised object at our deepest level, thus making a pervasive and self-destructive sense of guilt always possible.

When, during the first months of life, it becomes possible to perceive that the bad breast, that harmful and tyrannising object, is no other than the same well-loved and protective breast, then depression and remorse will appear inside us. Through our aggression we have endangered all the goodness, which, at the same time, we were part of and were surrounded by. The need for atonement will come with this remorse, trying somehow to repair the inflicted harm. The sense of guilt then, not in persecution but in repair mode, tries to establish new object-relations by renouncing the most primitive and destructive drives.

From our earliest days, love and hate are, thus, causing a sense of guilt, a persecuting and depressive sense of guilt, a self-destructing and a healing sense of guilt. They are there in the kingdom of the unknown, and from there they act upon us. The split that the infant experiences between the good breast and the bad breast belongs to what Klein has called the "paranoid–schizoid position", in which, through a complex interplay of projections and introjections, the objects are split as either totally good or bad. Later on, with the realisation that the same object both frustrates and gratifies, comes the depressive position. The sense of guilt and anxiety stemming from previous aggressive phantasies lead to the desire for reparation, and, at the same time, a differentiation is made between internal and external worlds.

However, the conjunction of love and hate will still produce another key stage in structuring the guilt feelings, a stage in which guilt will appear as indissolubly associated with the norm, the prohibition, and the law. It is the infantile oedipal situation, familiar to us after our earlier exposure to Freudian texts.

No one remembers when this happened. It was a time and place when history did not yet exist. Prohibition was there. This was the original prohibition, which will spawn all later prohibitions. The mother (or the father) was excluded from the field of desire. So, infantile omnipotence was mortally wounded in its ambition of total and exclusive love. Against the wish of being everything for the mother, the father emerges as the symbolic instance from which prohibition stems.

"Men have always known that they once possessed a primal father and killed him" (Freud, 1939a, p. 101), Freud tells us in reference to his "scientific myth", the primal father's murder. In effect, as in that prehistoric myth, everything happened in that time and place that nobody can remember. Love and hate gave birth to law and, in the same process, that small animal born from a man and a woman became a human subject. At that moment, history begins, and a fully ignored continent sinks into the unconscious ocean. Nothing, however, is entirely extinguished. Everything remains active: desire, love, hate, murder . . . and guilt, the sense of guilt that we will never know exactly where it was born or whose name it bears.

The father, representing prohibition and law, rejected and "murdered" in the battlefield, builds his tomb at the heart of our desire and from there he imposes a substitute, heir, and representative. That is the superego; an eternally open eye in our interior that, without ever blinking, keeps watch, proposes models, and punishes the transgression of its norms and ideals. The law is, thus, fixed at the deepest levels of our being. The threats against our misconducts will no longer be needed, and neither will instruction on what is "good" or "bad", or to be chastened or punished for transgression or negligence; nobody will be needed to call us to great ideals. Everything is inside, the overseer, the voice of good and evil, the punisher of transgressions, the call to great ideals. The father, beyond the echo of paternal and social ideas and judgements, will establish his seat of power in the kingdom of things forgotten or "unknown". From there, he will dictate his law, propose the models, punish transgression by instilling guilt feelings, and a lack of fit with his models by means of inferiority feelings (Freud, 1923b, pp. 19–36).

As internalised representative of the father, the superego observes, punishes, and presents an ideal to be followed. But the superego is, at the same time, a powerful "reaction formation", which means an instinctive renunciation. Freud points out two consequences: the desexualisation of the Eros drive, which turns towards cultural aims, and the redirection of the aggressive drive towards the subject himself in the form of remorse.

The relationship between guilt and the death instinct is thoroughly analysed by Freud in the short but dense article, "The economic problem of masochism" (Freud, 1924c). There, he warns of the danger from self-destructive drives, which, in alliance with sexual drives, lead to a masochistic sexualisation of morality: " Masochism creates a temptation to perform 'sinful' actions, which must then be expiated by the reproaches of the sadistic conscience" (Freud, 1924c, p. 169).

The function of "Ideal" that Freud attributes to the superego in *The Ego and the Id* (1923b) had already been described in his essay "On narcissism: an introduction" (1914c). It is worth pointing out the relationship that this work establishes between moral conscience and narcissism. The infantile narcissistic libido is not passed totally to the adult to allow investment in objects external to his ego. A great part of it is transformed in the creation of an ego-ideal, which is close to the actual ego and compares it with the Ideal: if the requirements of this Ideal are excessive, the ego will easily fall into neurosis (Freud, 1914c, pp. 93–99). He used similar terms in "'Civilized' sexual morality and modern nervous illness": "All who wish to be more noble-minded than their constitution allows fall victims to neurosis" (Freud, 1908d, p. 191).

Confession of guilt: conversion or destruction?

From these summarily described situations, the sense of guilt can perform very diverse functions in us. In effect, the sense of guilt constitutes a basic structure for a person's integration and for his access to reality and to the world of values. Therefore, we need that psychic structure that will cause inner discomfort when our behaviour strays from what we set as an ethical or religious ideal. The harm we can cause to ourselves or to others can only be registered as such by means of guilt feelings in the same way that physical pain constitutes an alert signal for the injured organism. Not all guilt feelings, therefore, can be considered pathological.

We are, in large measure, made by guilt. It has presided over the most critical moments in our development as human beings. The first stages in the integration of the ego, access to symbolic order and to language, our passage, in short, from nature to culture has relied on the sense of guilt as a key element for this process. It would, therefore, be naïve to try to free ourselves from something that has constituted us and still does. Without a sense of guilt, we would wander about in physical reality without temporal and spatial references.

Knowing how to feel guilt in certain occasions is, thus, a sign of maturity. "Nobody wants guilt" goes the popular saying. We frequently tend to deny it or to project it outside us, blaming other people or circumstances for our woes and for the limitations we do not wish to assume. Learning to endure the displeasure caused by a healthy self-criticism is a challenge we all have to face in order to achieve a state of maturity. It is also an indispensable condition for our progress on the path of faith. Without acknowledgement of guilt, there would be no possibility of change or transformation. Neither would there be a possibility of conversion.

The recognition of guilt can become an agonising task, so sometimes defences are raised in an effort to try to ignore it (Grinberg, 1992, pp. 153–154; Klein et al., 1955; Money-Kyrle, 1952; Parsons, 2003). But, as Anna Freud affirms, "True morality begins when the internalized criticism, now embodied in the standard exacted by the superego, coincides with the ego's perception of its own fault" (Freud, A., 1993, p. 119). (From a non-Freudian perspective, Jung warns of the dangers present in the denial of guilt. Particularly clarifying is the article "After the catastrophe" (Jung, 1945, pp. 194–207).)

There is, in effect, a depressive sense of guilt that emerges as an expression of the harm we have done: harm inflicted on another person, the rupture of an encounter, loss of our love, and loss of the values we have chosen to preside over our lives and our behaviour. It is a productive sense of guilt that comes from discovering the deception that might have inadvertently installed itself in our lives. In St Ignatius Loyola's words, it is a kind of guilt feeling which sheds "tears that move to love" (1914, Rules for perceiving . . . Third Rule (316)), that is, a dynamic of conversion and change.

This conscious sense of guilt looks primarily to the future, and avoids exhausting all its energy in painstakingly going over the infractions of the past. It is a sense of guilt at the service of life instincts, and, therefore, expresses a deep desire to continue living further and better.

But guilt can also create a self-destructive cycle, often disguised as the necessities and demands of faith. It is an unrelenting sense of guilt (therefore anguished rather than sad or depressive), and is also fruitless. It is that which, again in St Ignatius's words, sheds "bitter tears" (1914, First Week, Fifth Exercise (69)). It does not express the desire to live, but, rather, shows a destructive dynamic of self-depreciation and death.

That kind of guilt feeling does not really consider the harm inflicted. It knows only of the danger of losing the love of the other, in this case, God (as if God would love us for what we are and not for what He is), or in the harm done to our own ideal image. It is, therefore, an egocentric sense of guilt that locks up the individual inside himself. In parallel, his spiritual life stays polarised in an obsession with narcissistic perfection that we will explore later on. God and his Kingdom are not really present, much though the subject prefers to think otherwise. Finally, the subject ends up living for his sense of guilt, or, as would be expressed by the dynamics of the law described by Paul, for himself and no longer "for Christ Jesus who died for us and was raised again" (2 Corinthians 5: 15).

These double dynamics of guilt find, in the Gospel, a great, living illustration: Peter and Judas, as two modes of the double dynamics that can be unleashed by guilt feelings.

Both have broken their alliance with Jesus. Both broke their link with him, one by denial and the other by treason. Neither of them turned out to be a psychopath, that is, a subject who, by some king of superego deficit, is indifferent to the harm he might inflict. Both fall prey to remorse for what they did, and both are inside a dynamic that would want to erase what they had previously done. Peter cries bitterly, Judas gives back the silver pieces to the leading priests, also confessing explicitly his guilt (Matthew 26: 75, 27: 3). But the final outcome is diametrically opposed. Peter seems to feel cleansed by his tears, "bitter" initially, "moving to love" afterwards. Those of Judas are exclusively "bitter" and self-destructing. Peter suffers from Jesus' penetrating gaze as he turns (Luke 22: 61). Judas's pain seems to come only from his own observance of his soiled image. The outcome for one is life, a life initially frustrated and then transformed by the re-encounter. For the other, the outcome is death, suicide, as the maximum expression of the self-destructing dynamic that guilt unleashes so many times.

In the Christian experience, then, there is a time for conversion and a time for joy and engagement. In our faith experience, there should be moments when the consciousness of harm (by action or by omission) is present in us and moves us to transform and change in the same way as happens in any healthy and deep interpersonal relationship. But the problem comes, as indicated at the start of the present chapter, when the whole experience of faith is invaded by feelings of guilt and its many varied manifestations, which are often subtly diverse.

The problem arises when the God we face sends back to us a negative reflection of ourselves, when coming into His presence results almost immediately in dissatisfaction or self-reproach. When His presence does not raise joy, or barely does. When God does not usher in life and delight and, instead, is a permanent messenger of death and misfortune.

Mea culpa, mea culpa, mea maxima culpa

With deep intuition, Freud says,

> If civilization is a necessary course of development from the family to humanity as a whole, then – as a result of the inborn conflict arising from ambivalence, of the eternal struggle between the trends of love and death – there is inextricably bound up with it an increase of the sense of guilt. (Freud, 1930a, p. 133)

Born from the repression of instinctive animal life, civilisation is forced to convert all the aggressiveness developed by an inhibited and repressed individual into a sense of guilt.

According to Freud (in very close similarity to Nietzsche's position), in the ensemble of cultural creations, the religious phenomenon is the one that presents wider connections with the sense of guilt. In Freud's analysis of religion, the sense of guilt appears as the more relevant unconscious element, the one that sets in motion the creation of gods and demons, rites and prayers, sacrifices and oblations. As we have seen in the earlier chapters of this book, the two great pillars of the psychoanalysis of religion are the themes of consolation and of ambivalence/guilt. Of these, it is the latter that signifies the most specifically psychoanalytic contribution to the study of the origin and development of religiousness.

Guilt, in its most conscious acknowledgement, emerges in terms of sin, remorse, transgression, pardon, law, or moral conscience. But in its deeper and wider dimensions, at a purely unconscious level, it is revealed in terms that, at first sight, seem to have little or no relation to guilt. At the clinical level, this is evident for the psychiatrist or therapist. At other levels, this unconscious character of guilt appears by means of certain beliefs and dogmas, certain rituals and liturgies, praxis, propositions of spiritual or ascetic ideals. The feelings of guilt pose, therefore, a series of questions that go way beyond the ethical and moral area. The whole religious experience, as much in thought as in feeling, can be bound intimately to this sense of guilt.

This is the starting point for what should be the core of the present chapter: how the sense of guilt, in its unconscious character, has progressively invaded, coloured, distorted, and, many times, perverted the Christian experience. In the melodic diversity of discourses on faith, in dogmatic theological treatises, or in popular religious expressions; in the different tonalities of the moral attitudes and behaviours, conservative or progressive in tone; in the various ritual or liturgical rhythms, orthodox or heterodox; in the diverse spirituality themes or ascetic cadences, a kind of constant *basso continuo* can be heard, an iterative background, a compulsive, repetitive murmur that somehow intones *mea culpa, mea culpa, mea maxima culpa*. These are the traps that the unconscious sets for faith.

This unconscious side of guilt should be emphasised because it is not generally taken into account as much as it should be. The ego does not resign itself to the displacement out of its own centre that the unconscious represents. It tends to believe that what it does not think or feel simply does not exist. Narcissistic omnipotence easily betrays us with denials that sometimes manifest as frenzied behaviour.

The sense of guilt which, from birth, protects us from total annihilation phantasies, the sense of guilt born out of a "murder" which is foundation of our growth into a human subject, is there as an echo of that primal murder, punctuating the diverse events of our history, in that place of which we know nothing. The prohibition is internalised, but denied as internalised, inevitably resulting in concealment of the truth. Our egos struggle to trace what happens in the unconscious, partly because certain elements of the ego itself are also unconscious (the unconscious character of the superego, and, therefore, of guilt feelings, is analysed by Freud in *The Ego and the Id* (1923b). He insists again on this character in the fourth lecture of *New Introductory Lectures on Psycho-Analysis*, entitled "The dissection of the psychical personality" (Freud, 1933a, pp. 57–80)).

Perhaps the first task to be addressed by that ego would be the humble acknowledgement that it is not fully lord and master of its own behaviour, of its thoughts and its feelings, but, rather, as Freud put it, is a poor diplomat who has to keep the peace among severe, tyrannical, and contrary masters (Freud, 1933a, p. 77). The degree of success in accomplishing that task will determine the degree of truth, authenticity, and liberty it might provide us.

Perhaps we should also recognise that the religious experience constitutes one of the more propitious spaces to enable those strategies of guilt with the power to induce neurosis. From there, beliefs and dogmas, rites, spiritual and moral practices, and life habits could be strongly conditioned, even to the point of losing their original meanings.

There are significant reasons why we should question the extent to which the Christian message has been tainted by the subject of guilt and to what degree it is serving to propagate its unconscious endeavours rather than the message of Jesus of Nazareth. A number of elements indicate that we have frequently fallen into the traps of guilt, and that guilt, disguised in Christian apparel, has succeeded in making us kneel before its own gods and demons.

Sin, love, and death

Our God has suffered serious deformities caused by the pathologies of guilt. His message has progressively resembled the primal murder drama, as described by Freud in *Totem and Taboo*: there is an original sin against the father that unleashes the full dynamics of guilt and atonement. In those dynamics, everything is magnified (the offended God, the offence, and the atonement), but in them nothing is ever fully resolved.

Certain representations of the Christian God have, in effect, been coming closer to the image of that imaginary father described by Freud: mighty, strong, and originator of every law, in whose presence one must assume a precarious "it's you or me" attitude. He is a father without beginning or end, because he is the owner of the origin and does not know death. He is the image of omnipotence described in the previous chapter.

Admired father, therefore, but hated father also, because total power and total pleasure belongs solely to him. In short, God, embracing totality in a dream, against the unavoidable outbreak of the deepest emotional ambivalence of love and hate, and, in consequence, of a permanent sense of guilt and permanent atonement (Domínguez-Morano, 2006, pp. 86–94; Rosolato, 1969, pp. 66–108; Rubenstein, 1971).

"We have committed an original sin against the Father, a sin which should be washed away with a death, the death of His own Son, this being the only way we can find the path to reconciliation". This could be a summary of the Anselmian theology of redemption as it was formulated in the work *Cur Deus Homo* (Anselmo of Canterbury, 1929). Insistence on such faith formulations and the polarisation it produces taint the Christian message in a way that resembles the phantasmatic world of guilt. It is the original sin of the "primal father's murder" that, at the unconscious level, left us demanding atonement, a need for pardon, and an urge for reconciliation with the "dead father".

A purely expiatory conception of Jesus' death is, thus, set in motion (particularly after Saint Anselm), giving away the strategies of unconscious guilt rather than the data underscored by revelation. It is a tragic conception of salvation, in which reconciliation with the Father comes only through reparation in the flesh of a crucified and sadistically executed brother. This has markedly polarised the presentation of the Christian message. Jesus' death, in this view, suggests a God who needs blood for forgiveness, and not as a consequence of Jesus' uncompromising denunciation of the religious foundations of the society of his time, and of the perverted human relationships stemming from them. It has been said that the death was necessary, wished for, "pleasant" to God, because His clemency was impotent and tied up by inexorable justice. Therefore, the sacrifice was needed, the Son's immolation. As the Eucharistic Prayer reads, "the sacrifice which restores man to your friendship".

The father in the parable of the lost son (Luke 15: 11–32) is hardly recognisable here. He did not need prior acknowledgement of guilt by the son, or a reproach extolling his own grief, and even less so as a condition for the restoration of friendship. There is not a single drop of blood in the parables of pardon (Luke 15: 1–32), except that of a calf killed as supreme expression of feasting and joy at the re-encounter.

It seems as if our unconscious mind is not willing to accept God's unrestricted generosity. Something pushes us to sacrifice, to kill something in ourselves as prior atonement for the re-encounter, because we do not conceive that the other does not need something from us in order to forgive and approach us. Perhaps because, from our infantile omnipotence and from our hidden emotional ambivalence, we might have thought that with our sin (as we might have been told at some point) "we have killed God" (you have to be really omnipotent to do such a thing!). Projecting, then, our notions unto God, we deem it necessary to kill something in us by way of sacrifice: the amputation of something very dear, burning an object or abstaining from some pleasure. (Our aim is not to disregard any religious or Christian meaning to the sacrificial ritual, but to give warning about the dangers entailed in framing it in relation with God as a kind of self-mutilation. Sacrifice as an expression of freedom for the creatures can effectively have a place and a meaning as symbolic exchange in an experience of faith (Vergote, 1978, pp. 156–162).) Once again it looks as if the relationship with God becomes established in an impossible "you or me" situation, and, from there, the affirmation of one necessarily implies the denial of the other. Again, the traps of the omnipotent God, already mentioned in the previous chapter.

Early on, Christianity proposed a conception of salvation with a more pessimistic and dramatic tone than those brought out in Jesus' preaching. The sacrificial and expiatory dimension of his death gradually took prominence, thus displacing another conception of God and His relationship with men, expressed certainly in more optimistic and also salvific terms, but in a very different sense (Castillo, 1986, pp. 47–81; Diéguez, 1981; Estrada, 2003, pp. 137–180; Fiddes, 1988, pp. 46–76; Pihlström, 2014, pp. 81–101; Sesboüé, 1988, pp. 327–356).

That expiatory conception of Jesus' death, appearing in later New Testament writings, must be considered as secondary and subordinated to the conception in earlier writings, closer, therefore, to Jesus himself. It should not be imposed, as has happened, on the others, nullifying the most important meanings of the death of the Lord. (The work of Schillebeeckx (1979), tells us about the origin and meaning of the three basic conceptions existing in the New Testament regarding the death of Jesus: (a) the eschatological prophet–martyr, (b) the divine plan for salvation, and (c) the expiatory death.)

In this regard, Duquoc thinks that we have received a contradictory legacy, partly due to the reality of Jesus' scandalous death, which left no option but to search the Old Testament for ways to make that death more understandable and acceptable. The God's Servant songs (Isiah 52: 13–53, 12) appeared to be the most suitable for that. The death as sacrifice and atonement began to be more prominent, "but at the price of enhancing dimensions ignored by the preaching and the actions of Jesus" (Duquoc, 1978, translated for this edition).

The concept of salvation was, in this way, progressively being reduced exclusively to "salvation from": salvation from sin, salvation from evil, salvation from death, salvation from hardship, salvation from the past. A sense of "salvation for", which seems more in line with the Gospel's preaching, was progressively losing favour: salvation for goodness, for going out of our own centre for the sake of the Kingdom. Salvation for life, understood as a project to change reality towards a Kingdom of God, worthy of man, salvation for progress and thrust for the future.

Salvation, captured in the web of guilt, became individual and egocentric, anxious and permanently threatened. But, as González Faus so insightfully writes,

> God is salvation in the renouncement of it, because He replaces (or compensates for) the illusion of having projected (your wish) by having to risk everything . . . If you search for God as salvation just for your self-affirmation, you will only find yourself. (González Faus, 2006, p. 15)

Thus, the greatness of Jesus of Nazareth has been reduced to "Christ-for-individual salvation". In all this we find a kind of morbid obsession with death and pardon, love and hate, rebellion and obedience, where the great psychological themes of guilt, rather than the evangelical ones, resound in simultaneously light and dark tones. In this way, Jesus' sacrifice, which was an existential sacrifice, a donation of his own life in extreme fidelity to God, is degraded to a mere ritual expiatory sacrifice. Christ is reduced to the role of scapegoat of our guilt, a salvation paradigm with great religious resonances, simultaneously psychological and from the Old Testament, but still a paradigm, we should admit, surpassed by the new mentality of the Gospels.

We have no doubt that preaching the message thus reduced has had, and will ever have, great success and drawing power. The themes of guilt ensure that. Certain rites and celebrations of popular piety (which can be fairly explained as "rites of the father's death") make it clear. (From a psychoanalytical point of view, we have interpreted the Semana Santa (Holy Week) celebrations in Andalusia, which seem to highlight the deep ambivalence before God in the never-ending celebration of a Father ("Nuestro Padre Jesús") who dies at the cross, never fully succeeding in resurrection (Domínguez-Morano, 1985, pp. 131–175).) But we should ask *why, what for,* and *before whom* we make people kneel by setting this sense of guilt in them. We should do it because, in effect, the price can be as high as that of perversion of the message and of keeping persons in an infantile and neurotic state. Perhaps this has been the most serious trap that the unconscious has set for faith.

This way of conceiving God and Jesus' salvation also generates an impregnation of the guilt feelings to the whole Gospel's message. A floating sense of guilt contaminates the Good News with a gloomy, sombre, and suffocating mood. The beatitudes, for instance, at the nuclear core of the message, are, thus, no longer about Jesus' felicitations and greetings to the followers of the Kingdom who set themselves those utopian values, but turns instead into the expression of a law (!) which cannot by any means be obeyed and, therefore, leads only to self-censorship and reproach. In the Christian community the reading of the beatitudes does not usually cause the joy of belonging in the Kingdom. Instead, it usually causes anxiety about "failure"(!), inferiority because of impotence in the face of the ideal, or the narcissistic wound connected with that unattainable "perfection". Legalism, as an expression of a faith dominated by the sense of guilt, results, then, in a narcissistic closure that worships the law as a mirror instead of worshipping God.

The calls for authenticity on the Sermon on Mount ("anyone who looks at a woman lustfully has already committed adultery with her in his heart", Matthew 5: 28) no longer seems like an invitation to truth and sincerity and instead comes to imply an omni-vigilant God who, from within the individual, morbidly scrutinises every wish and thought. God has, thus, turned into the heir of the dead father; that is, in the superego who dwells in our unconscious. Nothing escapes God; He sees and controls absolutely everything . . . We are no longer before that God "greater than our hearts" (1 John 3: 20) who, because He is God, in Fuertes' expression: "He cannot be morbid". (In the actual words of the poet: "*Contesta oh Dios hermoso/ que por ser Vos quien sois / no puedes ser morboso*".)

With these representations of God, it is quite evident, from a psychoanalytical viewpoint, that it is impossible to avoid a certain way of facing sexuality. There is an unavoidable logic uniting morals and dogma. Especially telling in this respect is Pohier's chapter titled "Recherches sur le fondements de la morale sexuelle chrétienne" (Pohier, 1972, pp. 173–223).

The birth of the law interiorised by the superego in the unconscious is closely linked to the vicissitudes of sexuality. The prohibition of incest constitutes the origin and foundation of all further prohibitions. This implies that sexuality will always take a decisive role in the strategies of guilt. Of that, we have plentiful evidence.

Sexuality, especially sensible of the sense of guilt and, hence, of religion, has to be denied time and time again in the dogmatic positions we have described. From there, one of the more grotesque distortions of the Good News has occurred: in giving sexual behaviour a central space in the moral life of believers, the Gospel has been morbidly erotised. The denial of sexuality and its consequent overvaluation constitutes one of the more grotesque traps that the unconscious has set for faith. The sense of guilt, paradoxically, has raised a monument to sexuality at the centre of the Christian experience, since the denial of sex leads to its solemnisation and enshrinement. We shall approach all this when, in Chapter Eight, we will ask ourselves about sexuality in the New Testament ensemble.

But if sexuality presents problems, aggressiveness does even more. If sexual drives are linked to the birth of the sense of guilt, aggressive drives are as well, even much more so. That is why religious man finds himself frequently at a loss as how to deal with his hostile drives. The path he generally finds is that of turning those drives on himself. But we should not forget how that is precisely the basic mechanism in the origin of the feelings of guilt, because it is there that self-reproach, remorse, and self-censorship originate.

Love brings problems, but hate brings them out even more. Thus, any possibility of aggressive expression is often denied, ignoring that aggressiveness is a dimension of life that does not have to be simply identified with pure destructiveness, abuse, or cruelty. Conflict, struggle, and violence (however understood) are systematically denied, sometimes even before being identified, recognised, or differentiated according to their value in their existence, and valued or discriminated according to a certain value hierarchy. The Gospel is, thus, unctuously sweetened and distorted.

Klein showed us how hate-induced anxiety is very intense from the first moments of life. That is why frequently the slightest trace of conflict makes us nervous. We all have terrible phantasies of what might happen if our aggressiveness is unleashed.

However, the gravity lies in how easily, from this situation, Christian love is falsified in a way that is quite frequent in ecclesial discourse. A "chemically pure" love is preached, which by eliminating (in psychoanalytical terms, "denying") all conflict, becomes a great lie and the most powerful alibi against a reality which, in itself, is unavoidably conflictive. That was certainly not the way Jesus behaved, as shown by the Gospel accounts describing the continuous conflict He faced, and which He Himself generated by announcing the Kingdom.

We should question, for instance, if love for the enemy implies that he would no longer be felt as such, as enemy, and, hence, as an object of aggressiveness. That is, felt and recognised, even if not exercised, aggressiveness. Denying such feelings, it could hardly be said that the enemy is such and that our relation with him would be a loving one. Imploding our aggression (or thinking we have by means of some odd artifice), we have turned the enemy into someone kind and friendly. From there, things are easy. But the problem is that by denying aggression, we progressively achieve the most perfect and sometimes sophisticated self-destruction. This way, a stench of death invades the Christian experience. An amazing ineffectiveness of Christian love in transforming reality (which necessarily implies conflict, contradiction, and struggle) is the other face of the coin. Proper elaboration of our violence does not mean forgetting that the Gospel has enemies and that identifying and recognising them as such should be a continual task; that is, if love for the enemy is not a pretext, and if it is true that "the Kingdom of Heaven has been subjected to violence, and violent people have been raiding it" (Matthew 11: 12). Although there are divergences about the interpretation and possible translation of this text (we shall return to this matter in Chapter Ten), there is no doubt that it is possible to offer a good amount of data from the New Testament to demonstrate the existence of personal and community conflicts accepted and confronted as such (Cf. v. gr. Galatians 2: 11–14 (Peter–Paul confrontation); Acts 15: 36–41 (conflict and separation of Paul and Barnabas); Acts 11: 1–18 (confrontation Paul–Jerusalem community), etc.)

It is not surprising that the image of the omnipotent God has driven us to a salvation message obsessively polaridsed in a purely expiatory conception of salvation and that, from there, sexuality and aggressiveness, love and death, have shaped the Christian experience. Guilt completes, as we have seen early on, a perfect triad with the sexual and aggressive drives.

The obsessive impregnation of rites

As we have analysed in the first chapter on the relationship established by Freud between neurosis and religion, it was precisely obsessive neurosis that made possible a deep interpretation of religious behaviour. In the rites that characterise this type of neurotic disorder, Freud found, in effect, a striking similarity with religious practices (Freud, 1907b, pp. 117–127; Fitz, 1990, pp. 141–147). This similarity has also been widely recognised by psychiatry and clinical psychology in general. It is not rare that even the patients themselves, without any previous psychoanalytical knowledge, describe their complicated obsessive ceremonies as a kind of religious rite. As we know, from this analogy Freud went on to identify obsessive neurosis as the most important key for his whole analysis of religious behaviour (Cf. the section headed "The process analogy" in Chapter Two of the present work; Domínguez-Morano, 1991, pp. 349–364).

The basic point of coincidence between obsessive rituals and religious practices was placed early on the feelings of unconscious guilt that take root in obsessive and pious individuals alike. That guilt, derived from repression of intense instinctual movements, unleashes a series of magical and ritualistic behaviour patterns as defence strategies.

When the contents of faith move towards those poles, towards conceptions of God that call up emotional ambivalence and, with it, a compulsion to guilt, rebellion, and pardon, then religious practice will approximate this obsessive logic. Sacramental practice will change to a somewhat sophisticated way of appeasing guilt feelings and spiritual life will become a privileged ground for the development of narcissistic perfectionism. We are dealing with the magic of rites and the triumph of mirrors.

The resonance of guilt structures upon Christian drama manifests as expression and representation in the life of the sacraments and their rituals. Often, in those rituals, the body itself joins the word, bringing to light the drama of guilt. On the other hand, the Roman Catholic doctrine of *ex opera operato*, insufficiently understood, has helped to form a magical conception of sacramental practice (Hierzenberger, 1969; Tornos, 1987). The symbolic dimension yields to the formal rigidity of rites: repeating invariably time and again the same words, the same gestures, the same signs, and the same chants. An example could be the obsessive implications that can be attached to repetitive prayers such as the Rosary (cf. Carroll, 1987, pp. 486–498).

Spontaneity in expression is taken away. Forms are sacralised and so, as described by Freud, "the petty ceremonials of religious practice gradually become the essential thing and push aside the underlying thoughts" (Freud, 1907b, p. 126). We are in a situation, well analysed by Castillo in his work on the sacraments, in which rite and magic dominates (Castillo, 1986, pp. 140–164; Vergote, 1978, pp. 129–146).

But the most grave concern, however, is not a mere matter of forms and attitudes in the sacramental practice. It is concern about the contents themselves, and how they can gradually change and distance themselves from the original meanings, through unconscious displacements. The sacramental theology itself seems to have undergone a malign transformation, in which it has grown intertwined with the unconscious themes of guilt. A detailed approach to each of the sacraments, beyond our present purpose, might be, no doubt, an excellent method to detect the latent guilt strategies found within the great themes of the faith experience. Let us examine two of the most commonly practised: the Eucharist and the sacramental confession.

As remarked in this chapter's introduction, from the very first salutation to God, prayer takes the form of admission of sin and a request for forgiveness: *mea culpa, mea culpa, mea maxima culpa*. All along its development, acts of celebration and thanksgiving have also been tinged by the obsession with sin, purification, and pardon. Bread is no longer the meal that creates brotherhood and wine is no longer the sharing of Jesus' death experience. In too many theologies and catechisms, bread and wine are turned into purifying elements that magically wash away sin, and came about mainly to "fortify" the purpose of inner cleanliness.

Frequently, those acts of remembrance suffer from a great omission: they forget that the pardon was already granted by God in order to eliminate anxiety arising from guilt and help, instead, to usher in the reality of His Kingdom. The Eucharist, joyous expression of gratitude, has been transformed to the point of frequently becoming a monument to the sense of guilt. The offering of gratitude has been buried by the weight of guilt (the invasion of guilt in the Eucharistic liturgy can be evaluated in the important documentation collected by Jungmann, 1952).

The sacrament of reconciliation has turned into the sacrament of penance and "confession", a term with so many unconscious resonances, which, therefore, has even acquired a certain clinical and psychopathological character. The "compulsion to confession" has rightly been described as a symptom closely related to feelings of guilt. It would seem that, in the sacrament of "confession", we had the sense of guilt speaking "live". The huge formal variation that the sacrament of reconciliation has adopted throughout history shows, in effect, the progressive emphasis on feelings of guilt which has taken place in Christian experience as a whole.

The trap that the unconscious has set for the experience of conversion is clearly visible, too. The inner change in which one looks to a new future is turned into a withdrawal into oneself that tries to calibrate the degree of responsibility for the past (the reference to God and His Kingdom turns up as self-reference linked to a sullied narcissism). The consolidation of obsessive attitudes, the objectification of the sense of guilt, the false illusions of reconciliation that quell and disguise deep aggressive drives, the complicity between penitent and confessor, the masochist satisfaction in the anxiety derived from guilt, and so on, are just some of the more remarkable traits that became part of the ritual of confession. In the sacrament of reconciliation, the traps of guilt are plain. A good part of the Christian community seems to have become aware of it and perhaps this is behind the huge present crisis in the practice of this sacrament (Morandi, 1983, pp. 231–243).

But if the sacramental practice is perverted into a magical rite for the appeasement of guilt, the ethical dimension of faith and spiritual life on the whole, placed in those spaces so close to obsession, easily becomes a perfect narcissistic hideaway.

The mirror of the ideal and the law

The superego, as heir and representation of the "dead father", has a say on any moral decision and any proposal of an ideal. But its voice, born as an intense reaction formation against sexual and aggressive drives, can grow distant in meaning from what the Christian praxis proposes. In a very dense article, Jesuit psychoanalyst Beirnaert (1970, pp. 364–375) discusses the questions which psychoanalysis poses to the moralist complete with the radicality such questions possess, so frequently left aside. Indeed, from its origins and evolution, the superego can place its dynamics and goals in very diverse sites from those that, on a rational level, constitute our objectives and our values. In fact, our particular history might have incorporated, through successive socio-cultural identifications, a whole series of norms, values, ideals, projects, goals, etc., which hardly correspond with the ideals and values of the Gospel. All this can be extremely delicate; therefore, it must be the target for deep and continual analysis. We can feel guilty without sin (like the scrupulous person) and we can also have sinned without feeling guilty ("Lord, when did we see you hungry or thirsty or . . . and did not help you?" the damned ask themselves in Matthew 25: 44).

Unless we pay attention, the superego voice can eventually impose itself on us, with all its mundane and anti-evangelical impregnations, and cause our praxis of faith to become purely submission to its powers. Our food will be to fulfil its will, the will of that "dead father" who dwells in the unconscious and not the will of the "living father" who dwells in heaven. It will be difficult to know which voice and command we should answer to (the functions of this necessary task of examination and discernment in an Ignatian understanding of our world are explored in an earlier work: Domínguez-Morano, 2003, pp. 117–134).

Only by their fruits shall we know if we are following the dark unconscious imperatives or if our alleged moral ideals articulate and develop above and beyond them. The morbid withdrawal within oneself, the narcissistic omnipotence feeling from the achieved "perfection", the rigid intolerance of oneself or others, the spiral of self-reproach and dissatisfaction, the unwillingness to reassess any law or ideal, these are some of the traits that indicate a total submission to the superego and are, therefore, signs to keep in mind when learning to detect which will we are answering to in our specific praxis.

On the passionate path to virtue, the world frequently disappears. Being saintly, living in purity, avoiding those humiliating behavioural slips that are so easy to fall into, strengthening your soul with that intense invigorating prayer, examining your conscience carefully; in this way, with a continuous vigilance, you go full speed ahead. But you are headed, unfortunately in many cases, towards forgetting the world and others. Thus we enter the *sancta sanctorum* hall of mirrors where our image is multiplied in a celebration of sacred self-eroticism. "We are good and perfect. Our Father will be happy and therefore He presents us with this spiritual sweet consolation. Our Father loves us as a reward for our diligent virtue". Our Father who is in . . .; where, in effect, is that Father?

But this idyllic mirage easily falls apart. The confines of virtue become suffocating. The mirrors suddenly start to reflect scorned and hated images. Sin, stain, pettiness, impotence, carelessness, and indolence seem to grow. "We are bad, imperfect and negligent; small, very small. We'll never reach the ideal which our Father proposes." The world remains out of touch. It becomes a pretext to continue on the passionate and tortuous road to virtue.

Paradoxically, the sense of guilt increases with virtue. "It is precisely those people who have carried saintliness further who reproach themselves with the worst sinfulness" (Freud, 1930a, p. 126). The reason is not surprising within the dynamics of guilt. Submission to the superego, representing the "dead father", entails repression of hostile drives and turning against oneself in the form of self-blame and the need for punishment. The crime is continual since the instincts are also. There is no possible solution. The misfortune is permanent (García Reinoso, 1977: the author tries to revive this Freudian line of research regarding guilt, which implies a dialectic situation; the greater the goodness, the greater the "internal authority").

In this situation, something extremely important has occurred; we have forgotten that what primarily matters in Christian faith is not to be a saint, but to follow Jesus. We have not been called (neither were the Apostles called) to dedicate ourselves to an ascetic school of perfection (Jesus was not an ascetic hermit, and neither did he present himself as such). But, instead, we are called to join Jesus on a mission to transform reality into the Kingdom of God, assuming his destiny as a willingness to suffer the cross. Therefore, is not so much a question of imitating Jesus, but of following in his footsteps. What is important is not to stare at ourselves in the mirror, but to look at the path of the one we wish to follow.

Furthermore, it is important to take into account that the law that is dictated by the representative of the "dead father", that is, the ideal he proposes, does not recognise time or history but knows how to take over the laws and the ideals which arise through various opportunities. That is why the law, being timeless, is able to accommodate the fashion of any time.

From there, the enslaving practice of virtue can appear in the more traditional, more moderate, modes or in the more progressive and revolutionary ones. What matters is the existence of the law which, taken as an absolute, becomes unquestionable. The whole world submits to that law or that ideal. Whether to live it as an inner spirituality or as outer engagement is, from that perspective, insignificant. The myths of traditional morality can be replaced by others, both exactly opposite and correlative, that possess an odd structural correspondence and identity. Outer engagement can hide the same morbid withdrawal within oneself, the same narcissistic feeling of omnipotence, and the same unwillingness to question the law or ideal itself (Beirnaert, 1964, pp. 33–44, 73–94).

We should ask if certain Christian groups have not, in effect, suffered a kind of displacement of the locations of the sense of guilt, going from inner spirituality to the anxiety of engagement, retaining the same compulsive traits ("we have to commit ourselves, we have to commit ourselves"). The absolute ideal can fall mercilessly upon us and on those around us. With the absolute ideal, we encounter the same ineffectiveness when trying to modify and transform reality towards the Kingdom of God, even if that reality is the only one we are aiming for, in theory.

In the same way, we should reflect on the formation and subsequent disintegration of engaged Christian groups that, in the end, experience the bitterness of having achieved nothing. Taken in by a certain ideology, the members create anxiety in others with their accusations and then fall prey to an ideological absolute, and end up broken upon discovering that they have the same inner problems previously rejected for the sake of the commitment which was consuming them. Reality does not allow itself to be changed when what draws us to it is either submission, or eternal rebellion against the paternal phantasmatic images that are embedded within ourselves.

Image of God and sense of guilt

The sense of guilt has moulded us from birth. Guilt has taken us from nature to culture. Thanks to the sense of guilt, we have been able to open up to reality and its values. But the sense of guilt can easily set traps, defaulting on its duties. Religion, inextricably united at birth with feelings of guilt, is where the sense of guilt can make life most difficult for us. The Christian faith can also turn into its accomplice and become entangled in its more toxic aspects. In this way, enclosed within the labyrinths of the unconscious, faith can turn into the executioner in the service of the death instincts, in this way betraying the deepest aspects of religion's liberating message.

This perversion of the Gospel can happen in some of the ways we have tried to illustrate in this chapter. Christian experience is invaded by a floating malaise, sadness, anxiety, and regret, so that often it is difficult to recognise within it the message of Good News.

Christ freed us from the agent of death and condemnation, represented by the law (2 Corinthians 3: 7–9): agent of death since it makes man self-centred in a desperate reach for salvation (Romans 7). That is why God wants us free from the anxiety of sin, in order to make possible in us a fertile encounter with which to transform life. In the Gospel, sin is, thus, left as something from the past, as if resolved. Freed from the labyrinths of guilt, it becomes possible to adhere to the Kingdom beyond the desperate attempt for personal salvation. For salvation, being true to one's own conscience is enough (Matthew 25: 31–46). Jesus came to show us how to go beyond that. While entangled by law, sin, and guilt, it will be impossible to find the way to our freedom and to the freedom of others, to self-acceptance and self-love, and to the acceptance and love of others. Ahead, we face a great task; to transform reality into the Kingdom and it will not be feasible while we are trapped by guilt.

The great God, larger than our conscience, the living and joyous God, the free and liberating God, has been constrained to the dimension of our conscience and unconsciousness. Turned into a God of death and sadness, an oppressed and oppressing God through "the grace" of guilt. God freed us from sin . . . it is time to free God from our sense of guilt.

We have endorsed our fear and anxiety by using God's signature, making Him an author of endless prohibitions that are often nothing more than the prohibitions of our unconscious against the instincts that are feared. We have given our fears the rank of divine laws. As an antidote to our poorly contained desires, we have fabricated a controlling God. Our wounded narcissism has created a God who functions as a crutch for our missing absolutes. To ensure submission to our dark ideals, we resort to an exigent, never satisfied God. God suffocates in our laws, grieves over our intransigent demands, dies in our self-aggressions, feels scorned by many of our religious motivations.

A God of life has revealed Himself to us, and our sense of guilt has turned Him into a God of death. It is very important that we free God from our sense of guilt, that we give life back to Him. We could, in this way, discover and create a God of joy, a God of play, a God of body, a God of battle, a God of sex, a God of freedom. God does not fear any of these things. God is the fulfilment of all these human realities. If we do not take them away from Him to hand them over to the demons, life will be possible, and with it, the labour of our deepest longing: that of happiness.

PART III

SEX, POWER, AND MONEY

CHAPTER EIGHT

The bonds of flesh

Psychoanalysis, among other human sciences, has shown that sexuality in its broadest sense assumes a very important place in our lives. The whole of our interpersonal relationships, including those of families, couples, and even community and pastoral relationships, are, thus, affected by our sexual–emotional dynamics.

It is also true that our ideals and our life projects are strongly conditioned by the inner world of desires, which takes shape through the years. Our specific libidinal structure and particular conscious or unconscious demands can, thus, favour or reinforce our goals in life. But they can also, at times, hinder or cast doubt on the direction and purpose of our life projects. We have all seen what happens when our deepest emotions have not been properly heard or taken into account; the life projects we had undertaken, perhaps too naïvely, can fall to pieces, sometimes dramatically.

Nobody is guaranteed a stable and final balance in this matter. Neither the most stable couple, nor the most successful celibate, nor the most integrated community are completely assured of their balance and stability. Thus, few dimensions in life have such a determining presence in the ensemble of our life experiences.

On the other hand, we all know how sexual behaviour is frequently a focus of concern, anxiety, and conflict for many people. Sexual behaviour has become, for many believers, as mentioned in the previous chapter, a relevant point when reviewing their relationship with God and the moral rectitude in their life, sometimes even to the extent of placing the problems of sexuality at the centre of their Christian experience.

Sexuality and psychoanalysis

Psychoanalysis has certainly caused a revolution in the understanding of sexuality. Against a "biologistic" definition that narrowly equates sexuality to genitality and procreation, psychoanalysis has looked into a whole ensemble of pleasure-producing phantasies and activities, present since childhood, that are not limited to the fulfilment of a physiological need. Genitality and procreation can be viewed as the tip of the iceberg, with the majority of its matter hidden beneath the surface. In essence, sexuality is a life force seeking a total pleasurable fusion encounter. Viewed as such, it is no longer seen as a luxury or a pleasure given in exchange for the burden attached to procreation.

When speaking about sexuality, psychoanalysis diverges from the designation of instinct, in order to emphasise its character of drive.[1] Instinct, unlike drive, implies an unlearned, biologically acquired behaviour; an instinct addresses automatically, almost mechanically, a very precise object and is triggered by well-determined stimuli. It has a precise neurological and muscular basis. But, as we climb up the biological scale, instinct progressively loses its rigidity and gains flexibility. On reaching the human species, it blossoms into drive. We break through the old biological constraints, allowing the historical and biographic influences to have a say.

The whole process has huge consequences for the understanding of human sexuality: the drive is no longer about the satisfaction of the previously determined goals and objects, as with instincts. In this way, sexuality "spreads" and permeates the whole being, to the point of giving basis to the assertion that everything in the human being has a sexual dimension, even if nothing can be understood as pure and exclusively sexual. As Merleau-Ponty expresses, from a point of view different from psychoanalysis, there is osmosis between sexuality and existence, a reciprocal influence between the sexuality of human beings and the way they conceive life (Merleau-Ponty, 1975, pp. 171–191). (On the psychoanalytic interpretation of sexuality: Freud, 1905d, 1907c, 1908c,d, 1914c, 1923e. A good, perhaps too concise, summary of the theories of Freud, Klein, Reich, and Lacan can be found in Simon, 1975.)

Achieving "maturity" and balance between all those forces present in sexuality is one of the greatest hopes in any person's life. Not an easy matter, indeed, and many mistakes can be made along the way. In addition, ideological contamination can make the task still more difficult (I have addressed the issue of sexuality and affective maturity in a work entitled *Los registros del deseo*, Domínguez-Morano, 2001a).

Perhaps we should remember that the very concept of "maturity" is ambiguous and fairly relative. Maturity, in effect, is nothing but a never fully reached ideal, which, on the other hand, lends itself to taking in a whole series of omnipotent phantasies of an infantile character. It could be said that nobody fully reaches maturity and total integration of his affective and sexual world. A series of more or less effective defence barriers will always be present and maturity will, in consequence, be only relative, depending on how well the subject articulates the defences and drives. Neurotic and perverse elements always play a part, to varying degrees, in our libidinal organisation. The acceptance of these neurotic or perverse elements, with their unavoidable conflicts, can also be used as a guideline to evaluate the "maturity" of a person.

There are certainly risks in substituting the ideals of "maturity" for those of sanctity, and the danger of falling into the same narcissistic trap of seclusion that, in other times, was common in the ascetic realms of spirituality. That would also limit an individual's success in two important areas needed for balanced personal growth: the capacity to work (in the broadest and richest sense), and his capacity to love and be loved (from the viewpoints of each subject, according to his particular personality structure).

The institutions should also be more cautious when assessing their members' affective maturity. Too frequently, motivations far from the properly psychological come into play. Often, these contain the secret intention of making the supposed affective "maturity" meet the objectives and goals of the group itself, which might also not be very "mature".

In any case, psychoanalysis has given us a broad perspective on the conflictive possibilities that the long and complex road of libidinal evolution can lead to. Neurosis, perversion, and integration are the three possible final destinations Freud refers to.

Freud, in his *Three Essays* (1905d), presents the difficult problem of access to instinctual integration from the first situation, neurosis, which undoubtedly qualifies as "perverse" and "polymorphous". In other words, infantile sexuality is characterised by the search for pleasure apart from genitality and independently of procreative aims. Also, sexuality appears in childhood multiplied in a whole series of drives, "partial drives", which hardly achieve integration. The repression of such drives gives rise to neurosis, while the failure of integration in a final organisation, which Freud calls "genital", would cause perversion.

That integration, which approaches the concept of "maturity", implies, among other things, the solution of the oedipal conflict by renouncement of the phantasies linked to parents (renouncement, we could say, of going in search of "fathers" and "mothers" throughout one's life). Second, it would involve the capacity to integrate the sensual and tender streams of sexuality in a relationship. Finally, it requires the capacity for an encounter with the other as a free and different "you" and not as a mere object of dependency, possession, or dominion. (Dependency and possession would correspond to the kinds of relationship typical of the first stages of libidinal evolution. In the first, the "oral stage", the personal relationship type basically articulates on the key of being "breast" or "mouth" towards the other. The relationship mode of possession would demonstrate the libido articulation of the "anal stage", in which the sadistic and masochistic elements are predominant.) In conclusion, "maturity" would coincide with the capacity to establish relationships, giving up the phantasy of becoming everything for the other, or for the other to become everything for oneself. That totality, which is the ultimate objective of sexuality, will have to be given up as a condition to enable the possibility of a real, positive, and joyous encounter with the other. (As mentioned in the chapter on praying, not even God can be seen as a total object who would fulfil the ultimate aspiration of desire, denying in this way the condition of our loneliness. The mystics, as we recalled there, recognised this better than anybody (Domínguez-Morano, 2016).)

Furthermore, we should add that sexuality, through its unavoidable unconscious connections, has a certain boundless and "transcendental" character. It is present in each one of us as a reality that is out of our hands, which holds us instead of us holding it. Hence, it appears as a reality threatening in its demands and, at the same time, as a reality that beckons us with promises of supreme gratification and happiness. In consequence, it is surrounded by fascination and terror. It seems to promise happiness, a plenitude that would never withhold affection, yet, at the same time, comes with the shadow of guilt, death, and destruction.

This invasive and threatening character of sexuality contributes to the need we all feel to defend ourselves from it. Otherwise, we could just do away with it all: couple, family, institution, even with the individual himself. In consequence, sexuality appears, on the one hand, as the supreme symbol of happiness, and, on the other hand, as the supreme symbol of prohibition and taboo. Sexuality cannot help but intersect with law and prohibition. We are quite far today from naïvely imagining a happy primitive life in a culture free from any sexual limitation.

Sexuality as a search for an impossible totality is analogous to the religious experience. As we explored in Chapter Six on the image of God, the religious and sexual experiences do not have dissimilar roots. The maternal Eros of infancy, as the search for an all-encompassing everything that would satiate any affective deprivation, constitutes the infrastructure of the future desire for God as totality (cf. Chapter Six of the present work, "The God of the child and the God of Jesus", particularly the section titled "The maternal totality as grounding of divinity"). From all this, the relationship between sexuality and religion is usually close and ambivalent. The history of religions is there to demonstrate how sexuality can reach a sacred status (fertility rites, sacred prostitution, etc.) or be considered a prime enemy of transcendence, precisely because of the totality it longs for. The taboo prohibitions appear, then, in order to prevent any competition with the gods (Bastide, 1950; Devereux, 1972; Lévi-Strauss, 1968; Malinowski, 1937; Mead, 1952).

In these general reflections, it should also be mentioned that sexuality has, without any doubt, a sociological or, more specifically, sociopolitical dimension. Throughout civilisation, sexuality has appeared as a privileged symbol of power. Impotence defines someone who is "unable", in both senses of the word. The thing is that sexuality appears, even before any other human dimension, as "the privileged basis for self-vindication against another who has the privileges one would like to possess and who prevents our access" (Pohier, 1972, p. 192, translated for this edition). This explains the close relationship between the exercise of power and sexual repression. The latter can fulfil a function that is not only economic or socio-political, as announced by Reich's early works, but aims to convert the repressively trained subjects into obedient elements and vassals of constituted power. Therefore, any institution that hopes to firmly impose its power on others will take a repressive stance on sexuality for the same reason. Most types of political dictatorships or institutional tyrannies have intuitively applied these methods. We shall revisit this in the final pages of this chapter.

The reflections outlined above have the single purpose of highlighting the importance of sexuality for the whole individual and for collective life. Therefore, we cannot avoid wondering which role the Gospels assign to this important dimension of life.

As we have seen, psychoanalysis has opened new perspectives on many dimensions of sexuality; this could bring new insights with which to perhaps glimpse aspects of the Gospel texts that, up to now, might have gone unnoticed. The role of the family in the configuration of erotic life, the father's function as representative of sexual prohibition, or the phantasies linked to our masculine or feminine condition, are all elements about which we now have a great amount of information and can provide surprising perspectives if, through them, we undertake a new interpretation of Jesus' message. The following chapter is dedicated to this attempt.

A surprising silence

A reality with such implications for personal and social life encourages one to search within Jesus' message for a source of direction and guidance. However, upon first reading of the Gospel texts, we are surprised at the secondary place sexual issues occupy. Certainly, there are neither indications of sacredness nor taboo (that is why it is surprising to find theses such as those of Jacobelli (1990) trying to assign the character of a sacred sign to sexuality). But we are also forced to admit that the relevant references available are so scarce that the believer can hardly use them to construct a thorough and precise frame of reference as guidance for behaviour on such a slippery road.

It is quite obvious that, in Jesus' message, sexuality does not occupy a sacred space where the subject can find a privileged place for his encounter with God. On the other hand, sexual behaviour, regardless of the fascination it can exert, does not appear as an obstacle to the believer's recognition of God as the only absolute. Most of the exegetes acknowledge that the New Testament does not offer complete and systematic teaching on sexual sins, and certainly the authors are far from giving a privileged place to sexuality in their pastoral concerns (Fuchs, 1995; Humbert, 1970, pp. 182–183). The central interests are concentrated elsewhere: apparently, what can most hinder man's journey towards God is not sexuality, but, rather, injustice, money, legalism, pharisaic hypocrisy, and even, in certain cases, religious practices themselves.

The absence of concern about sexual behaviour can even be found shocking. Let us consider, for instance, that something as significant as Jesus' celibacy is not even explicitly mentioned in any New Testament writing. This is especially surprising if we consider that it belongs to a cultural framework in which family and fertility were regarded as privileged spaces for God's presence and benediction. Celibacy, however, used to be regarded as a sign of divine curse, or as a religious inconsistency, not well taken in Judaist communities. For instance, we have the case of Rabbi Simeon Ben Azzai in the first century CE, who, because he remained unmarried, had to endure the reprobation that "he preached well but did not practise his own preaching" (Vermes, 1977, pp. 108–109). In parallel, no precise information is given on the marital status of Jesus' followers. We can gather that at least the majority were married, since Paul, when mentioning the rights he was freely giving up, writes, "Don't we have the right to take a believing wife along with us, as do the other apostles and the Lord's brothers and Cephas?" (1 Corinthians 9: 5). Yet, it is presented as a question that the New Testament authors do not seem to be concerned about.

On the other hand, it is meaningful that Paul does not draw any theological or moral principle from Jesus' celibacy when he tries to lay the foundation for the condition of virginity, and, when answering a query about marital status, he carefully differentiates what is the

Lord's command from what is just his own opinion (1 Corinthians 7: 1–16).

However, it is not only the matter of marital status. There are many other questions surrounding sexuality which deeply worry many Christians and on which Jesus says nothing. For instance, we have no explicit references in the Gospel on behaviour issues such as masturbation, homosexuality, or on sexual relationships before marriage, issues which so frequently worry and torment the conscience of many believers. (We have limited these reflections on the theme of sexuality to the Gospels. We have consciously left aside other New Testament writings in which there are changes, sometimes significant. Once again, however, we should recall that basic hermeneutical criterion which sets the primacy of the Gospels' texts in the evaluation and interpretation of all the other writings of the New Testament.)

No doubt all this is surprising and can even awaken the suspicion that such silence is hiding an unconscious denial of sexuality, since the best repression is precisely that of declaring the repressed non-existent. Something similar happens in certain circles in which silence on sexuality indicates its denial and condemnation.

Yet, it is also obvious that the Gospel silence on sexuality is not generalised silence. It is silent on some specific issues, but is also clearly assertive on other matters that, directly or indirectly, have an impact on the world of sexuality. We are compelled to think that the Gospel silence on the matter does not come from fear of sexuality, but from the freedom to properly contextualise sexual behaviour. This silence is extremely eloquent if we look at it in the wider context of what we are told about sexuality, not at the level of specific behaviour, but, rather, in the ways in which it is channelled and configured.

Jesus, or the "passion" (epithymia) for the Kingdom

The term "epithymia" meant originally the direct drive towards food and sexual satisfaction, or simply desire in general. This was the sense used by the evangelists in relation to hunger (Luke 15: 16), longing (Luke 22: 15) or even the desire for God's word or revelation (Matthew 13: 17) (Kosnik, 1977, pp. 24–32. There, we are advised how the concept of *epithymia* in St Paul changed its meaning under Stoic influence and became equated with the fruit of sin. The Stoic aversion to "passion" kept its influence in ethical Christian thinking from St Paul's time until the present day).

When we speak of Christ's "passion" for the Kingdom, we do it with full awareness of the term we are using. In doing so, we want to express that Jesus' life is presented in the Gospel as completely focused on the attainment of an "object" (in the psychoanalytical sense, object is the correlative of love, the aim in the search for totality) which, in his case, we can identify as the establishment of the Kingdom of God. If the total absence of data on Jesus' sexual situation compels us to leave it out of specific historical research, we can venture from his general behaviour that there is in Jesus a "passion" that absorbs him, frees him, channels all his psychical energy, and becomes the essence of his joy and personal fulfilment.

Starting from this "passion", Jesus' behaviour as described in the Gospel tellingly reveals a position on sexuality that would fit that of the man who has found total freedom in relation to it. Jesus' behaviour in interpersonal relationships is hugely illustrative of that freedom. There is no person from whom Jesus feels the need to protect himself. He accepts social misfits, publicans, and sinners with an openness which provokes scandal. A woman widely known as a sinner weeps at his feet, wipes them with her hair, covers them with kisses, and anoints them with perfumed ointment. Jesus did not ignore, as the Pharisee thought, that the woman was a sinner, but since her love was so great as to break the taboo that marginalised her socially, Jesus sides with her against the religious professional (Luke 7: 36–50). This action confirms that there is something graver than misplaced sexual behaviour: lack of love.

Only from a free position towards sexuality is it at all possible to break the taboos around it and to proclaim that the "impure" can earn a place in the Kingdom before those who conform to current sexual standards (Matthew 21: 32). Reich, the master of the so-called "social revolution", rightly said that Jesus was the prototype of a free man who expressed in his behaviour a personality in which the deepest vital needs are resolved. For Reich, neurotic men could not stand Christ because his freedom at all levels was intolerable to them. Neurotic and blinkered men killed Life in murdering Christ (Reich, 1953).

Jesus did not present himself as an enemy of the body, preaching sacrifice and privation. He was neither a hermit nor an Essenian, nor did he present himself as such. He even caused surprise and shock with his refusal to participate in an ascetic or sacrificed life. Neither himself nor his disciples observed fasting (Mark 2: 18–19), and he was called a glutton and a drunkard (Matthew 11: 19). The cross he asked his followers to bear and which he bore himself until death was the sign of his total devotion and his fidelity to what he loved to the extreme. His passion for the Kingdom drove him to deny himself until the end and to let himself rot as the grain of wheat. His life, his work, and his love gave meaning to his death and not the other way around. His end was the supreme demonstration of how much he had loved and the expression of total fidelity to that object of love.

From this passion for the Kingdom, Jesus' celibacy becomes an ideal for all those who would "have made themselves eunuchs for the sake of the kingdom of heaven" (Matthew 19: 12). From there, we can rightly understand the place that the Gospel reserves for sexuality. That place comes, as we shall see, from the deep subversion of social values that the Kingdom of God sets in motion.

We do not intend to present here an overview of the diverse ways of approaching sexuality, or delve into the complex issue of the Christian sense of virginity. Suffice to say that Jesus' behaviour in this regard constitutes a paradigm for any call to virginity or celibacy. It eloquently illustrates what psychoanalysis has called "sublimation" (the possibility of experiencing sexuality with a change of its objects and aims). Sublimation entails many difficulties, both in its theoretical understanding and in its practical exercise, which we will not explore here (there is information and a bibliography on them in Domínguez-Morano, 2001a, pp. 241–267).

Establishing the Kingdom, as Jesus advocated, implies, in effect, a radical change of all the systems of values in which society finds support. As anthropologist Magli asserts, no revolution has ever tried to carry out a project such as that of Jesus of Nazareth. No genius we have known, she tells us, has ever tried to totally change the cultural system, since the genius operates generally in a single sphere of culture or society: the arts, politics, ethics, economics, etc. The substantial difference between the genius and Jesus is that the latter broke the cultural model in which he lived, battering and destroying with blunt logic the diverse relationships that bound and institutionalised it. Jesus questioned the very structure of sacred things, not only denying certain rites or certain laws, but fundamentally changing the religious categories and the social structures supported by them (Magli, 1982, pp. 27–33).

The proposal of the Kingdom of God implies a disruption of social values that has unavoidable impacts on certain approaches to sexuality. It is not only a matter of sexual behaviour or prescriptions. It is, rather, a questioning of the fundamental structures in which sexuality operates: the family, the father's role, and the woman's place.

Only from this perspective shall we be able to understand what the Gospel says about sexuality. Otherwise, we would just remain in a state of surprise at the silence on the matter, or else trapped in the analysis of the few terms directly related to sexual behaviour. Unfortunately, this is what usually happens, producing, at best, a loss of the great horizons we could contemplate. Once again, "we can't see the wood for the trees".

Jesus and desacralisation of the family

The family is, no doubt, where sexuality first takes shape and direction. During infancy, family relationships mould the fundamental attitudes towards sexuality. Also, through those relationships, in the complex interplay of positive and negative identifications, the psychosexual masculine and feminine role configuration is achieved.

Even more important is the fact that the same parental figures constitute the first love objects targeted by that infant sexuality. Hence, the first basic prohibition on sexuality is embodied also in the parental figures. Thus, the "bonds of flesh" have, in humankind, a basic double meaning; on the one hand, "bonds of blood", attached to a history, a family saga, and, on the other hand, "bonds of flesh", attached by libido to certain love objects.

Thus, the family is the place in which sexuality clashes for the first and primal time with limitation, prohibition, the law. The "bonds of blood" are forbidden as "bonds of flesh". In consequence, sexuality carries an indelible mark with the name of the father's figure. That figure will remain as the symbol of law and prohibition, unavoidably limiting desire.

As can be seen, the family is the privileged space in which the fundamental attitudes are born and developed. The parent's sheltering, protection, and affection or, at the other end of the spectrum, the parent's indifference, apathy, and aggressiveness, give shape to the affections, emotions, feelings, and, in general, to the balance or imbalance of the future subject. That is why the links of love, the most fundamental prohibitions, the most important bonds of the person are focused on the members of his own family. Thus, the family node both limits and contains the affective space so fundamental in society. Furthermore, these affective relationships determine and guide the individual's other relationships, such as those in economic, religious, or ideological spheres.

So, it is understandable that any social institution would show a keen interest in maintaining and defending this first node of relationships. Via family life, the individual conforms to the patterns and norms of behaviour of each culture. Because of its affective implications, it is the most effective instrument for transmitting the values, criteria, and conventions that are imprinted on each subject, who becomes a transmitter in his turn. So, the family is the manner in which each culture and civilisation perpetuates itself; an essential means for historic continuity. As we shall see later, it also helps the future adult to believe in, and submit to, authority.

However, the family is also, for the same reasons, a focal point for ambiguity, psychic mutilation, oppression, and conflict. All negative values are also assimilated through it. The gravest affective imbalances are equally forged there. It can become, using the expression of a psychotherapy patient, a "neurosis-producing factory", and might even be, according to the anti-psychiatry family theoretician Cooper, "the territory for the most violent crimes of our society" (Cooper, 2006, p. 9. Other works on the psycho-social problems in the family are Lacan, 1938; Laing, 1971; Salvador Bertrán, 2009).

So, the price for maintaining the family institution at all costs can be quite high. However, the social, political, and religious institutions always seem ready to pay it. There is talk of upholding and improving the family, while always assuming that the model is unquestionable.

Now, Jesus' position towards the family is surprising and even disconcerting. Accustomed, as we are, to consider the family as an untouchable institution, many passages in the Gospels shock our sensibilities. We forget that for Jesus, family is not something that must be preserved at all costs, as we often tend to think, and neither is it sacrosanct; a sacred and absolute duty.

Jesus came to bring a new order in human relationships, to which the "bonds of flesh" are subject (Mark 3: 31–35; Matthew 10: 37; Luke 14: 26). A new system of parentage is thus opened, setting aside the biological order. A new community of the Kingdom takes centre stage, and the bonds of the spirit prevail over the bonds of the flesh. From this moment on, the family will have a place in the Kingdom of God, as long as the bonds of flesh are informed and structured by those of the spirit. But if the bonds of the flesh try to maintain their primacy or enter into conflict with the bonds of the spirit, the family will become disqualified.

On the one hand, Jesus sees the family bonds as a reference model for the new communitarian family. Jesus uses the examples of family and general human relationships and the situations they entail as parables to highlight the meaning of his message (for instance, Matthew 22: 2–3; 24: 19; John 16: 21; Luke 16: 27; Mark 10: 19; Matthew 7: 9, etc.).

But, on the other hand, family bonds are radically called into question when they oppose the values that must inspire the new community. Since the family represents and transmits the dominant social values of that culture, the conflict between family values and the values of the Kingdom comes into open conflict. In so far as the family unit represents and fosters the social values of owning a lot, climbing the social ladder, and outshining others, family bonds amount to a chain which Jesus' followers are called to break.

That is why the fundamental message of the Gospel implies a drastic confrontation with what the family usually is and represents. In some way, the conflict is unavoidable. This was the case for Jesus himself, whose relatives thought he was out of his mind because he was not pursuing the right kind of success, was not living for himself, but with total submission to a life of service, because in his own town, among his relatives and in his own home, he announced the impossibility of being a prophet (Mark 6: 1–6; Matthew 13: 55–58; Luke 4: 16–24). With all that, Jesus asserted publicly and openly the substitution of communitarian relationships for his family. His mother and his brothers are those that, like him, listen and are faithful to the only paternity possible on earth (Mark 3: 31–35; Matthew 12: 46–50; Luke 8: 19–21). The womb that bears and the breast that nurses, the biological relations, are replaced by listening to the word and by its fulfilment, that is, the bonds of the spirit (Luke 11: 27).

The establishment of the Kingdom collides with the dominant values of society; that is why the confrontation is going to affect the very core of the family institution. The division of the family, so threatening for the social framework, was announced by Jesus and assumed as an unavoidable condition for the establishment of other, more humane, relationships: parents and children will clash; brothers will denounce each other and will be delivered to death (Matthew 10: 21; Mark 13: 12; Luke 21: 16). War will break out between family members because of Jesus (Luke 12: 51–53; Matthew 10: 34–36). He proclaimed himself as a necessarily higher object of love than those of the family: father and mother cannot be loved more than himself (Matthew 10: 37–38 par; Luke 14: 26–27). That is why those who follow him abandon their parents and, with them, all their relatives (Matthew 4: 20–22; Mark 1: 20, Luke 5: 11).

Such is Jesus' radicality. It is a radicality that invites deep scrutiny of the sacralising attitude which society easily adopts towards the family. For Jesus, the fact that the family serves as a vehicle, a guarantor, and a constraint for sexuality does not mean it cannot be questioned. There is something more important than the control and direction of sexuality between established margins. Those margins, which simultaneously serve to interiorise dominant social values, can be used to perpetuate values that oppose those of the Gospel. That is why Jesus does not view the family as an absolute and sacred institution. From the moment that the family represents and perpetuates oppressive relationships, it turns into another structure that the Kingdom has to contest. Because not even the holiest values the family can transmit justify, in the eyes of the Gospel, the violation of values such as radical equality, liberty, and autonomy, devotion and service, so frequently infringed by the family institution. From the moment that the family prevents or hinders the individual's freedom, and, hence, his disposition towards the Kingdom, Jesus opposes the family. The idea of family division and the loss of control of sexuality did not paralyse him with fear, as is often rationalised. Instead, he demystified and put into perspective that basic structure in which sexuality is given shape and primary focus.

Jesus: moving beyond the father

For Jesus' followers, the nuclear family takes second place to the faith community as the primary form of relationship. The bonds of flesh lose their primacy, but, in addition, in the new structure, the relationships based on ties of filiation are redefined. Everybody, fathers, mothers, and children (bonds of the flesh), are called to become spiritual brothers and sisters (bonds of the spirit), which makes all of them children of the Father in heaven. All this means that the Christian is called to become an adult for whom the father and the mother become brother and sister, friends, through the bonds of the spirit. Fatherhood and motherhood, the bonds of the flesh, have to be overcome. "Woman", not "mother" is the only way Jesus addresses Mary in the Gospel, a totally uncommon way for a son to address his mother in the literature of the time (Brown, R. E., 1979, pp. 898–916; Mateos & Barreto, 1979, p. 150).

If the family structure is dependent on the communal structure, an even greater effort must be made to overcome the definition of the father figure therein. There is no place for the father in the Christian community (Mark 10: 24–31). We shall dwell on this important matter throughout the next chapter. Now, however, we are interested in highlighting that, by trying to go beyond any given father figure, Jesus is pointedly questioning a critical aspect of sexuality.

If the family is the primary place where sexuality is shaped and channelled, the father figure plays a key role in limiting desire and possible objects of love. The bonds of the flesh are forbidden as bonds of libidinal love. That is why the father figure, as we have seen all along, exerts in the family the role of the first representative of prohibition and law. Only in this way will the subject be able to see himself as such, that is, awakened to a reality that forbids total and immediate wish fulfilment, and called also to acknowledge a basic lack, which nobody or nothing will ever quench.

Yet, if the father incarnates and represents a primary and necessary repression of sexuality (the prohibition of incest), he is also going to represent the basis for that fundamental instance of the psyche, the superego, which, as analysed in the previous chapter, will dwell inside the subject, watching and censoring all instinctual activity. The superego is the internalised father figure, and, at the same time, the basis for the faith the individual will place in authority in the future, and for later seeking of paternal figures. In the course of its development, the superego, in effect, assimilates the influence of those people who have occupied the parent's place: educators, professors, and idealised role models. Thus are born the "great men", the leaders of the masses, the great authorities who establish the dynamics of submission that we focus on in the next chapter.

The human heart can suffer nostalgia for the human father and also a temptation to submit to others holding a paternal role and demanding submission, adoration, and control. In this dynamic, which is the subject of our present interest, repression of sexuality plays a decisive role. If the father acquired power by placing himself as the prohibition and the law of the child's sexual desires, in a similar way any authority that aims effectively to dominate others will recognise sexual prohibition as an excellent way to maintain the authority it desires. That is the deep-seated reason that sexual repression is such a key instrument in any kind of tyranny or dictatorship. Any repression of this kind weakens the ego and reinforces the superego and, hence, authority. As in hypnosis, childhood-like conditions are achieved: an attitude either so imposing and intimidating, or so tender and protective, that the hypnotised subject gives up his own ego. But, in its turn, there is also a dialectical relationship between the superego and power: the greater the density of the superego, the weaker and easier it is to handle the ego; the weaker the ego, the greater is its need for the superego and authority.

Moving on from the father figure, as Jesus proposed, takes on new salience here. Overcoming that is, first of all, a necessity for attaining an adult position. Fighting against the tendency to remain attached to the parental figures as a means of protection, Jesus proclaims the need for a personal autonomy to make dedication to the Kingdom possible. Somehow, every Christian must ask their parents why they are searching for him or her, as Jesus did in the temple. By choosing to stay in Jerusalem without warning, he shows his independence and liberty from family authority. As the psychoanalyst Dolto suggests, Jesus, in the temple, divests his parents of the unavoidable possessive dimension that parenthood entails, and shows his will to begin an adult life. This adult man knows only one final and inviolable relationship, that of the sole Father in heaven, an absolute relationship, which, precisely for this reason, questions any instance of paternal authority (Dolto, 1977a, pp. 35–40).

But it is not enough to become autonomous in relation to our parents. With even more reason, any type of paternal projection on other social figures must be overcome. Nobody on earth can claim paternal authority. Nobody can exert paternal power or protection functions in the Christian community. "But you are not to be called rabbi, for you have one teacher, and you are all brothers. And call no man your father on earth, for you have one Father, who is in heaven. Neither be called instructors, for you have one instructor, the Christ" (Matthew 23: 8–10).

He who follows Jesus leaves his father behind and, with him, all protection and authority over him. By forfeiting everything "he shall receive a hundredfold now . . . and in the world to come eternal life". But the father's place will remain forever empty. In Jesus' words, during this time, a person will receive a hundred times more: houses, and brethren, and sisters, and mothers, and children, and lands; all of it in the Christian community: *the father is the only thing he will not find a hundred times* (Mark 10: 29–31). This omission in the Gospel is intriguing and meaningful in relation to the rewards for Jesus' followers. No doubt it is more significant than a mere oversight by the evangelist. It is way of saying that, in the new order of relationships, the father figure as a symbol of imposition and power has no place. Nobody can assume this role in order to exercise power over others.

In the Kingdom's new order of relationships, the only bond is that of brotherhood in mutual service. This is how Jesus related to his own people. That was the reason for making a clean break with the role of lord and master by washing the feet of his disciples. This was a rupture that, as often occurs, created a backlash among his people. Peter rejects categorically that egalitarian message; he is not ready to accept that break with the asymmetric relationship between master and disciple; he needs to be subservient, he needs somebody above him to submit to, and from whom to receive protection and security. He will have to accept that, in Jesus' community, there is no place for a pedestal because there, as in true friendship, the distance between the ideal and the real must be short.

The distance is great between servant and master, between teacher and disciple, because one knows, has power, and the other does not: "a servant does not know his master's business". But Jesus has communicated everything to his people, and, therefore, creates a new type of relationship based on equality, that is why he can call them "friends" (John 15: 15). Within this friendship, there is no place for a law.

In effect, perhaps friendship is the only type of human relationship not socially legislated. Love between spouses, the relationship between parents and children, and that of brothers and relatives, are legislated. In friendship, though, the relationship is maintained or broken solely by the individuals' free decision, and is based on the state of the friendship itself. It is love springing from freedom, that grows within unrestricted attraction and is maintained by the sole force of a freely accepted fidelity, delivered between those who feel bonded by that model form of human relationship. It is love, free of any price or interest. That is why "there is no greater love than to lay down one's life for one's friends" (John 15: 13), because the pinnacle of love coincides with the apogee of freedom (Domínguez-Morano, 2001a, pp. 209–240).

In the community of the Kingdom, therefore, there is no place for relationships which are not defined by freedom and, thus, by overcoming the father figure (Rahner, 1977, pp. 98–103; we shall offer more important bibliographic information on this theme in the next chapter). The Christian should not nostalgically search and long for the father. The father figure dwelling inside the psyche of the person must be buried. Only in this way can he read his own story as a future to be fulfilled. So he has to free himself from the law as a symbol of paternal imposition or irrational superego demands. Instead, he is called to freedom, with the capacity of discernment in relation to his own conscience, expressing his personal autonomy with mature and rational control of the instincts.

It is not possible to put a hand to the plough in the task of accepting the Kingdom as commitment to the future and to look back to bid farewell to the father, because, in doing so, that father from the past lives on inside the subject. The father's place must remain empty; a space that enables the individual to know himself and gives him autonomy and liberty. That is why we must "let the dead bury their own dead".

This overcoming of the father to which Jesus invites Christians, even if not obvious at first sight, clearly alludes to the spirit of freedom that must preside over their lives and, more particularly, their relation with sexuality. That is understandable if we take into account the close relationship which psychoanalysis has shown exists between the realm of the paternal and the exercise of sexuality itself.

Jesus, liberator of women

In any type of society in which the family represents a sacred space revolving around the father figure, the masculine element becomes, in itself, a fundamental privilege. Human essence will be represented by masculine values, manly power, in paternity. So the Hebrew man said his daily prayer thanking God "for not creating me a woman" (Swidler, 2007). Having children, and male children, was considered the highest wealth; not having them, the lowest poverty. "Everybody is happy when a boy is born; everybody is sad when a girl is born", goes a rabbinical saying.

The woman, deprived of the human essence of masculinity, remained or remains marginalised. Her vital function lies in complying with the man's requests, sacralised as the family itself. For her sexual function, the woman becomes the man's object and her existence is reduced to the biology of her body: to be wife and mother.

When the woman is objectified in this way and constrained to her biological functions, she loses her voice and her word. The object does not speak and does not wish. So, the woman's role is to be responsive to the voice and the desire of the only subject, the male. The denial of her sexuality through her confinement to the tender and affective world of motherhood leads to an investment of her own body as the only love object allowed, and, hence, to a markedly narcissistic position. Furthermore, this feminine narcissism is socially fed and favoured in order to make her the erotic object of the male, whom she has to seduce and attract passively. Only thus can she take the sole role left to her: wife and mother. When the woman assumes the function of erotic object, she has to spend all her energy in keeping herself as such: young, attractive, "feminine", and pleasant to the male. But, in addition, all that has to be done passively. Her initiative must be kept secret. Any expression of her own sexual wishes makes her suspect, because it has been socially agreed that the only position for a woman other than that of mother is that of the prostitute. Thus, everything leads to a dangerous split between the expressions of sexuality *vs.* expressions of tenderness. The denial of the first is used for the excessive development of the second, resulting in many problems, with consequences for the male also (Chasseguet-Smirgel, 1964; Devereux, 1982; Domínguez-Morano, 2012; Ruitenbeck, 1967; Schneider, 2004).

In Jesus' times, even more than today, the unique glory that a woman could have at her disposal was to possess a fertile body (Carr, 2003; Gómez Acebo, 2012; León, 2012; Magli, 1987; Marconi, 2008; Schüssler Fiorenza, 1983; Swidler, 2007). That is why Jesus' mother was flattered when a village woman said, "Blessed is the womb that bore you and the breasts at which you nursed!" (Luke 11: 27). However, in the Kingdom of God, the woman's confinement to her biological functions experiences a radical change. The bonds of flesh and blood are no longer her sole glory; now she can listen to the word of God and actively respond to it. The woman is, beyond her body, also called to listen to God's message on history and to respond with her voice as the subject she is, and, therefore, as the bearer of an initiative and an expressed desire.

Since the woman is the bearer of a desire and a word, she is no longer, according to Jesus, an object to possess, an instrument to use, or a property to own or destroy. Hence, the position he took on divorce, provoking scandal among those around him. It did not take much to repudiate a wife and solicit divorce: the sighting of a more beautiful woman, the wife's careless burning of the food, the appearance of a wart, or even bad breath, were all valid reasons (López-Azpitarte, 1981, p. 469). When the woman is not a subject, she can be replaced without difficulty or objection by another equivalent object. It is against this situation, more than against divorce (at least, as it is regulated in our present time) that Jesus firmly reacts, defending the wife from her husband's capriciousness. "The two will be one", equal in conditions and rights: the disciples' reaction shows clearly how unpopular Jesus' position is: "If this is the situation between a husband and wife, it is better not to marry" (Matthew 19: 1–12). It is the reaction of the wounded narcissistic male. Sperm is no longer the privileged essence of the human being (along these lines, Magli analyses the condition of women, both in the study on *Gesú du Nazaret*, 1981, and in *La Madonna*, 1987).

The woman who is no longer chained to her biological functions recovers her voice, her speech, in this way gaining an important role in establishing the Kingdom of God. For this reason, women went with Jesus regularly "from one town and village to another, proclaiming the good news of the Kingdom of God". Walking with the Twelve were Mary Magdalene, Joanna, the wife of Chuza, Susanna, "and many others" who "were helping to support them out of their own means" (Luke 8: 1–3). This, of course, caused scandal and unease, or, at the very least, astonishment, as demonstrated by the disciples when they found Jesus speaking alone with the Samaritan woman: they "were surprised to find him talking with a woman" (John 4: 27). It was, in effect, considered undignified for a religious master to speak in public with women. Male arrogance had marginalised them alongside slaves and children.

While marginalised, they are preferred by Jesus. He reveals himself explicitly as Messiah to the Samaritan woman, so that she begins sowing the word herself: "Many of the Samaritans from that town believed in him because of the woman's testimony" (John 4: 39). Equally, women are the first witnesses of the resurrection and the ones who proclaim the central good news of the faith: "And go quickly, and tell his disciples that he is risen from the dead" (Matthew 28: 7).

One of the main reasons why women have been, and are still, socially marginalised and belittled is because of the awakening of a series of unconscious phantasies, which frequently manifest in the male. For the man, feminine genital sexuality often provokes intense and threatening castration phantasies. When the woman is seen as a mutilated being, it is necessary to move her far aside in her difference. She causes fear, and an effective way of easing that fear is to abase her condition. The threatened phallic supremacy is, thus, reinforced. Because of this type of unconscious motivations, the phenomenon of menstruation and blood are, at both the individual and collective level, loaded with powerful taboos that try to keep those distressing phantasies at bay (Freud, 1918a). Because of their state of impurity, women must be removed and hidden.

That was how women with chronic bleeding behaved in the times of the gospel, being cautious to go unnoticed, avoiding any attention. Ritually speaking, a woman was impure; psychologically, she could not recognise herself as a woman worthy of a man's gaze. Because of her feminine condition, she was banned from considering herself a subject of desire; moreover, because of her haemorrhage, she even could not consider herself an object of a man's desire. However, while in hiding, she displays a want, an intense longing that compels her to reach out and touch, by any means, the hem of Jesus' garment. That gesture becomes a prayer that obtains a response. However, Jesus does not accept the woman's taboo-perpetrated meekness. So, against his usual habit, he seems to give the miracle a complete display of publicity: "Who touched me?" The woman is called to emerge from her place of hiding, to break the taboo of marginalisation, to end the complicity between her shame and social banishment. She is called by that man to have faith in herself as a woman (Luke 8: 43–48; Dolto, 1977, pp. 105–123).

When pondering a woman's position in the Kingdom, Mary, Jesus' mother, obviously and logically takes a central role in the Christian message (Domínguez-Morano, 2001b). The social fabric needs references to help give form and strength to the desired social models. So, it is not strange that Mary's figure has been manipulated based on those social models, producing, in consequence, a displacement of the Marian profile towards the poles of the feminine model prevalent in Western culture. The woman, who is called socially to deny her wish and reduce her existence to the roles of wife and mother, has determined an image of Mary essentially viewed from this perspective. Mary's virginity has been used to reinforce an image of a woman that denies her wish and focuses almost exclusively on tenderness and motherhood. With that, the Christological accent on virginity has been extremely distorted. Instead of considering that virginity as an expression of God's unique intervention in history, going beyond the bonds of blood and flesh, the biological and corporal dimension has been tendentiously emphasised, exalting a chaste purity capable of avoiding the pitfalls of sexuality. What society wants from women has deformed the Christological accents in Mary's image, and, in turn, that image has been used as the model which perpetuates and reinforces the model of a woman who denies her sexuality (the virgin), and limits herself to the womb that bears and the breast that nurses (the mother). (Magli centres her 1987 work, *La Madonna,* on these matters. After reviewing the New Testament data on Mary, she analyses the cultural build-up of the Virgin as the model woman.)

The masculine phantasy of the mother–virgin, which permeates the history of religion, finds its resonance here (Jones, 1974, Volume I, pp. 198–210, and pp. 266–357). We forget that Mary was blessed not for her maternal biology, but for having listened to God's word and putting it into practice. She has been the symbol of an Israel faithful to God's word, the woman who hoped with unbreakable faith for the fulfilment of the promise and who proclaimed that God had already intervened in history: "he has brought down the mighty from their thrones and exalted those of humble estate. He has filled the hungry with good things" (Luke 1: 46–55). She is a woman who rejoices, not for being set free from her sexuality, but because God begins to build His Kingdom by eliminating inequality between men. (The role Jesus assigns to women in the creation of the Kingdom of God certainly leads to questions about the role of women inside the Church. There is, at present, ample bibliography on the subject. In particular, we could point to the following studies: Countryman, 1988; Gómez Acebo, 2012; León, 2012; Pintos, 1990.)

Flesh and spirit

The foundations of human sexuality have been deeply affected by Jesus' revolution. The Gospel is not concerned with specific sexual behaviour, but, rather, with the basic structures in which sexuality develops and where the main alienations take place. Jesus' message is not silent regarding the basic structures of the idolised family, whether it be the father as a sign of oppression, or with marginalised women. In reality, the Gospel says little about matters of sexuality. What happens is that our concept of sexuality betrays us when we consider it from the perspective of biology, reduced, therefore, to the corporal dimension and its possible contacts. In this respect, the Gospel certainly tells us very little. Jesus' message, we repeat, is not concerned with specific sexual behaviour, in the same way that issues related to physiological functions are not central to the psychological studies of sexuality.

Beyond sexuality, and this side of love, there is sexuality as desire, with a corporal support that love does not essentially need, but implying at the same time references that set it clear of the pure satisfaction of a biological need. These affective implications of sexuality are what the Gospel tries to activate. It could be asserted from this perspective, therefore, that the silence of the Gospel on specific sexual behaviour cries out, proclaiming the most decisive points of sexuality.

Where the treasure is, there your heart will be also. And the treasure, for Jesus' followers, is in the establishment of the Kingdom of God. In other words, in the passion to transform an unhappy and unjust social system into a community of equal brothers and sisters for whom there is only one Father in heaven. The person dedicated to this passion is the person who, moved by the Spirit, is free towards everything and, therefore, called to be free in sexual matters. For that person, sexual behaviour is neither very important nor very problematic. He or she will not be able to serve both God and sex; but also not to serve God and a law barring one from one's own sexuality. The Christian is not "circumcised", marked in sex by a law.

If Jesus' message does not offer us a code on sexual ethics, it is because he has set the foundations for a mature state in which freedom replaces law and love must have the last word. With this, the matter of specific sexual behaviour is left in our own hands as adults who, through faith's discernment, find the supreme guide to conduct our lives. This discernment consists in the experience of love that invades the believer's affective life and raises in him a sensibility and a penetrating knowledge, discovering what pleases the Lord. The only test to verify the truth in his discernment is the fruit of the Spirit: love for your neighbour in his diverse manifestations (Castillo, 1983, pp. 150–155).

Therefore, no sexual behaviour can ever, under any pretext, constitute an attempt against the other. Sexuality, on its own, even in the widest, broadest sense we can assign to it, is not love. But for a follower of Jesus, who lives in service to others, his sexual behaviour is guaranteed to be "pure". If love is missing, his abstinence or sexual behaviour will lend itself to all types of "impurities", regardless of how much they are blessed or backed by any specific norm. If love is missing, sexuality will be a domain especially inclined to all types of manipulation, blackmail, and oppression of others. We could find the case of those who, in Yourcenar's expression, "extol purity; they don't know how much trouble purity can contain" ("font l'éloge de la pureté; ils ne savent pas combien la pureté peut contenir de trouble") (Yourcenar, 1978, p. 40).

On the contrary, for one who lives in the dynamic of the Spirit, sexuality becomes, at different levels and registers, the engine of any encounter with life. Integrated in the broader frame of love, he will avoid the traps of the "loves that kill" by possessiveness or the "sexual perversion" most clearly condemned by Jesus: that of the pharisaic narcissism of those who are actually in love with themselves, and channel their libidinal energy in self-contemplation of their religious life. As we know, prostitutes are entering the Kingdom of God ahead of them (Matthew 21: 31).

The Spirit is guiding us towards the whole truth and awareness of the Father. Therefore, if we are really possessed by the Spirit of Jesus, we shall know God the Father, the one of Jesus of Nazareth, who, unlike the God born from folds of flesh, is not essentially concerned by sexual behaviour.

An unsolved problem in the Church

Frequently in our Church an echo from certain discourses on sexuality can be heard which, in the end, says, "God does not like man to make love". Such discourse implies a previous image of God and an earlier image of sexuality, too. Both images, psychoanalytically suspicious, are nearer to unconscious oedipal structures than to Jesus' message. God appears as public enemy number one of pleasure, or at least as especially suspicious of it. Through Jesus' teachings, it should become obvious that that version of God should be called Laius (the name of Oedipus' father in the Greek tragedy), and not the name of the "God-Love", which is the proper name for Jesus' Father and our sole Father.

The search for, and attainment of, pleasure has been a decisive element in our psychic development towards maturity. We should, then, feel especially grateful to pleasure without the need to view it, as often happens, with mistrust and suspicion. It is true that there is the risk of confusing it with happiness itself, of making it absolute. But that should not lead us, as frequently occurs in Church discourse, to its devaluation and its constant subordination to other values, as if pleasure in itself would not be worth attaining.

There is spontaneous talk of "legitimate pleasures" without feeling the necessity to speak of "legitimate emotions" or "legitimate memories" (Pohier, 1972, pp. 177–178). Even Jacobelli, in her questionable attempt at making sexual pleasure somehow sacred in her work titled *Risus Paschallis* (1990), reveals something significant in this respect in the book's subtitle: *Il fondamento teologico del piacere sessuale* ("Theological foundation of sexual pleasure"). Why would sexual pleasure need a theological foundation, more so than intellectual or artistic pleasure, or other dimensions of personality such as, for instance, memory or will? It seems to be that sexual pleasure, unlike other human dimensions, needs legitimation, authorisation and, in sum, constraints. Thus, we touch upon a really serious problem in the present Church.

There is no doubt that the ways of thinking about and experiencing sexuality in our Western societies have gone through far-reaching changes. In a certain way, these changes have had an impact to some degree in almost all socio-cultural strata, expressing themselves in diverse mental categories depending on the social sector concerned.

But the common denominator is that most people can no longer accommodate taboo-tainted and repressive ways of approaching sex. The proof is all around us; we see it daily in social media. In Spain, because of the socio-cultural conditions during Franco's dictatorship, the change has been even more marked. That new way of thinking about and experiencing sexuality keeps evolving day by day, spreading across a growing number of social sectors. Problems related to sexual information and education, masturbation, premarital relations, homosexuality, the couple, birth control, celibacy, etc., are approached and experienced in many different ways.

The factors unleashing such significant changes in the concept and experience of sexuality are very diverse and perhaps not always well known. Sometimes, they are accompanied by the intervention of elements unrelated to sexuality. No doubt, one of the most significant in our present society has been the longer life span; a couple's life is considerably longer and their interests and concerns have logically focused more on good communication rather than procreation, which, in the past, would have absorbed all their energy. Thus, sexuality is a reality that must be given new meanings.

If a typical marriage in the nineteenth century lasted about thirty years, the main part of it would have been devoted to breeding about six children, on average. At present, a marriage can easily last fifty or sixty years, with just a few of those years dedicated to child breeding, since the average number of children per couple is usually no more than two or three (caused, in part, by the huge fall in birth and infant mortality). The life of couples has changed. Concerns about child breeding matters recede into the background.

Substantial economic changes, such as the shift to industrial and urban habitats, have also had a significant impact on the family structure and in the function of marriage and of the couple. Methods of contraception (independent of the moral judgement they might deserve) are also available, altering the ways of experiencing sexual relationships for most couples in our society.

The human sciences (and especially psychoanalysis, as we saw earlier) have brought a revolution in the concept of sexuality, which has become part of the mental structure of a large part of the population. Psycho-physiology itself has led to a view of human sexuality that is much more interdependent of the central nervous system and, therefore, of the environment, putting in a reduced perspective the role of the mere biologic and procreating instinct (Wolman & Money, 1980).

A similar change in perspective, brought about by ethnographic studies and cultural anthropology, has changed the ways and means of experiencing and thinking about sexuality, by showing us the great diversity of experiences in humans across time and space (Lévi-Strauss, 1949; Malinowski, 1937; Mead, 1952).

The critical social analysis of the family, undertaken as much from Marxist views as from anti-psychiatry ones, has equally permeated broad social spheres, breaking the monolithic and *quasi*-sacred idea generally held about this important social institution (Cooper, 2006; Engels, 1972: Laing, 1971). The so-called "sexual revolution", advocated by Freudian–Marxist Reich and brought up to date by the student movements in the 1980s, was also a sudden blow to traditional ideas on sexual morality (Reich, 1942, 1945; Marcuse, 1987).

In addition to all these elements, another important change has been the progressive secularisation of our Western societies. Obviously, many sexual behaviour patterns have, in the past, survived through the power of certain socially valid and individually internalised religious images. With the philosophy of "God is dead" and, above all, with the practical atheism or agnosticism of the masses, many pillars holding up traditions of sexual behaviour have collapsed. Cearly, this matter raises many questions on a theoretical level and, perhaps, also temptations on the practical level. All the intimate and complex relationships between sexuality and the image of God we have analysed before are fully present at this point.

The unquestionable fact is that the ideas and models of sexual behaviour have been transformed in contemporary society and that, in spite of a certain neo-puritanical nostalgia emerging in North American society (that played such an important role in the transformations), it does seem difficult to imagine a return to the models in force half a century ago.

All these changes have, obviously, had a very deep impact on the moral ideas of Catholic believers. There is no need to go to progressive Christian communities to see the change in attitudes, clearly divergent from those officially held by the Church, that many Christians show on such themes as masturbation, premarital relations, contraception, etc.

As Pohier asserts, these changes cannot be dismissed as just an expression of laxity in the community of believers (Pohier, 1972, pp. 226–246). We all know that sometimes many Christians adopt behaviour not accepted by traditional morals only after great inner suffering and with great honesty and a clean attitude of approach. The deep analysis of their personal and social reality, their sincere reflection in God, and the guidance of other believers (ministerial or lay) have led them, painfully but clearly, to adopt a new behaviour in these matters. On other occasions, the decision is taken and the position adopted peacefully, with the conviction of their own honesty and that, particularly in this field, the last word must be from their own discernment and not from an authority external to their own conscience.

But our interest now is that, no matter what ethical judgement we might declare, the issue remains, posing a problem that goes beyond the realm of morality and which becomes a grave pastoral problem.

Many Christians do not understand how the Church shows such a rigid and inflexible character in this matter, while in other areas of its moral, pastoral, or liturgical action it has been able to make very important transformations. Ecclesiastical sexual morality seems to hold a special status, kept separate from other areas of human behaviour. In matters of sexuality, the Church has consolidated traditional morality and, in certain circles, the "no small matter" doctrine keeps being asserted. A caress is as grave as sexual abuse. Effectively, in matters of sexuality, the Church is confronted with an unsolved problem.

Pohier reminds us that during the Second Vatican Council, in a wave of optimism and freedom of expression that the Church has rarely experienced, the three topics that were excluded from discussion in the council hall referred to sexuality: the use of contraceptives, the celibacy of priests, and the status of remarried divorcées. Later on, the history throughout the preparation of the Humane Vitae encyclical is revealing and very well known. The later Synods have been characterised by unchanging positions whenever matters related to sexuality have been revisited.

It is as if something is blocking any attempt to make changes in this domain, in spite of the important movements and extensive questioning produced both outside and inside faith communities. Moreover, if we consider what was previously said about the role that the Gospel gives to sexuality, we shall have to conclude that, unless it is just a matter of stubbornness (not likely in an institution that has otherwise shown such fine intelligence), many other important questions are involved here: questions which otherwise would go far beyond the personal conscious positions of those who chair the institution.

The deep implications that sexuality shares with other dimensions in life might, in effect, give us a clue to understanding this striking mystery. A whole series of representations about God, salvation, and sin can really be at play concerning sexuality.

We have already been able to confirm, in earlier chapters, the role that sexuality (understood in the broadest sense that psychoanalysis has shown) plays in the development of the human psyche and the impact it effects in the configuration of images of the father, the law, and, hence, of morals and religion. Sexuality, aggression, guilt, and reparation are concepts that psychoanalysis has forced us to consider within intimate relationships. From there, the important analysis looked at earlier regarding the image of God, soteriology, sin, etc., is necessarily concerned by the ideas we might have on sexuality. Beyond a moral question, we find ourselves faced with a series of important dogmatic matters (Castillo, 2009, 2010, 2016).

We must again recall Pohier's legacy. He insists time and again on the close ties between moral questions and dogma. We have these moral principles because we have this dogma and *vice versa,* he has repeated many times (he insists particularly on these ideas in his 1972 essay, pp. 171–223). In consequence, the change in sexual morality finds particular resistances that are, in large part, unconscious and certainly spill over the personal reality of this or that church official. It is a much deeper matter.

But there is another point we need to make, to which Pohier perhaps does not pay enough attention in his analysis of the problem. We remarked at the beginning of the present chapter that sexuality also maintains an intimate relation with the sociological and sociopolitical dimension, more particularly with the exercise of power. Reich showed (with one of those accurate intuitions spread across his whole strange body of work) that sexual repression often has the goal of creating docile subjects and vassals of established power. This is the same intuition that political tyrannies of any designation have always had. The domination of the most intimate space of the individual means the practical domination of the whole person. It implies the coercion of the source of his wishes and of his power of expression, as well as the prevention of any type of self-affirmation against the law or against power.

When considering the overcoming of the father that Jesus encourages, we remembered how the father acquires his power by positioning himself as prohibition and law against the child's sexual desires. In consequence, we also mentioned that any authority that aspires to an effective domination over others will find an essential foothold in the prohibition of sexuality.

In the light of the knowledge gained from psychoanalytical research, it is impossible not to suspect that the ecclesiastical institution's resistance to revising its approaches to sexuality is related to these other important questions. The temptation can be to maintain a secret domination over the mass of believers through the control of that intimate area of personality. The close relation existing between sexuality and guilt feelings might also attempt to maintain the believers in a position of submission (possibly in a totally unconscious way) and weakening of their own self. The sense of guilt brings people to their knees; but we have once again to ask ourselves, before whom do they kneel, is it before the God of Jesus of Nazareth or before their own sacralised superego and its representatives?

The problem is grave, not only from the moral perspective but, perhaps particularly, from that of pastoral work; the masses understand less and less, and more frequently make fun of the Church's positions in this matter. The believers are gradually growing apart, theoretically and practically, from hierarchy, a distancing of fact in the end. In consequence, we have a grave, unsolved ecclesiastical problem. And the issue of power is also caught in between. Our attention will turn to this in the next chapter.

Note

1. Translator's note. The author refers in his note in the Spanish original to the fact that the excellent translation into Spanish by López-Ballesteros of Freud's Complete Works fails to properly translate "trieb" as "pulsión" and uses "instinto" instead. It is, remarkably, the same problem that occurs in Strachey's *Standard Edition* on the translation of "trieb" as "instinct". Only after the French translation of

"trieb" as "pulsion" did the word "pulsión" become common in Spanish for "trieb". In the present translation of *Belief after Freud*, as explained in the Translator's note to Chapter Two, we have followed the "instinct" option taken by Nicholson-Smith when translating Laplanche and Pontalis's *The Language of Psycho-Analysis*. However, in the present chapter, we need to use the word "drive" for "pulsión" in the Spanish original.

CHAPTER NINE

Do not call anyone father

The relationships of authority and obedience constitute a problem area in the Church's theory and praxis. The difficult task of articulating Christian freedom with submission to certain laws and regulations, or being true to one's own conscience with the availability required by the religious institutions, poses problems not easily solved, and which create a permanent source of conflicts in ecclesiastical life. Biblical, ecclesiological and dogmatic studies have frequently focused on a whole series of nuclear problems that surface when trying to conciliate those two necessary poles: Christian freedom and Christian obedience (Estrada, 1988, 2008, pp. 251–302; Müller, 1966; Rahner, 1977).

On the other hand, psychology, using different methodological approaches, has done research to illuminate this type of human behaviour, its motivations and psychical effects. Perhaps these studies might throw sufficient light on a problem that frequently has psychological implications, even though the psychological motivations have often been disguised with theological or spiritual reasoning.

For the post-Freudian believer, the theme of obedience to authority is especially worthy of suspicion because of the possibility of covering up deep infantile positions and disguised temptations.

Psychoanalysis has shown that the denial of our own wish in favour of submitting to authority figures, as well as the imposition of that wish on others, can produce a series of unconscious reactions related to significant experiences from our childhood.

Our approach in this chapter, however, is not exclusively psychoanalytical. Contributions from other experimental and social psychologies are employed to help us in the attempt to reach a comprehensive understanding of the mechanisms at play in the exercise of authority.

The necessary relationships of obedience

There is no unanimity when defining the obedience relationships. For some, obedience takes place when a subject modifies his behaviour with the purpose of submitting to the orders of a legitimate authority (Levine & Pavelchak, 1985). Others define it as conformity to rules and orders (English & English, 1958, s.v. "Obedience"). However, it is worth highlighting that with obedience, at the time of decision-making, the subject's own wish is relinquished to the desire of somebody else on whom authority is bestowed. For this reason, conformism has been considered a close relative of obedience, in so far as it requires a reduction of personal initiative and acceptance of a course taken by others (Asch, 1952, 1956). Someone else's desire is imposed, voiding or setting the subject's own desire aside.

We should not insist on the need for relationships based on obedience in individual and social life, even if it means a certain wound to our narcissism, which so often dreams of absolute liberty in relation to others. It is evident that responsibility requires respect for the laws and standards needed for the common good, and that certain anarchical views mask the temptation of omnipotence that we shall explore further regarding certain types of authoritarian personalities a little later.

From a strictly biological point of view, birds, amphibians, and mammals exhibit the need for hierarchical structures, which, in the human species, has an analogy in authority systems (Marler, 1967; Tinbergen, 1953). In a social network, a hierarchical organisation contributes to a better defence against the dangers of life and brings, through functional delimitations, stability and harmony to human relations. We all know how, on certain occasions, a challenge to authority can provoke violence, dangerous for the stability of the group or community. We have to conclude, therefore, that behaviour related to obedience has been shaped by issues that concern survival itself.

Along these lines, we should also mention the importance that psychoanalysis gives to obedience-based relationships in the formation, development, and stability of the human subject. Clinical experience has shown, in effect, that the absence of authority frequently results in significant disorders such as ego-weakness, anxiety, predisposition to neurosis, and even to psychosis (Dolto, 1977b; Lebovici & Soulé, 2007).

It is similarly revealing that Freud even attributed the increase of neurosis in our modern societies to the loss of authority associated with the weakening of religion, in spite of the judgement the latter deserved in his view (Freud, 1910d, p. 146). At another level, it is worth remembering too that Freud himself places on *obedience and patient submission to the doctor's advice* a great part of the effectiveness which may offer the psychoanalytic treatment (Freud, 1916–1917, p. 15).

Obedience, then, necessary for the development of personality, and often indispensable in maintaining social stability, is, however, quite a complex type of personal relationship, with widely varying motivations that can lead to very diverse results, even destructive ones, at both individual and collective levels. We shall explore that in the subsequent pages.

Examination of obedience in the psychology laboratory

In the social psychology field, there is a publication on some experimental research, done at Yale University, regarding obedience to authority, which could very well be called a classic work. Its description features in any social psychology handbook that focuses on the subject. The book's author, Stanley Milgram, gives a detailed account in *Obedience to Authority: An Experimental View* (Milgram, 1979).

The study, which is based on a full controversy and much new research, dares to provocatively pose the question of the huge individual and social dangers that might ensue from obedience to authority relationships. That is why this research, without doubt, serves as a serious warning that should be taken into account at the start of any reflection on this type of human relationship.

Milgram's research aimed to study the limits of obedience in a situation that involved inflicting pain upon another human being. To this end, small three-person groups were formed: a teacher, a learner, and the experimenter. Only the first of them, the teacher, was unaware of the true conditions of the experiment. That person was recruited through advertisements asking people to take part in a study about memory and learning.

During the experiment, the person in the role of teacher read to the learner a list of two-word phrases (for example, "blue box", "beautiful day", "wild duck" . . .). Subsequently, he read just a series of single words ("box", "day", "duck" . . .) that the learner had then to associate with the corresponding words on the first list. Each error was apparently punished by a fifteen-volt electric discharge, and could be progressively increased to 450 volts. The person performing the role of learner faked pain in proportion to the assumed level of discharge. Every time the teacher expressed doubt or the wish to stop, the experimenter ordered him to continue. These orders were formulated on a scale of increasing authoritarian tone, from saying, "Please, go on" to stating, "There is no choice, you have to continue" (Milgram, 1979, pp. 25–34).

In that situation, the person performing the role of teacher is torn by the conflict between two incompatible demands: the experimenter's authority and the learner's pleas. The result of the basic experiment is shocking: of forty "teacher" subjects, twenty-six made it to the end in spite of the moans, screams, yells, agonised complaints, and even, later on, supposed fainting of the person in the role of learner (Milgram, 1979, p. 63).

The experiment, much discussed and analysed in social psychology circles, was repeated later with many modifications, trying to dissect the intervening variables. The results, with variations, continue to demonstrate how far an individual will go before saying no to authority. In another experiment, for instance, it was discovered that some nurses were willing to administer virtually dangerous drugs to a hospital's patients under orders from an unknown doctor. Others were willing to touch a snake they believed to be poisonous and put their hand in a container filled with supposed acid. All these people, before the experiment, would have declared that on no condition would they lend themselves to such behaviour.

In the theoretic analysis that Milgram carries out in the experiment, he makes a distinction between two different psychological conditions for the subject who obeys: one when he considers himself to be in a state of *autonomy*, the other when he finds himself in the *agentic* state. In the first case, he feels responsible for his actions and uses his own conscience as a guide for behaviour. In the other state, when he sees himself as part of a hierarchical structure, he thinks that those "above" are responsible for their actions and he adheres solely to the received orders. His own conscience is left aside. In this case, blame does not ensue from his action but from his obedience or disobedience (Milgram, 1974, pp. 168–175). It is well known that it was precisely this type of exculpatory reasoning that excused the actions of the agents of extermination in the Nazi concentration camps, or in the detonation of atomic bombs, or atrocities of the Vietnam War, etc. But, well before these extreme examples, it was evident that such a dynamic of transferring responsibility to the hierarchical structure happens frequently inside our own ecclesiastical relationships, causing, no doubt, very significant perversions in the sense of responsibility and in Christian freedom, which we shall look into later. Milgram concludes that if humanity needs obedience to survive, the need for the capacity to evaluate authority is *even greater*.

Obedience and early loves

If we leave the experimental level and go to the psychodynamic analysis of the motivations that, to varying degrees, lend themselves to obedience, we would have to distinguish two main cores, both rooted in the infantile affective world. The first is intimately linked to the primary defenceless condition in which we enter this world.

That state of defenceless, in effect, will force us to live in total subordination to the people who look after us and on whom not only will our survival depend, but who will establish our basic trust in life, our deep feelings of autonomy, or our capacity for later personal initiative (cf., on this subject, the development outline offered by Erikson in his already classical *Childhood and Society*, particularly Chapter Seven, "Eight ages of man" (Erikson, 1965, pp. 239–266). The relationships with the theme of obedience are shown by Dominian, 1976).

From this biologically determined dependency situation, obedience is one of the basic modes available to solve our defencelessness. During infancy, obeying is a *matter of life and death*. On the other hand, obedience, combined with infantile feelings of omnipotence, takes on a magical character, which the child believes can ensure his protection. "If we obey, the dilemmas of our lives are solved" is the latent undertone that seems to play out during those first moments of our existence.

Additionally, in the first years of life, obedience is one of the best ways of ensuring a positive self-image. Something, let us not forget, almost as determining as survival itself.

In effect, obeying reassures us that we are good, appreciated, and safe objects. In contrast, not obeying brings very negative feelings, hard for the ego to endure, such as being bad, hurtful, unworthy to ourselves and to others.

Any sign of love the adult gives the child has the same effect as milk for the nursling. In consequence, the child loses his self-esteem when he believes he has lost the adults' love, and recovers it when he thinks he has regained that love. According to Fenichel, this is what makes children "obedient and trainable" (Fenichel, 1973, pp. 59–63). Their need for love is so great that they are ready to give up as much satisfaction as needed just to be promised that love or to avoid the threat of its withdrawal.

Nobody is free from having these early life experiences reactivated during certain moments of adult life. The nostalgia for the powerful beings who saved us in exchange for our obedience endures in one way or another as a residue of our infantile past. On the other hand, social institutions seem instinctively to sense these longings that, as we have seen, are biologically predetermined. As did the adults of our childhood, they also promise us protection in exchange for our docility. "If you obey you'll be protected", they seem to hint. With that implicit assurance, the authorities of this world present themselves with the arrogance of a God.

Through these dynamics, there is an attempt, sometimes desperate, to present ourselves as "good children for mum". Because the mother, even if far away or gone, survives in our psyche as an internalised object that caresses us and helps us feel that we are good and valuable, or threatens us with the withdrawal of her love; consequently, our feelings towards ourselves will automatically change to unworthiness and self-contempt.

Some people seem to be structurally marked by this dynamic in their relationships of obedience. For them, obeying guarantees good decision-making. Responsibility will never be theirs; it will always rest with those above them, in whom they place their full trust. Their leaders and superiors are, thus, invested with the omnipotence that, in their childhood, they assigned to those formidable beings who cared for them when they were in a state of helplessness. A *phantasy of totality* supports these modes of infantile relations with those above. As Freud told us regarding religion, these situations imply an assignment of infantile omnipotence; but, instead of doing it in favour of the gods, here it is done in favour of the bosses and superiors, who, like the parents during childhood, are invested with all the power and knowledge. As García Callado says (1990, p. 305), insisting in this omnipotent character nested in infantile obedience relationships, authority becomes for these individuals "a kind of purveyor–protector–guide that feeds and directs the sense of the ego" (translated for this edition).

In this context, obedience, of course, loses all adaptive capacity and responds exclusively to a purely subjective need. To the subject, it is not the specific content of the order received that matters, but the *desire* of the order giver, with the objective aims left at another level. The Milgram experiment mentioned earlier highlights how true this can be.

Psychoanalysis has shown the deep bond between authority and love (Freud, 1915–1917, p. 445). The motivations that frequently lead to submissiveness and credulous docility in relation to authority are, in effect, libidinal in character. As in front of a hypnotist, the presence of authority figures can weaken judgement, and, in a similar way, by means of emotional bonds rooted in past infantile dependency. This is what makes Freud conclude, "the credulity of love becomes an important, if not the most fundamental, source of authority" (Freud, 1905d, p. 150).

The first loves of our lives, loves predetermined by the extreme need with which we humans are born, become the main impetus for adopting submissive attitudes towards those authority figures in which we can find a protective power. Thus, *defencelessness–love–*

obedience are key to the dynamics of certain types of submissiveness in the face of authority.

The ambivalence of submission or rebellion

The psychodynamic analysis of the relationship with authority now leads us to another set of motivations, also rooted in the distant past of childhood. In them, permanent submission or rebellion in the face of authority can make up the two faces of the same coin: the aspiration to hold the reins of omnipotence.

The primal feeling we have analysed of radical infantile dependency on the parents fades into a feeling in which fear and rivalry come into play. The child, after a certain time, begins to fear the power of the parents, who seem to have great capacity to persuade, give orders, punish, praise, or manipulate. In particular, the father figure becomes, in the oedipal situation, an authoritarian figure and an object of competition. Emotional ambivalence, that simultaneous double stream of love and hostility, permeates the entire relationship with the parents.

Freud has insisted on the permanence of those ambivalent relationships towards the parental figures and in their early displacements towards other authority figures. The child, he tells us, goes from viewing his parents as the only source of faith and authority to doubting the unique and incomparable qualities he had assigned to them (Freud, 1909d, p. 237). Soon he will start to transfer the lofty ideals he had projected on them to other figures and representations of authority, the teacher being one of the earliest and most privileged among them. Also with these new symbols of power, he will address his ambivalent feelings in a mix of admiration and respect on the one hand, and competition and hostility on the other. Our attitude towards them, Freud tells us, "is, after all, an ambivalent one since our reverence for them regularly conceals a component of hostile rebellion" (Freud, 1930e, p. 207).

Both rebellion and propitiation remain inside the psyche and the external objects can be used as "witnesses" of these internal fights. For instance, as we already remarked, Dostoyevsky's figure showed Freud the existence of internal debate between submission and rebellion towards the father figure, which finally ended up in a position of total submission to secular and religious authority, "veneration both for the Tsar and for the God of the Christians" (Freud, 1928b, pp. 171–172). In contrast, Freud views Leonardo da Vinci as someone whose freedom from parental figures fostered his research activities, wisely reasoning that "he who appeals to authority when there is a difference of opinion works with his memory rather than with his reason" (Freud, 1910c, p. 122).

So, the diverse articulation which, in each person, is made on the positive (love) or negative (hostility) poles of emotional ambivalence will condition, in some measure, the rebellious or submissive position when confronting future representations of authority.

The question of totality, however, will always be present when the relationship with these authority figures is marked by these aprioristic characters of constant submission or rebellion, which seem to operate regardless of the actual content. A question of totality is, we know, typical of the unsolved oedipal structure, since that oedipal situation can be overcome only by renouncing the omnipotence of desire and by accepting a limited, contingent, plainly human position, we could say. It requires accepting the father's fallibility and the permanent loss of the omnipotence and omniscience once assigned to him, with the secret hope of winning it back some day for oneself.

The position of necessary rebellion, of *a priori* refusal to award value to the approaches of authority, seems, in effect, first of all a "personal matter", an insurmountable opposition between the power holder and the powerless: power hides that phantasy of omnipotence and plays out in a kind of indissoluble "you or me" scenario. "You are not the one who knows and the one who can; I am the one," the eternal rebel seems to say. "I do not grant you the omnipotence that my father once tried to take away from me." It becomes impossible to lend credence to whoever has any authority status. (One of the motives analysed by Freud as a source of eternal rebellion against authority is the reaction to being deceived on sexual matters and to the intimidation frequently applied to children in religious matters (cf. Freud, 1907c, p. 137).) Power, in these cases, is usually the most hated and, at the same time, the most deeply loved and desired.

Rebellion, obviously, should be approached as the other face of infantile dependency. The rebel needs authority in order to exist, as much as the submissive person does. Neither one nor the other has reached the necessary, though always painful, liberation from the parents' authority. On this matter, Freud says, "there is a class of neurotics whose condition is recognizably determined by their having failed in this task" (liberation from their parents' authority) (Freud, 1909c, p. 237). According to him, this liberation from the parents, which is most pronounced during adolescence, creates "the opposition, which is so important for the progress of civilization, between the new generation and the old" (Freud, 1905d, p. 227, 1915–1917, pp. 336–337).

For the submissive person, self-assertion of the ego brings a real danger. That is why he prefers to assign the assertion of his narcissistic omnipotence ideal to the figures "above" him, who, in this way, are invested with all-powerfulness. The boss, the teacher, the superior, like the imaginary father of childhood, knows everything and can do anything. The temptation here is to use omnipotence in his favour by means of identifying with those figures who are invested with all power and knowledge. Even more so if those figures are also considered as spokespersons for God's will. Omnipotence is, thus, guaranteed, bringing to life itself a security with clear signs of fetishism.

However, a deeper analysis shows that not even for the submissive person is the emotional ambivalence towards authority figures totally resolved. Beneath so much reverence, responsibility, and obedience, the hostile dimension against the imaginary parents survives more or less disguised or displaced as other behaviour. Beirnaert has described with wonderful precision the unconscious dynamics that usually develops in this type of situation (Beirnaert, 1987, pp. 112–115).

Against the hostile pole (active though unrecognised), a series of defences develop, trying to reduce its harmful potential. The most effective of these defences consists in building up a number of "reaction formations"; that is, a number of behaviour patterns characterised by being the precise opposite of those desired. In this way, the idealisation of the boss, superior, or teacher progressively builds up, precisely in defence of the hidden aggressiveness felt against them. This results in the "cult of personality" situation, a very emotional and barely rational one. Rationalisations of a religious character, as history shows, lend themselves particularly well to serving as justifiers for that progressive dynamic towards sacralisation of power.

Omnipotence is denied to those in power, but unconsciously desired in systematic rebellion. Omnipotence is granted also to powerful bosses, teachers, or superiors with the desire of taking part in the power structure by means of submissive identification with them. In both cases, we witness the refusal to face the subject's own responsibility, including the possibility of making mistakes, which is, however, the necessary price we must pay in order to stay true to our own desire.

The temptations of obedience

"We know that in the mass of mankind there is a powerful need for an authority who can be admired, before whom one bows down, by whom one is ruled and perhaps even ill-treated" (Freud, 1939a, p. 109). This assertion by Freud, although provocative, nevertheless delivers a considerable dose of truth. There are many human situations that seem actually to confirm such a scandalous reality. The relationships based on obedience can tempt us to evade our own desire and ease the weight of our responsibility. Psychoanalysis has unveiled many of the strings which move that strange need frequently felt by human beings.

As we have seen, obedience lends itself to dreadful fascinations, particularly associated with our infantile past. Perhaps for this reason, acquiring the capacity to be free in the face of authority representations (free to accept the authority one considers appropriate or sidestep it when fidelity to one's own conscience requires it) constitutes one of the most difficult tasks, perhaps never fully accomplished. Perhaps also for the same reason, it is one of the most liberating tasks we can undertake in our lives: the freedom to live without regard to how we are viewed, either negatively or positively, without being trapped by a complacency that leads us to aim to be a "good subject", or by the bitter anger of being barred from the spheres where the strings of power are pulled.

The temptations offered by the relationships of obedience have, in effect, a force that, for many, becomes simply irresistible. The diverse structure and strength of our egos have to be counted as one of the most important variables that feature at the time of relating with authority figures. Certain cognitive, emotional, and attitudinal elements seem to come into play, as we learn in the studies which have researched the profile of the conformist individual.

The most important traits noted for this type of personality are the following.

1. In their cognitive functions, they present a tendency to rigidity and even poverty of ideas. They are usually individuals of lower intelligence.
2. Regarding the motivational and emotional functioning, the conformists show less strength in their egos and in their capacity to endure stress. They show a higher degree of anxiety.
3. In their self-image, they suffer feelings of inferiority. They are generally less intuitive and less realistic when assessing their self-image.
4. In their interpersonal relationships, they usually feel more anxiety with others. They are more passive, more prone to suggestion, and, in general, they are more dependent on fellow human beings, at the same time feeling more uneasy and reluctant about them.
5. In the areas of attitudes and values, the conformist leans towards moralistic attitudes and traditional values with a low tolerance of ambiguity on those grounds. (Krech et al., 1972, pp. 533–534).

An ego weakened by the continuous efforts to keep at bay its own repressed instinctual contents, will provide, according to Freud, fertile ground for total surrendering to authority in its search for external support (Freud, 1910d, p. 146).

In a wider sense than the one we have analysed up to now, attentive reading of Freud's *Group Psychology and the Analysis of the Ego* could bring to light important insights on what the relations with authorities constitute at a collective level. The need to be loved, guided, advised, directed, and even reprimanded by a boss can be activated at any time inside a social group as a stratagem to replace the individual ego-ideal with that of an admired father, protector of all the members (Freud, 1921c, pp. 67–143, 117–128). In this way, Freud makes us conscious of the bonds of libidinal origin, which are latent in the relationship with authority figures. Matters of love effectively get in the way.

Times of crisis seem clearly to increase this need of strong figures to worship and admire. It is the temptation of finding oneself in front of that image which Freud analysed so well in "The great man" (Freud, 1939a, pp. 107–111): the temptation to surrender to the longing for the omnipotent father imagined in the childhood years.

From another angle, studies from social psychology have shown how individuals and groups tend to react favourably to any type of warlord when they have insecure personalities or when circumstances in life place them in a position of doubt or ambiguity. Hitler, it has been rightly said, was also a creation of the wishes of the majority of his citizens. As Ansbacher expresses in his study on this theme, it was "a creation of psycho-sociological character" (Ansbacher, 1948). The Frankfurt school, as we know, has also amply analysed the psychosocial conditions of the Nazi surge. We shall look into that further on.

The temptations of conformity in obedience relationships can be the stronger as the opposition behaviour against authority has at least two very important brakes. On the one hand, disobedience has an internal constraint that can be significant: the feelings of guilt. The Milgram study mentioned earlier is also expressive in this respect. The subjects who refused to keep torturing the other person by applying electrical shocks were those who truly felt guilty, not the ones who maintained their obedience to the end.

> The price of disobedience was a gnawing sense that one has been faithless. Even though he has chosen the morally correct action, the subject remains troubled by the disruption of the social order he brought about, and cannot fully dispel the feeling that he has deserted a cause to which he had pledged support. It is he, and not the obedient subject, who experiences the burden of his action. (Milgram, 1979, pp. 163–164)

On the other hand, in disobedience we can also find an important external brake, which can go from a sanction (sometimes more decisive) to rejection by the other and, potentially, by the group as well.

In obedience, in contrast, instead of brakes we easily find a significant accelerator; by means of obedience, we can have the security of being well-regarded by those above us (important gratification) and, therefore, also enjoying the approval of our own internal superego.

The exercise of authority

The concept of authority is known to be one of the most polemical among social scientists. Schützenberger defines it as the power, pressure, influence, or ascendance exercised by one individual towards another, or on a group or crowd (Schützenberger, 1971). Sillamy defines authority as influence exerted on others in order to elicit certain behaviour from them. Authoritarianism occurs when an individual is capable of imposing his will on others without experiencing any type of contradiction (Sillamy, 1980). In effect, the forms under which authority can be expressed can be very diverse. We rightly speak of moral, social, hierarchical, academic, professional, judicial, military, or religious authority. Also well known is the distinction made by Max Weber, accounting for the basis of the type of legitimacy granted, including a legal–rational type of authority, another based on tradition, and last, one based on charisma.

From the field of psychology, and particularly from psychoanalysis, the exercise of authority has been analysed as a type of behaviour that can easily trigger very primitive mechanisms, generally of an unconscious character. The exercise of authority, so necessary for development of social life and of the groups that make it up, constitutes, like that of obedience, an extremely hazardous ground for interpersonal relationships.

When we command, a whole world of desires and fears is awoken in us, even if frequently outside our own consciousness.

From childhood, exercising new powers or capacities can provide satisfaction; the pleasure of walking, working, organising, managing, or handling issues or people. But, in addition to this natural satisfaction, power brings another, more purely narcissistic, pleasure: not commanding, but *being the one who commands*. As Gallimard puts it, to be like God, to take His place, has always been the temptation for our sinful nature (Gallimard, 1963, pp. 5–9). In effect, it does not seem to be Eros, but Narcissus who is the patron saint of power; we could conclude that the supposed eroticism of power is, in essence, a narcissistic type of eroticism.

Love of power, or, as we shall also see later on, the fear of exercising it justly, can be an important hurdle for individuals and groups. Particularly the thirst for power, and a despotic use of it, has frequently been the object of attention from the social psychologist and the psychoanalyst. Socio-political motives have determined in large measure such special attention.

The studies of the group known as the Frankfurt School on the "authoritarian personality" appeared as a necessary reflection after the savage phenomenon lived through in the Europe of Nazism. Adorno offered us a precise and well-defined profile of such a type of psychological structure (Adorno, 1975, pp. 474–479; Zamora, 2004, pp. 108–116). This model of personality, full of prejudice and a clear slave of the most conventional beliefs, seems to feel secure only when the people who display it find a place on the social scale. Submissive, respectful, and obliging to those above them, they will always be ready to treat those they consider below them in a dictatorial, rude, and scornful way. The authority figures give them a kind of guarantee of immunity (forgetting that they can be abandoned at any time), so they feel threatened by any criticism against the power structures; it amounts to a serious threat to the foundation and basis of their lives that they have constructed. Fromm echoed this idea when he said that, for these types of people, there are only two sexes: the powerful and the powerless (Fromm, 1982b, p. 192).

Fromm's analysis of authoritarianism in his *Escape from Freedom* undoubtedly contains the core of ideas most widely shared among us on this theme and one of the best contributions in the otherwise questionable work of this author. For him, authoritarianism represents one of the mechanisms of escape that a person sets up due to his fear of freedom and of the feelings of loneliness and powerlessness that freedom frequently entails (Caparrós, 1975).

The sadomasochistic dimensions that prevail in the "authoritarian character" stand as defences in order to get rid of the individual ego and of its attitude of freedom towards life (Adorno, 1975, p. 477). Within this context, the will for power appears as the most significant expression of sadism. Yet, at the same time, Fromm points up that, in the "authoritarian character", we find a power that is not rooted in force but in weakness, since it comes up as a desperate attempt to gain a force that it really lacks. When an individual is truly powerful, he does not feel any need to exercise his power over others. It is true, as rightly expressed by Mounier, that authoritarianism is nothing but the energy of the weak (Mounier, 1947, pp. 527–528).

Klein and her school, from a more properly psychoanalytical approach, have shed light on the weaknesses hidden behind authoritarianism. Their analysis has shown how *love for power derives from a direct attempt to control inner dangers*. From this perspective, the most feared is found in the uncontrollable character of our own impulses and, in particular, of the destructive ones. In the face of these, we feel genuinely "uncared for". To embrace, then, an omnipotence phantasy is an "effective" way to avoid the danger and anxiety set in motion by our own helplessness. By means of that omnipotence phantasy, the subject believes he can control all potentially painful situations and so have access to everything useful and desirable, both inside and outside himself. That omnipotence phantasy, through which he achieves security, acquires an especially aggressive character in its quest for power—power which will be the more tyrannical and dictatorial the greater his security needs.

Riviere and Klein explained how, in certain circumstances, that omnipotence and power phantasy is attempted not by way of aggressive dominion over the others, but through love. In particular, they refer to the manner of intervention of certain religious leaders in which this modality of omnipotent control of others could be perceived. But a deeper analysis would reveal that, in reality, love in these cases is a only a way to mask a desire for power, always selfish in nature and without the least degree of interest in others (Klein & Riviere, 1964).

The resolve to gain prestige and overpower others seems to be due, in effect, to a need to fight internal fears outside oneself. Within this whole set of primitive fears and anxieties which the person longing for power tries to deny through the control of others, unconscious feelings of guilt play a crucial role. As demonstrated by Fenichel, the more power a person has, the less he feels he needs to justify himself. We know very well that the increase in self-esteem considerably reduces the feelings of guilt. Therefore, the person filled with power (real or imagined) feels himself to be so important and precious that he will suffer hardly any feelings of guilt. Furthermore, he feels he is able to determine, without any reference other than his own ego, what is good and what is bad (Fenichel, 1973, pp. 639–640). In the extreme, his abuse of others can create a vicious circle of guilt and guilt denial by means of the increase in power, which might lead to perverse tyrannies, as the recent history of humanity has, unfortunately, witnessed.

On other occasions, these feelings of guilt that the person tries to control through the use of authority leads to the projection of that same guilt on others. We then come upon the sadly well-known figure of the paranoiac ruler who progressively and pathologically comes to mistrust his own subjects. The danger he believes others present for him leads him to adopt continuous measures of defence and control towards all others (Freud took a very early stand on this in his letters to Fliess (see Masson, 1986, Draft N, dated 31st May 1897)).

But we have also mentioned the danger which can surface when he who is socially called to perform an authority role fears the use of that power he has been granted to influence (not to dominate) others. Thus, we find the case of the person who relinquishes the responsibility he has accepted for fear of a real or imagined conflict.

In these very "democratic" times of ours, holding a special position such as chief or superior can bring problems. The phantasy of being excluded from, and even rejected by, the group can lead to deplorable ways of exercising authority, for both individuals and groups. These are the other "temptations" of authority: that of playing the role of friend, obsessively determined to be "just another team member", or that of the paternalist who, without asking, stubbornly presents himself as beneficial to the others, treating them as if they were children. (These temptations were also analysed by Gallimard, 1963.)

For some, as we have seen before, the exercise of authority can unconsciously compare with holding the father's position, seizing his functions and his power. That unrecognised aggressiveness can inhibit the determination needed to create a structure that the group might need at a given time. Commanding can be problematic also for those who maintain unconscious infantile desires of ripping power away from those above them, or for the people that seem unconsciously to associate initiative with transgression.

Between the will for power and the need for submission, very strong complicities can, of course, be established. In our analysis of obedience, we mentioned that some people need to be submissive in order to obtain a feeling of security. Many social institutions use this biologically determined longing to obtain protection in exchange of obedience in their favour. "If you obey you will be protected," they seem to say. Educators and authorities coincide in the use of the time-tested technique of delivering "narcissistic supplies" of love and protection in exchange for our obedience. This position, says Fenichel, is shared by all the gods and all the authorities. "It is true," he tells us, "there are great differences between an almighty God, or a modern employer, and a mother who feeds her baby; but nevertheless it is the similarity between them that explains the psychological effectiveness of authority" (Fenichel, 1973, p. 628).

In a very similar way, it is worth mentioning Legendre's ideas referring to the latent libidinal dynamism of many Western institutions, among which the author highlights the Roman Catholic Church. The bonds between the subjects and their censors are bonds of love, since the censor, offering all his power and knowledge as an act of love for his protégés, is not considered a tyrant against whom one should turn, but a loved servant. Love establishes, in this way, the great complicity in authority's and obedience's stratagems (Legendre, 1974).

"Those who exercise authority over them call themselves benefactors" (Luke 22: 25). That is precisely the great triumph of whoever manages to transfer to himself the introjected father image: to make others call him benefactor. The superego does not only work for control and repression of the instincts, but, additionally, to propose socially approved ideals and goals. If fear is felt only towards authority, that fear would be less effective than the fear felt when, at the same time, that authority is loved as the embodiment of the self's own ideals and goals. That function is the one that creates that peculiar and irrational relationship that confers to the fear of authority the necessary force for the repression process. Violating the prohibitions of power not only entails the fear of punishment, but also the loss of esteem by that instance which embodies the self's own ideals, the content of all that one would want to be.

Towards a society of brothers

If we pause to analyse where the most significant changes are taking place in the area of interpersonal relations in our Western societies, we should, no doubt, point out that, with the changes in the man–woman relationships, it is in the longing for an egalitarian society where we find the deeper changes. The ideals of equality, liberty, and fraternity mark, in effect, an indisputable milestone for modernity.

These changes, in a broad psychosocial sense, as also happen at the individual level, experience resistances, fixations, even regressions, that, at certain moments, seem to block and endanger the unleashed process. With good reason, there is talk of reactionary movements in the groups. Movements which, when touching on the themes of authority and obedience, should be named as "nostalgia for the father" (as opposed to "rebellion against the father", so popular in the 1960s). Against the vertigo induced by the idea of a future open to our own desires and determined, as much as possible, by our own responsibility, springs up the nostalgia for a firm and decisive word that guides our step and fixes the goals we should obediently follow. We have already noted how social psychology warns of how this danger is especially important in social situations of crisis or ambiguity.

These resistances, fixations, and also regressions, which are, in fact, occurring, are not able to block, or even do away with, certain processes of higher amplitude and intensity, which point towards the conquest of a society based on the fundamental equality of all human beings.

The processes in favour of autonomy and responsibility permeate all social strata: from the level of international affairs, with the decolonisation processes, or at the national level with devolution of autonomy to the regions, to those of commerce, industry, business, or collective professional organisations, we find similar movements towards autonomy and progressive gain of liberty. In all these areas, authority is divested of its aura of omnipotence from earlier times. On the other hand, as González Faus so rightly affirms, recent historical experiences such as those of Nazism or Stalinism have created in us a kind of "authority trauma" which needs to be taken into account when trying to understand our collective psychologies (González Faus, 1990, p. 247)

That high appraisal of personal freedom is undoubtedly what brought down the Berlin Wall, that has fuelled the significant changes made in all the Eastern European countries, and what encouraged the aborted student revolution in China.

On another level, but no less salient, the authority in the family itself, so important for the introjection of the power relation keys, is questioned from many different angles and, in fact, is being experienced in very different ways from those of earlier times. Nowadays, education is advocating the importance of giving children a sense of personal worth which must be obtained by means of progressive separation and growing autonomy from their elders, avoiding fear of punishment or of feeling stifled by power-invested figures (Dominian, 1976, pp. 121–122, who remarks that a system of education that is working towards equality does not mean falling for the impossible idea of an absolute equality; the goal of equality relative to personal values needs to recognise the differences in physical, intellectual, emotional, etc., capacities).

It is evident that these new ways of dealing with family authority and questioning patriarchal authoritarianism, regardless of how they may be judged, are there to stay as a fact of our daily experience and have a direct impact on our ways of relating to power. We are, it has been said, on the way to a fatherless society (cf. Mendel, 1968; as we know, this work became a central point for ideas constantly handled during those years; reflections on that are contained in Rof Carballo, 1987, pp. 323–327).

Obviously, these far-reaching changes in relation to authority, at diverse but very broad levels, are lived and evaluated in a very different manner according to each person's ideology and personality structure. As could be expected, the authoritarian figures we analysed before react badly to the loss of automatic respect for authority that was given in earlier times. They will hardly understand that the nonconformists, the reformers, the pioneers represent the engine of change and progress.

Yet, the march towards a society of equals, a society of brothers, where the cult of personality is not present, where authority would be just a social function and not a narcissistic complacency, where obedience would be to respect and dedicated service and not the submission of one man to another, constitutes a process which is currently under way, which is hardly reversible, and which the Christian (and so we enter into another type of reflection) must welcome with joy because he, too, has received a crucial invitation not to call anybody father or teacher, as we saw in the previous chapter.

The Christian in the face of obedience and authority

We must begin with a reaffirmation: the term "obedience" is not used in the Gospel to describe the interpersonal relations within the community. This fact is clear and eloquent. "Obedience" applies only to the relationship with God or to Jesus' command of natural elements or demons (Mark 1: 27, 4: 41). This obedience to God has a basic sense of "listening" (as shown by its Greek root, *hyp-akoè*, and Latin, *ob-audire*) and can lead otherwise to disobedience against men and even to transgression of religious rules. Thus, Jesus does not obey certain prescriptions of Jewish law and traditions of the time (Mark 2: 18–28; 3: 2–6; 7: 2–3) and his disciples express clearly the need to obey God ahead of men, even when they represent religious authority (Acts 4: 19).

It should, then, be understood that the extreme obedience shown by Jesus to his Father drove him to be, and to appear, religiously disobedient and that the same attitude would make sense for those who follow him. One wonders why (unless explained by ideology) the term disobedience (in addition to obedience) does not appear in the dictionaries of biblical theology. There is certainly no lack of New Testament writings to comment on.

These critical facts about Jesus' words and actions in the Gospel are, naturally, the ones to be used as basic hermeneutical reference when reading all the other texts in the New Testament referring to matters of obedience. Therefore, they should never be interpreted in a way that infringes, even minimally, the radical principles of equality that characterised the interpersonal relationships in the Christian community.

In that Christian community, it has to be stated, in terms of clear psychoanalytic reference, that the place of the father should remain empty. Father, teacher, or director, are not Christian words in so far as they are used to describe a type of interpersonal relationship inside the community. Only God can take that place. As we have seen in the previous chapter, a follower of Jesus is called to go beyond any "nostalgia for the father" and avoid the temptations that obedience and authority can offer as ways to evade responsibility and desire. This entails, as we have seen, totally giving up infantile thought, which is formed in terms of totality; giving up, too, the belief that the all-power or the all-knowledge (and, hence, total security) is available to us.

A relationship in which somebody would claim to be father or teacher to the believer would mean a relationship in which the radical equality we are called to would be under attack.

The Church—it is said—is not a democracy. True. But this should never be understood as a justification for authoritarianism and abuse inside the community. It is not a democracy and still less an absolute monarchy; it is—it should be—much more than a democracy, a fraternity in which attentive listening, respect for the other's differences, the search for his benefit above and beyond ideas and institutions, should prevail over "mundane" types of relationships, in which, as we know "rulers . . . lord it over them, and their superiors act like tyrants over them" (Mark 10: 42). And we cannot and should not believe we are being of service to others when what we are actually doing is being controlling and disrespectful (cf. along these lines, the excellent study by Estrada, 1985, pp. 53–97).

As González Faus has conveyed, Jesus denounced the existing authorities because they expected to obtain justification just by calling themselves benefactors or service providers without, in fact, *exercising* service. In the Christian community, however, there is recourse to authority only as the *last* instance (Matthew 18: 15–17) but not as first, even less sole, instance. Jesus himself, who had full authority to command demons, was a model in his exercise of authority as an authentic service, trying not to command men, but, rather, converting their freedom. He who confessed to holding "all power in heaven and earth," González Faus also says,

> tried to speak not by dictating, but by convincing others so that the great authority of his word would not spring from outside (from the law or the appeal to God Himself), as with scribes and Pharisees, but from within. (González Faus, 1990, p. 265, translated for this edition)

From Jesus' example, the Christian community has the great responsibility of showing to the world a way of exercising authority and obedience in which full emphasis is given to the principles of service, respect, maturity, availability, and integrity, which were the signs of Jesus' authority. Unfortunately, this responsibility has, apparently, not been understood.

Obedience and authority in the Church

"In the realm of authority, the global Christian community has failed in the right reading of the signs of the times" (Dominian, 1976, p. 130). This statement can serve well to reflect on how obedience and authority are exercised inside our Roman Catholic Church.

Certainly, one of the great signs of the times, as we have seen, is the aspiration to create a society of equals in which any type of domination by man over man is eradicated. The sense of personal autonomy is an evident achievement of our society. The whole world is engaged on a large-scale transformation to replace relationships of dependency with relationships of equality, at the level of nations, societies, families, etc. Church rulers, however, seem to live unaware of these changes and to show little sensitivity towards this evident "sign of the times".

Moreover, the Church has even shown misgivings, mistrust, and even condemnation of certain important socio-cultural achievements, such as popular sovereignty and personal freedom. Pehaps, as Laboa thinks, because they feared that their acceptance could influence the Church by demanding greater participation in decision-making from the community of believers (Laboa, 1990, pp. 291–302).

But then we find ourselves in a dangerously incoherent situation. Because, as Cabarrús says, on the one hand, the Church presents itself as the herald of liberties, especially in nations with socialist or totalitarian regimes, but, on the other hand, "champions an inquisitorial line in its own depths and with its 'most faithful children'" (Cabarrús, 1990, pp. 32–44, translated for this edition). Too frequently, its ways of exercising authority constitute, in consequence, an authentic contradiction in terms. Our society can hardly understand some of the decision-making procedures in the Church community. Hence, scandals frequently arise within the ranks of believers, and non-believers too, sensitive to what they rightly consider to be the moral conquest of our times. We know—and we should blush about it—that the media echo these sentiments, expressing their disapproval or shock and pointing to the Churches' progressive erosion in credibility, in a world that works so hard to attain its liberties.

The Kingdom of God has been associated with an authoritarian system, which, by using authority not as competent service, but as domination, has generated fear and feelings of guilt quite alien to Jesus of Nazareth's message, and to what his message should inspire. In the Christian community, the typical characteristics of the lack of emotional maturity during childhood have been encouraged and favoured, perpetuating, in this way, immaturity in its diverse structures, in particular in the clerical position.

> In a certain sense the worst sin a Christian, Bishop or common man or woman, can commit is to search satisfaction of his own need of emotional security by trying for the extension of the Kingdom of God in authoritarian terms. (Dominian, 1976, pp. 131–132)

In a particularly excruciating way, the German theologian Drewermann has recently carried out, with the help of deep psychology, an important critical analysis on relationships of ecclesiastical obedience (Drewermann, 1989, pp. 426–479). For him, the Church overemphasises the availability and submission of an individual's will to the superior's will. All the accent is on the advantage of dependency through the renouncement of the subject's own wish and own will. A quite incoherent situation is thus reached: on the one hand, the subject's own will is identified with mere subjectivity, which should be given up; on the other hand, with the superior's will, different hermeneutics are used, since his wish is imposed as the objective reference. This gives birth to the dangerous illusion of a community without subjects, in which the group, represented by the superior, becomes ideologised and the superior's will is identified with God's will (regarding the understanding of God's will, we point to the excellent study by Franco, 1983, pp. 3–21). The libidinal load on the capacity to command relates in this way to the absolute denial of will by the subject (through the use of slogans referring to Jesus' self-denial in martyrdom, etc.). There is, thus, a huge asymmetry between the superior's omnipotence and the subject's powerlessness, diminished by the encouragement of feelings of self-denial. The dreadful result, according to Drewermann's analysis, is the elevation of infantile submission to the category of a theological virtue.

Drewermann's work is provocative and has stirred up significant controversy (González Faus et al., 1996). But there is no doubt, at least regarding the point we are analysing, that he has hit the nail on the head as to the many pathological elements acting in the relationships of authority and obedience in the Church community. Other authors, from different angles, have also highlighted this rendering of obedience in the Church as an absolute, wrongly equating it to a theological virtue.

In contrast with the pathogenic practices on authority and obedience, the need must be stressed for an exercise in loyalty and availability that would not generate subjects, but responsible and autonomous individuals. It would also be necessary to recover, as Drewermann would agree, a "theology of disobedience", based on Jesus Christ's attitude towards religious authorities, through discernment of one's conscience, in counterpoint with one's obedience to God. Denying this possibility would mean being unfaithful to the New Testament.

The vow of obedience

In service to the Kingdom, the best of Church tradition has seen in radical availability inside a group the basis to offer God a vow which, alongside poverty and chastity, has been called the "vow of obedience" (it seems obvious, for the above mentioned reasons, that this vow of obedience does not enjoy the same evangelical backing as poverty or chastity; in this respect, it is also meaningful that St Ignatius of Loyola and his first partners, very early on, had very clear views on the poverty and chastity vows while they only reached a conclusion on the obedience vow later on after a complex deliberation (cf. Sales, 1983, pp. 227–252). It is worth reflecting, even briefly, on the logic of this manner of consecration to God and His Kingdom, which implies the difficult renouncement of personal autonomy. Perhaps, from the reflection on this dimension of religious life, we shall be able to understand the deepest meaning of the Christian sense of obedience.

It is evident that the religious vow of obedience cannot be an exception to that fundamental call of the Christian message to encourage maturity, adult freedom, and what we could call, with psychoanalytical references, the necessary overcoming of the father. Therefore, the vow of obedience cannot dispense with a series of values without which there cannot be any personal maturation.

If the vow of obedience cannot be a way of renouncing personal responsibility and attainment of one's desire, if it cannot be understood as a way of ensuring an institutional protection or of submitting to imaginary parental figures as omnipotent, then its only possible meaning would be its function inside a fraternal community as a way of jointly discerning God's will. Besides giving unity to the group and making it available for the Kingdom, all the other things which have been said about obedience (so often permeating it with a strong spiritualistic scent, ranging from the taste of masochism to exaltation of an atrocious ascetic narcissism) should be suspected by the believer of infringing upon the most important values of his psyche and of his life of faith.

Within the specific fraternity in which a believer chooses to carry out his specific way of servicing the Kingdom, the "superior" (using the tradition-acclaimed term, which, however, properly seen, does not respond to a truly Christian mentality) expresses, on the one hand, the communion with that other great fraternity which is the complete Church, and, on the other hand, the communion with the specific fraternity which is the particular order or congregation.

Obedience, therefore, has to be understood in that context as a process, not easy certainly, of a *joint search for God's will*, a process which, to be carried out, requires an encounter and a dialogue between the individual and the superior. That dialogue, moreover, should never lose sight of the fact that it is inscribed in the assumption of a radical equality, regardless of the different functions inside the community; a dialogue of brothers who are sincerely searching for God's will as something that eludes both initially. Obedience, from this point of view, we could say is *a vow in duo* (at least), since, for its implementation, two parties are implicated, in contrast to what happens with the other vows of poverty and chastity.

Therefore, having the "sense of religious obedience" should be understood not only as the subject's capacity to renounce his own judgement, but also as the capacity of the superior to exercise authority in the only way permitted to a Christian: that is, as a competent service to the group, with an open availability also to suspend his own judgement in the course of the dialogue with the other. A different way to exercise authority should be seen also as an authentic "fault against the spirit of the obedience vow" on the part of the superior. As has been rightly said, obedience is co-action, without ever turning into coercion.

In consequence, the vow of religious obedience cannot relieve us from the responsibility of our own discernment as an essential part in that consequent search for God's will in dialogue and joint deliberation. Obedience, in this sense, makes discernment operative but can never replace it.

It becomes evident, too, that this previous discernment can occasionally lead one to hold a different or even contrary view to the one held by the religious authority, which will, however, be granted the last word (except in exceptional cases of "conscientious objection"). As Franco says on his study of obedience in St Ignatius of Loyola: "in the complex process of spiritual discretion, the superior is an element, but not the single one, not even always the last and most apposite one" (Franco, 1983, pp. 17, 21, translated for this edition).

St Ignatius of Loyola, who, in effect, has become the great master of the vow of religious obedience, always had an extremely clear view of this need for discernment as expression of the subject's own autonomy and responsibility. In addition, this discernment led him, at certain moments, to be open about his differences with the desires of papal authority, such as when the latter tried to appoint Francisco de Borja and Laynez as cardinals. St Ignatius considered that the same

Spirit who, for certain reasons, might move the Pope in one direction, could lead him in a contrary way for other diverse reasons. From that position, he also felt moved to make "all possible noise" in order that "the world might understand how the Company accepts such things", since, in the end, the papal will imposed itself (*Fontes narrativi*, II, 372). It is evident that the many misunderstandings stemming from the interpretation of Ignatian obedience would not have happened if attention had been paid to the governance and obedience praxis followed by St Ignatius (on Ignatius's intimate and personal relations concerning obedience, see the excellent psychoanalytical study by Meissner, 1992).

On the other hand, the implication of the subject's own desire and responsibility in the search for the will of God will be the necessary corrector for avoiding an understanding of obedience as a kind of magic act through which the objective content of the will of God is, automatically and almost mechanically, ascertained (on the origin of considering the Superior's voice as the voice of God, see Franco, 1983). Obedience, in effect, does not guarantee an understanding of God's will, even when superior and subordinate, challenging themselves and taking risks in that difficult task, subjectively get it right. Except, if obedience is understood as fetishism, we shall never possess an absolute certainty of objectively having got it right.

The vow of obedience, from this point of view, is a mediation that expresses and, at the same time, strengthens our availability for the Kingdom. For the same reason, it has an essential apostolic dimension and becomes an expression of our "freedom for", that is, our freedom in the option for the Kingdom of God. Moreover, it seems evident that if, in that option for the Kingdom as ultimate engine of availability, obedience was tainted, either for the one in command or the other in submission, it would become entangled in the pathological net and secretly serve the most infantile motivations that we have tried to unravel in the first part of the present work. From the moment in which obedience loses its pure *mediation* dimension to become an absolute finality in itself, it perverts the only meaning it can have from a psychological, social, and faith-related point of view.

Placed in this context of mediation, obedience brings unity to the group and expresses availability and the option for the Kingdom. From this position, it can be used to "lose oneself" in service to others, just as one in love "loses oneself" in the "object" dynamics one enters (in the Freudian distinction between narcissistic and object-libido, falling in love would be the best illustration of the "object choice" dynamics; madness, on the contrary, would best illustrate the other extreme of narcissistic libido (Freud, 1914c, pp. 69–102)). It would then express, in a quite eloquent way, the radical decentring to which Jesus invites all of his followers. When we lose sight of the commitment to the task of transformation through the Kingdom, obedience then comes to mean "losing oneself", but in the worst sense that can be given to the term.

The human value of personal autonomy can only be renounced when our task is just that of helping others. And only when the renouncement of this value is articulated in a higher value system, the Kingdom project, is that renouncement ethically valid and psychologically healthy. If this is not the case, obedience turns into an important source of human alienation, of psychic infantilism, and a fundamental attack on the radical equality to which we are all called when we enter the Christian community.

CHAPTER TEN

No one can serve two masters

A matter of love

Perhaps just a brief look at our relationship with money would be enough to make us realise that it is not always entirely logical or rational. It would seem that, in money matters, there is always "something more" than just money at play. Elements, hardly or not at all related with the real functions of money in our life, easily interfere. There is, in effect, a "something more" that seems to concern our emotions, an area which, in essence, escapes logic and rationality. It is a matter, then, of "love" or "lack of love", with all the blossoming of emotions that can arise from it: desires, fears, possession, rejection, guilt, etc.

If that somewhat "normal" dynamic "infrastructure" can be observed in ourselves or in any individual around us, we can also probably remember cases from life or literature in which irrationality seems to have prevailed in the most shocking and surprising way. The cases of absurd behaviour in this area can multiply almost without end: beggars who hide millions, people who resist changing thousands of coins, fellows who suffer anxiety at the idea of spending a ridiculously small amount of cash, but are capable of the biggest expenditures if done by credit card or bank cheques, and so on.

It could rightly be said that very few aspects of life are capable of producing such extreme rational and irrational responses within someone's personality. In no other area of behaviour can we use so many arithmetical calculations and in very few others can we also commit so many irrational blunders.

Perhaps that is the reason some men, applying the best of their rational capacity to the study of capital, have known how to recognise that undercurrent that flows below the merciless logic of money. John Maynard Keynes, one of the main figures of twentieth century economics, explains,

> The love of money as a possession—as distinguished from the love of money as a means to the enjoyments and realities of life—will be recognized for what it is, a somewhat disgusting morbidity, one of those semi-criminal, semi-pathological propensities which one hands over with a shudder to the specialists in mental disease. (Keynes, 1931, p. 369)

From the contact with mental illness and then its application to culture, psychoanalysis has learned to be particularly mistrustful of any type of discourse that pretends supreme rationality. Not surprisingly, therefore, it has also become interested in economic behaviour and has detected in its undertones hidden links with our individual past emotional history. The nature of capitalism, as Ferenczi expressed, is not purely utilitarian, but irrational and libidinal, too. Its thrust comes not just from practical matters, from the "reality principle", but integrates as well an irrational dimension that follows the primitive "pleasure principle" (Ferenczi, 1981, pp. 183–191).

As shown by psychoanalysis, our relationship with money also implies a "matter of love", or, in more Freudian terms, a libidinal, unconscious, and childhood-rooted question. This accounts for the fact that, as in issues related to sexuality, money provokes duplicity, false modesty, and hypocrisy. We are conscious that speaking about money can sometimes be as awkward as speaking about sexual matters (Freud, 1913c, p. 131).

A surprising relationship

The first to unravel the hidden relationships between the love of money and our infantile past was Freud himself, by offering, as on many other occasions, an interpretation which stirred up resistance and discomfort in the general public, often immediately and quasi-automatically.

The very content of the interpretation is especially likely to cause revulsion and rejection, since it involves, at the level of anal libido, a relationship between money and excrement. The physiological function of defecation, with its polarity of expulsion–retention, is established by Freud as the paradigm of relationships with outside objects (Laplanche & Pontalis, 1973).

In effect, Freud intuitively sensed this relationship from the early days of his research. We find it early on, in a letter dated 21 January, 1897, to his, at that time, closest friend and confidant, Wilhelm Fliess: the money which, in tales and legends, is turned into faeces, he says is merely transformed back into the substance from which it arose (Masson, 1986, p. 243).

He continued insisting on this surprising relationship as his analytical practice progressed in the knowledge of neurosis, and particularly of obsessive neurosis, so closely related, as we know, to the issues of the infantile anal stage (Freud, 1908b, pp. 167–175, 1913k, pp. 335–337, 1916–1917, pp. 314–316, 325–326, 1917c, pp. 128–131, 1933a, pp. 100–102, 106–110). In this way, one of what Freud called "conversions" (*Konversion*) takes place, by which a transposition (*Umsetzung*) of instinctual emotions is effected from certain erogenous zones to apparently foreign objects. But, what possibly can be the basis for proposing such an outrageous relationship between money and excrement? In his first writings on this theme, Freud approaches it as another of the antithetical relationships so dear to unconscious productions such as dreams, neurotic symptoms, etc. (Freud, 1908b, pp. 172–173). Later, however, he realises that it is not so much an antithetical relationship but, rather, one of analogy: starting from the narcissistic infantile situation, faeces have a very high value for children, difficult to understand by the adult, who is, through a series of reaction formations, too far removed from the primitive appreciation.

For the child, stool is something that, by virtue of coming out of his body, is highly valued as a part of himself. Helping to establish this relationship is the fact that just as the child is obliged for hygienic reasons to separate from his stool, money appears as the next a highly valued object. The relationship, Freud told us, can reach beyond money to other unconscious associations such as stool–gift–child–penis (Freud, 1917c, pp. 128–131).

Ferenczi, with the customary sharpness and depth of his studies, shows us the various steps that the child takes in order to carry out the sublimation of the anal content until the symbolic transmutation into money takes place. Thus, the faecal matter goes through a series of substitutions in which the primitive, self-erotic satisfaction related to defecation is progressively distorted: mud, sand, stone, marbles, and buttons, so satisfying for the child, facilitate the substitution of the odourless, dry, and hard for the fetid, wet, and soft. Money, presented from the outside as valuable, lends itself to the substitution for, and sublimation of, the primitive anal contents (Ferenczi, 1981, pp. 184–188). Through a complex process, this leads us to the Latin saying, "money does not stink" (*Pecunia non olet*).

Nevertheless, the association established by psychoanalysis between excrement and money can be shocking and also, for emotional reasons, incredible. It might seem unlikely that we could have valued what, from our adult viewpoint, we consider to be the very representation of the contemptible: faeces. So perhaps, before proceeding with other elements of this psychoanalytical investigation, it is worth remembering some data from anthropology that support the surprising Freudian interpretation.

Many symbols and legends, proverbs, and even religious rites remind us of the high value which, in diverse ways, has been conferred on anal contents and their relation with gold or money.

From the popular figure of the "Dukaten-Scheisser" or "Money Shitter", in German business, or, in a similar vein, the "goose that laid the golden eggs", the pictorial representations of erotic art (particularly caricatures), or Hieronymus Bosch in *The Paradise*, a painting in which we see a man defecating coins, all of them and many more clearly illustrate that popular wisdom and art have captured and reflected in countless ways the unconscious relationship that psychoanalysis has brought to light, providing an explanation (Jones, 1916, 1918, 1974, *Volume II*, pp. 22–109). The same relationship can be found in alchemy, when the "nigredo" and the obtainment of "aurum philosophicum" appear as two extremes in the transmutation process (Chevalier & Gheerbrant, 1969; Cirlot, 1968).

Many magic or religious rites also make the same appraisal of filth, investing it with important potentialities. Excrement frequently symbolises a sacred biological power inhabiting man that, once released, can be recovered somehow. Many primitive tribes are in the habit of devouring all kinds of filth, including their own. Faeces from sacred men (as in some parts of Tibet) acquire a high religious meaning and sometimes gold is presented as a sublimation of stool from a given god. The Aztec deity Tlazolteotl, whose name means "the coprophage" or "goddess of filth", is represented in a defecating position. The coprophagic rite has appeared also in various places throughout the history of religions (Bourkes, 1913; Mead, 1952).

In the same way, popular expressions attest to this frequent association between money and faeces. In German, for instance, haemorrhoids are called "golden veins" (*Goldener Ader*). Of the wealthy, we say they "stink of money", are "filthy rich" or, in contrast, of somebody without a penny, we say he is "cleaned out". Proverbs and sayings are also telling in this respect: "Money is the bladder of man, it cannot speak but can shout", or "gold coins are manure, but the face is worth a thousand gold pieces", as the Chinese say. *Aurum in stercore quaero,* sang Virgil the poet. And, in the old Spanish saying: "Gold made into coins, through how many sewers does it roll?"

Psychoanalysts have also not ignored the anal connotations of certain economic language expressions, such as "capital in circulation", "liquid money" and, more recently, "black money", or "laundering" or "cleaning" money (Brown, N. O., 1959, pp. 292–304).

The perverse love of money

Coming back to psychoanalytical research, it is worth looking into the established relationships between the dynamics of *possession,* so typical of the anal stage, and the feeling of *ownership,* which so significantly marks present Western societies, that will prevent us from remaining at the mere anecdotal level. Important emotional and social questions are linked to it. Fenichel was perhaps the best at unravelling those profound relationships (Fenichel, 1973, pp. 318–324).

When the child expels his faeces, a very precious substance for him, a part of his own body, he feels "this is something that should be inside my body, but is outside now, and I cannot put it back in". Then he calls it "mine", which, in that context, would mean: I declare it "symbolically-set-inside-my-body". In this case, ownership means things that, in fact, are outside, but symbolically are inside. In this way, they are endowed with "ego quality". So money, for many insecure people, becomes a fairly problematic matter: to lose money, to exchange it for something, or to give it away constitute acts of dispossession which they cannot consider a mere loss of an outside object but a loss of something which has previously been "incorporated"; that is, something intimately related with their egos. Such people will try to reassure themselves by possession and control of their money in the same way that the child, during his anal stage, can use the control of his defecation as a way of self-assertion within his environment.

When the paths to sublimation, described before in the Ferenczi analysis, fail, or when certain circumstances become very difficult for someone and force a regression to earlier stages of his emotional life, the attitudes towards money can become extremely irrational. The individual remains blocked in his primitive anal–erotic satisfactions and tends to revive them in a symptomatic way; that is, in a way that does not fit the real functions that money performs in life. To retain it or to expel it (to save or to spend, for instance) is not done as a function of real needs but as a function of unrecognised anal drives. It is the regressive relationship with money or ownership of objects that ends up permeated with same possessive (retentive) anal dynamics.

The collection of useless objects, the inability to get rid of obviously unusable junk, the conversion of time into "gold" maintaining the same hoarding attitude, are relatively frequent occurrences that express a kind of "perverse love" which can, of course, be disguised with the most colourful rationalisations.

Regarding the unhealthy ways of feeling ownership, clinical psychology could contribute countless cases. Without going as far as describing the psychotic patients who speak of their faeces as their wealth, their money, their gold, or their food, we find neurotics who, sometimes tragically, display the irrational dynamics hidden so often in behaviour related to money.

We are familiar with the case of the neurotic, particularly the obsessive one, who maintains a difficult relationship with money, mainly when it is time to pay for things. Abraham has shown the infantile dependency on the parents that is usually hidden in these subjects. Sometimes, however, they can surprise us by making sudden purchases, with the secret illusion of living a symbolic and wished-for independence, which they somehow know they lack (Abraham, 1916, pp. 299–302). Freud also pays tribute to the same sudden attacks of stinginess in the famous "Wolf Man" case: Freud, 1918b, pp. 72–73).

The ambiguous relations with money that can be maintained from a deficient resolution of anal conflicts often result in their being strongly permeated with guilt feelings. They can cause self-defeating behaviour and also (simultaneously monetary and psychodynamic) anti-economic behaviour: a person might, for instance, punish his unconscious anal–sadistic drives by wasting money or seeking out bankruptcy. The same kind of neurotic guilt also invades the behaviour of those who achieve a comfortable condition by reaching a certain economic level; this type of pleasure is denied internally to them because of the unconscious connections it has. Naturally, all that can be dressed up with beautiful rationalisations on the value of frugality or evangelical poverty.

Love of money, then, when it goes beyond its reality matching functions, expresses infantile emotional dimensions. We cannot forget that this love, with its essentially anal roots, lies in the pregenital area and this, psychoanalytically speaking, means a position in which narcissism dominates, preventing full emotional development; in other words, the full capacity to love (or hate), to overcome ambivalence, to obtain self-respect and consideration by others, and the capacity of sublimation in managing emotion, etc.

The perverse love of money is no longer a matter of "owning something", but of "owning self", with markedly centripetal dynamics. It is about enclosing oneself in a totality that denies outside references. That way, an individual tries to cover an internal lack and attain security, but he is really placing himself in the most insecure position that can be imagined, since, as Fromm affirms in his analysis of possession, "if I am what I have, and if what I have is lost, who then am I?" (Fromm, 1982a, p. 89).

Furthermore, even if the connection between the feelings of ownership and anal contents has been favoured in psychoanalytical interpretations, it is also important to take into account that it has not been the only one made. There is no reason to limit the connection between money and infantile libido exclusively to the anal area, even if the basic weight seems to be there. There is also a place, however, for relationships that display an infantile dimension of *oral* and even *phallic* character (Laplanche & Pontalis, 1973, "Oral and phallic stages").

Money, in effect, can also symbolise for someone a kind of food that can calm down certain oral anxieties or compensate for certain related deficiencies. In this respect, Fromm states that in the mid-twentieth century, the "hoarding" orientation, more characteristic of the anal stage, has lost ground to the "receptive orientation, in which the aim is to receive, to drink-in, to have always something new all the time, to live with a continuously open mouth, as it were" (Fromm, 1955). Money also can be used as a symbol of genital power, entailing apparently generous behaviour (expensive gifts, being philanthropic, etc.) which, in reality, tries to demonstrate a questionable "prowess" of another kind. (Norman Brown made us realise the genital and oedipal connotations Freud also assigns to the anal contents when he relates faeces not only to gifts or money, but also to penis or boy (Brown, N. O., 1959, pp. 334–340).)

If, underlying the relationship with money, there is a hidden matter of love, that love can be expressed through very diverse registers, from the most primary and infantile to the most evolved. Of course, regressions from one register to another can take place as a function of the particular emotional dynamics a person might experience on his present path. A diminished genitality can reinforce the anal functions, as happened with that person whose investments in the stock exchange increased each time he experienced a failure in love.

The psychosocial side of the problem

The previous interpretations can give the impression that psychoanalysis, once again, assigns an excessive role to the incidents in infantile libidinal life and its unconscious ramifications, particularly on a theme such as money, in which, we know, other types of interests, mainly socio-economic and political, mark the basic pattern.

We cannot, however, forget that the comparison between faeces and money does not (at least, it should not) attempt to derive reductively the constitution of economic dynamics from infantile libidinal dynamics. As Fenichel, one of the top level representatives of psychoanalytical theory and practice, tells us, deducing the real function of money from its neurotic use would be like supposing that the hidden sexual meaning the act of walking has for the hysteric reveals the sexual character of that function, abandoning on another level what it means as a way of moving on (Fenichel, 1973, pp. 544–545). But, as Ricoeur says about the Freudian interpretation of the possessive passion, there is no part of human existence that escapes the libidinal investment of love and hate. That interpretation is, however, perfectly compatible with other theories that restore its specific value to the economic sphere (Ricoeur, 1970, pp. 487–494).

Yet, in addition, this economic specificity must be considered, also from the psychoanalytical perspective, as a main component in determining behaviour in relation to money. It is precisely the economic dynamic that, in fact, in our society, usually favours the most regressive behaviour in relation to money. So, we could agree with Fenichel that it is, rather, the real function of money that influences and conditions anal eroticism, since social conditions largely determine the breadth and even the intensity of the retentive instinctual tendencies. Anal instincts change into the wish to acquire wealth only under specific social conditions (Fenichel, 1973, p. 545). (In a similar vein, see Fromm's ideas on "social character" which, on the matters we are analysing, should be valued well above his other areas of interpretation (Caparrós, 1975).)

As Tornos taught us in his philosophical anthropology course, human tendencies have a social configuration. In other words, there are typical ways of satisfying instincts, needs, and drives which are not biologically predetermined, but socially modelled. The way to satisfy aggressiveness, prestige, or power can vary considerably depending on the behaviour patterns that are proposed and gratified in the social environment (Bergler, 1951; Heinzelman, 1980). It seems evident that, in the ways of socially structuring instinctual tendencies, publicity plays a decisive role. "Marry for interest" read a recent advertisement, suggesting, in its double meaning, love of money ahead of the other most valued love: that of the couple. A brief analysis of the advertisements that surround us nowadays would give evidence of how the satisfaction of prestige is linked predominantly to monetary possession. We are familiar with the phenomenon of bankers taking the place of aristocrats in entertainment magazines.

This confirms Horney's idea: the possessive ambition propelled by our Western societies results in hostility as a tendency to deprive others, even to the point of turning the wish to despoil, embezzle, or thwart others in an authentic cultural norm (Horney, 1937, Chapter Ten).

In this respect, it is worth remembering the analysis made by Fromm (an author whom we value more as psycho-sociologist than as psychoanalyst). As we know, the psychoanalysis of Erich Fromm and of those called "culturalists" (K. Horney, H. S. Sullivan) tries to carry out an important revision of Freudian psychoanalysis. The distinction is then made between what must be considered "essential" and what looks "accidental" in Freud's thought. From this starting point, significant changes are undertaken in Freudian meta-psychology, such as the new assessment of the ego against the id and the superego, a lowering of the role assigned to the libido and the erotogenic zones by Freud, as well as a relativisation of the death instinct and of the Freudian approaches to the Oedipus complex. In contrast to all that, the role of the socio-cultural environment is significantly emphasised in the interpretation of repression or sublimation mechanisms. Thus, the ego and the environment become more relevant, lessening considerably the role of the unconscious. The "metapsychology" (Freud's term for the psychology placed behind consciousness) is mostly reduced to a "psychology of the ego" in a strongly sociological context. Marcuse (1987) is ruthless in his criticism of the culturalists in his lucid writing in the Epilogue of *Eros and Civilization.*

Nevertheless, Fromm emphasises the deep human alienation caused by Western consumerism. To consume is no longer a meaningful human experience, but a way to satisfy artificially stimulated phantasies, which are truly foreign to our real and concrete being. We eat and drink the phantasies fed to us by the media. To consume has become a goal in itself; an obviously compulsive and irrational goal, which replaces "being" with "having", even to the point of the perverse identification in which someone could truly say: I am what I consume (Fromm, 1982a, pp. 111–137)

From these consumption dynamics, productivity becomes the most important goal. A kind of productivity which deeply perverts the sense of progress itself, since really, as can be seen in Marcuse's analysis, it is a progress which ignores essential values like peace or human happiness (Marcuse, 1971, pp. 552–572). "We no longer give our surplus to God; the process of producing an ever-expanding surplus is in itself our God" wisely affirms Norman Brown (Brown, N. O, 1959, p. 296). We now come to the point where psychology makes an exit and theology takes its place, since we are fully in the land of religion and idolatry. But, thanks to psychoanalytical interpretation, we know what the idol is made of.

God or money

There is radical incompatibility between the passion for money and the passion for God. We cannot serve two masters at the same time (Matthew 6: 24, Luke 16: 13) (an exegetical analysis of the biblical maxim can be found in Carter, 2001). There is an incompatibility of a religious nature, because faith in God prevents idolatry, incompatibility of a moral nature, because it is not possible to serve love and selfishness at the same time, and incompatibility, too, of a psychodynamic nature, because it is not possible to feel a "passion" for the Kingdom and for money at the same time without tearing the subject apart.

The incompatibility between God and money in the Gospel is radical. It is not possible to love God, that is, generosity, devotion, solidarity, compassion, clemency, and, at the same time, love money, that is hoarding, accumulation, and the fundamentals of all injustice and lack of love: hunger, war, exploitation, death, etc. (Cavanaugh, 2008).

For Jesus' followers, love is not only a precept; it is the message itself. In consequence, the passion for money, which means a lack of love, stands not only as an ethical problem but also as a problem of belief, of faith, of religion. Loyalty to the single God is, thus, questioned; that is, the idolatrous character of money, marked in the Gospel by the term "Mammon" (the term's etymology is not clear; it seems to refer to "deposit", "provision", but Jesus' words seem to put it in the context of idolatry, with a meaning related to a refuge from existence (Rüger, 1973, pp. 127–131)).

The Gospel proposal on this is blunt and clear: Jesus, "though he was rich, yet for your sake he became poor" (2 Corinthians 8: 9) and had "no place to lay his head" (Matthew 8: 20). These sayings are not ambiguous. The choice of poverty is the basis and the condition for joining him in the work of the Kingdom: boats, nets, or office desk must be abandoned (Matthew 4: 20–22; 8: 18–20; 9: 9; Mark 10: 17–21). The creation of the new community, as the alternative to the world's perverse relationships, needs to break with what is the very basis of inequality and injustice (Kavanaugh, 2007).

At the core of Jesus' message we find God's revelation as Father and, from there, the proclamation of the equality and brotherhood of all human beings (Jeremías, 1965). In consequence, the creation of a community where sharing replaces hoarding, and which presents this as an alternative to the world's unjust relationships, constitutes one of the basic proposals in the proclamation of the Kingdom of God.

It is, then, understandable that work to extend the Kingdom is not possible by using what amounts to a denial of the equality message. Therefore, to fulfil the mission, one must go through the process of dispossession; "Do not get any gold or silver or copper to take with you in your belts" (Matthew 10: 9–10).

Moreover, the Gospel states that money is going to be one of the most powerful temptations for any of Jesus' followers: the power we assign to money, the force which the believer perceives money has in the creation and constitution of so many worldly powers, is going to lead him to believe that it also can be an exceptional instrument for the Kingdom's extension. That is the temptation. We know that Jesus was the first to suffer it (Matthew 4: 1–11).

It is worth emphasising this temptation, because it takes us straight to the issue of self-deception, so common in this environment. In reality, temptation is only that which, being one thing, can appear to the conscience as something quite different. The matter of money, as for anything where "a matter of love" is at play, is one of the most propitious places for a false conscience. We know how easily the most powerful rationalisations come up (such as St Ignatius's "second class of person" relative to the "ten thousands ducats") and open the way for certain economic–emotional dynamics without knowing where they will lead us.

Ultimately, the temptations of money arise from the panic caused by insecurity. Money, goods, and possessions appear then as a support, as firm ground under our feet. If we take into account the whole psychoanalytical interpretation made earlier, we could conclude that money is something more than firm ground; it is a protective shield, even more so, it is an internal object, body in the body, or, as Fenichel reminded us, something with "ego quality". The centripetal, retentive, hoarding dynamics of anal-eroticism and monetary possession have all the force of narcissism and infantile self-assertion. We are afraid of losing ground; so, we view money as a means to grip on to ourselves. The search for security is the basis of the temptation of money: "You have plenty of grain laid up for many years. Take life easy; eat, drink and be merry" (Luke 12: 19). Money stands for the dream of a secure existence.

Therefore, the first Beatitude tears apart this deception, uncovering the panic of insecurity. He who clings to money, thinking that this makes him greater and stronger, is not happy; happy is he who chooses to be poor, because, in this way, he feels and demonstrates that his security is in God and his happiness does not lie in owning oneself but in giving oneself. It is a gamble proposed to each one of Jesus' followers. Only through this experience can we find verification.

This obviously does not mean that ambivalence and ambiguity cannot also be present in our relationship with money. We cannot fall into Manichean totalities. Neither will conversion here be wholly fulfilled. But, at the same time, it also seems clear that those ambivalences and ambiguities must be consciously recognised as such, and the aims and goals should not be obscured with false rationalisations. It is necessary to know where one is and where one is not.

Along these lines, we could say that those "ten thousands ducats" which St Ignatius brings to our attention in the "three classes of persons" meditation compel us to take a position. In the text of his *Spiritual Exercises* (1914, 149–156), St Ignatius tries, as we know, to unravel the internal dynamics of the exercitant by means of the analysis of three subjects (the three "classes") who are in the position to opt for, or abstain from, God in their lives. In the proposed example, the alternative to God is "ten thousand ducats". The first of them seems to have opted for the money as lord, so he makes no effort for any change. The third opts decidedly for God as the only Lord, and, in doing so, he wins his freedom. But the second class of person, through an obvious rationalisation, tries to serve two lords at the same time. Ignatius shows the gravity of the matter, equating it to an attempt to manipulate God (Domínguez-Morano, 2003, pp. 139–161).

Those who "choose" to be poor

Instead of resorting to hoarding as an egotistical and hostile defence towards others, Jesus proposes sharing, as an opening to others and as a way to create a Christian community to be built as an alternative to oppressive interpersonal relationships. In a sharing type of relationship, the first narcissistic and aggressive self-assertion typical of the anal stage gives way to an open, kind, and warm attitude towards the other. Furthermore, where there is sharing, abundance follows, contrary to belief held by the fetishist who seeks security through hoarding. That is exactly what is meant in the accounts of the feeding of the five thousand (Mark 6: 30–46; Luke 9: 10–17; John 6: 1–15); a scant quantity, when shared, multiplies miraculously.

The choice of poverty signifies the freedom to put oneself at the service of the Kingdom. Getting rich, on the contrary, risks becoming deaf and blind towards Jesus' call. That is why it is so difficult for those who have money to enter the Kingdom (Mark 10: 23); their securities, their beloved objects, their libidinal dynamics point in a very different direction. Their love is placed in that dehumanised version of themselves which is their wealth. From there, it is very difficult to hear the call.

Yet, in the Gospel's message we find something that goes far beyond a mere ascetic renunciation of wealth. It is also a matter of freedom in relation to money. A freedom that, because of the primary emotional implications in play, is not easy at all. Money is an object that easily sends desire astray and ends up becoming its master. That freedom from possessions is, therefore, more complex than a question of having or not having money. This has to be affirmed, without, of course, mixing it up with hyperbole based on the classic and untenable spiritualistic reading of the first Beatitude.

This is not about taking advantage of the "poor in spirit" to legitimise material wealth; it is about the fact that a follower of Jesus, because he is conscious of the traps of money and its capacity to generate injustice and inequality, "chooses" to be poor. That choice is necessarily the fruit of freedom, of an internal capacity to have or not to have possessions. From that capacity, however, he chooses to be poor because he has divested money of its typical fascination and spell and has unmasked all the falsehood hidden in the security it is believed to bring.

It is evident that it is not enough to go without money to be an evangelical pauper. Even without it, it is still possible to be fascinated by it. That is one of the great traps generated by our consumerist society. The believer in Jesus can, however, allow himself the luxury of breaking the alabaster vial of very costly spikenard perfume in a "waste" of love. That is what Mary did (John 12: 1–11; Matthew 26:

6–13; Mark 14: 3–9). In those quantities, there is a real chance of solving very urgent cases of poverty. Judas, at the time, expressed some very logical thinking, but a logic that, at bottom, keeps faith in money, maintains belief in its power to change. Judas probably left his property to follow Jesus, but did not divest himself at the same time of the mind-set of money. Somehow, money kept being his "lord" (*Spiritual Exercises*, 1914, 155). Along these lines, we might recall the Ignatian meditation on the three "classes". The third one, the expression of the freedom of being in service to God, attests, "they have even no liking for it, to keep the thing acquired or not to keep it". Paradoxical as it might seem, it is possible maintain a "no liking to keep it" (155) as an expression of unconscious inner conflicts, and not as an expression of inner freedom in relation to those objects.

We should not forget that the Gospel teachings do not try to favour pauperism or be apologetic towards destitution or penury. We also know that Jesus used money (Luke 8: 2–3; John 12: 6). What matters is acquiring freedom from it in order to "choose" being poor as a condition for entering the Kingdom. As Rahner writes, in beautiful language on poverty,

> the mean, the stingy, the emaciated by destitution and lack of aspiration in his being, the undeveloped, the frugal, the man of petit-bourgeois measure, is certainly not the man that can give sense to the act of faith in poverty. (Rahner, 1962, pp. 74–105)

In these pages, Rahner makes very pertinent observations about poverty in religious life. A wealthy religious order, he tells us, cannot have poor members, but members who depend on the entirety of the community. However, neither dependency of material goods and property nor the lack of private property in the legal sense makes a man "poor". He will be an economically dependent man, and this can have respectable ascetic connotations, but is not equivalent to poverty.

In psychoanalytical terms, we can say that poverty is not the fruit of a "reaction formation" against the wish of having. In effect, it is worth remembering that the obsessive neurotic person is usually quite thrifty, extremely responsible with expenses and purchases. In fact, he can be very austere. But, in the dynamics of neurosis, that austerity can respond solely to a defensive mechanism through which the person adopts exactly the opposite behaviour of what he unconsciously desires. Of course, at the conscious level, everything is legitimised by means of all kinds of rationalisations. "Evangelical poverty" can be one of them. The poor person who does not have the psychological capacity to be rich is not the poor person of the Beatitudes (as he who does not have the psychological capacity to make love is not chaste or the "eunuch for the sake of the kingdom of heaven"). It is more likely that he will be a subject with a somewhat obsessive temper who, going against his repressed desire to possess, has developed, as a defence and control mechanism, a "reaction formation" opposite to that desire, which is something very far from what Paul says about himself in his letter to the Philippians:

> Not that I speak from want, for I have learned to be content in whatever circumstances I am. I know how to get along with humble means, and I also know how to live in prosperity; in any and every circumstance I have learned the secret of being filled and going hungry, both of having abundance and suffering need; I can do all things through Him who strengthens me. (Philippians 4: 11–13)

Poverty as opposed to wealth

To limit the existing relationships between the Gospel message and money to what has been said up to now would amount to a mutilation and a very gross simplification of the problems to their more individualistic dimensions. If we stop there (important as it might also be for the correct understanding of what remains to be said), we could very well be playing the god Mammon's game with his complex machinations. In effect, pontiffs preaching to their cults are not disturbed by those who acquire inner freedom from their god.

As we saw early on in this chapter, behaviour related to money is inseparably associated to the operating ways and manners of the social structures in which we live. In fact, economic factors usually foster the most regressive aspects of that behaviour within our society. In the end, social conditions determine the scope and even the intensity of the instinctual retention tendencies. The anal instincts, Fenichel reminded us, change into the desire to acquire wealth only under specific social conditions. Therefore, trying to free ourselves from the fascination of money, approaching the issue at a purely individual level would mean, also at that level, a serious misunderstanding of the issue. We know that evangelical poverty and current economic conditions are interdependent. Therefore, it can be asserted with good reason that the vow of poverty is the most socially significant, and what would have been considered in other times a sign of evangelical poverty, in today's Western society becomes a contradiction in terms. This happened, for instance, with mendicant behaviour. Poverty today is inseparable from an essential engagement in the fight against injustice and in the creation of a relevant symbol against the consumerism of our Western societies. This was the view taken by the XXXI General Congregation of the Society of Jesus in their decree on poverty (GC 31, Decree 12, 3–5).

In addition, a deep analysis of the relationship between Jesus' message and the economic power structures proves that the scope of that message is much larger than the sphere of the individual. Once again, a certain conception of soteriology is questioned here.

In the chapter on guilt and salvation, we spoke about the reduction the latter has suffered throughout history, until it was almost exclusively understood as a "salvation from"; a concept of salvation understood, in an especially dramatic tone, in the relationship of man with God. Above all, it was understood as an issue merely at the individual level, referring almost exclusively to the afterlife. For this way of understanding Jesus' salvation, what we have said until now on the question of money would be enough.

But we have given warning there that, against this restrictive and dramatic way of understanding salvation, there was another, which, rather than "salvation from", should be understood as "salvation for": salvation for a life understood as a project to transform reality into a Kingdom of God worthy of man; salvation as an impulse for both history and future (see the section titled "Sin, love and, death", in Chapter Seven). In this way, the relationship between the Gospel and money would grow and deepen.

It is absolutely certain that Jesus' message was primarily and directly a religious message. Once again it is necessary to affirm that Jesus did not come as a social reformer, and it is not possible to find texts in which Jesus makes specific socio-political proposals, and neither did he try to confer a particular socio-economic bent on his poverty. As Rahner says, Jesus' poverty is not primarily related to a social programme for the reform of economic situations, but as a consequence of the eschatological salvation situation (Rahner, 1962, p. 68). The Kingdom is already here and imposes a new way of understanding all aspects of this worldly dimension and any type of relationship with God and between men.

If, on the theme of sexuality, we said that the Gospel does not make concrete proposals on specific modes of sexual behaviour, but deeply subverts the structures in which sexuality emerges and develops, something very similar would need to be said about the believer's relationship with socio-economic structures. Jesus does not give us specific instructions or guidelines in this area of life (as important as they might be for us, as with sexuality). But the new eschatological reality of the Kingdom brings such a deep disruption in the understanding of man's relationship with God and with his fellow men that the socio-economic structures and spheres are immediately and radically implicated. All that through what is essentially a religious message.

A close analysis of the evangelical texts shows that, in fact, Jesus took a stand on socio-economic questions. To begin with, his own poverty should be understood as a shattering indictment of the socio-economic structures of his day. But, above all, it is from his proclamation of God's fatherhood, and of the consequent fundamental proclamation of equality between men that we must understand the far-reaching alteration of socio-economic structures that the realisation of the Kingdom pursues. From there, money, as a basic source of inequality and injustice, becomes a negative value that can even acquire an authentically satanic character. The ambition of wealth prevents brotherhood and, hence, the attainment of the Kingdom of God. From there we can understand that a follower of Jesus must leave everything behind and go in pursuit of him (Matthew 4: 20–22; 8: 18–20; 9:9; Mark 10: 17–21) and that the mission must be carried out from dispossession and not from the power of wealth (Matthew 10: 9–10). We must insist on this: it is not an ascetic matter, it is a matter of consistency with the message proclaiming the radical equality of all men and, therefore, the need to transform the structures which breed injustice.

From there, the choice of poverty automatically becomes a positive rejection and a battle against wealth. As Sobrino expresses so accurately with the antithetic terms used by St Ignatius ("poverty as opposed to wealth"), "to be in poverty is to have achieved it in opposition to wealth" (Sobrino, 1990, p. 113, translated for this edition). The exercise of compassion must place the Church in a state of poverty and, hence, against wealth as well.

It is not possible, in effect, to be against injustice, hunger, war, exploitation, drug trafficking and, at the same time, not be against the economic structures that generate, primarily in a brutal way, those devastating realities. It is not possible to preach about one true and living God, and, at the same time, as unfortunately happens in our Churches, be colluding with Mammon, who, no doubt, is the great idol that pulls the most important strings in our societies and who, like any idol, attracts the most damaging fascination and identifications. It is not possible to proclaim, in the Gospel's name, a demanding "social doctrine" and, at the same time, carry forward hidden alliances with the god that generates exploitation and death.

Violence and peace in the Kingdom

Here, we come back to a problem that we left outlined in Chapter Seven on guilt and salvation. We said that the Christian does not often know what to do with his aggressiveness and that generally this leads him to turn it against himself in the form of guilt, instead of directing it to the necessary fight for the attainment of the Kingdom. The Gospel has enemies, we said that also, and their unmasking and denunciation is an inescapable task for any believer.

During Jesus' times, in a society completely shaped by religion, that very religion, perversely understood, was the main obstacle for the revelation of the authentic face of God and of the dignity of man. That is why Jesus was implacable in his denouncement of it. The idolatry was that of the law and the hypocritical cult of God. In our secularised society, however, the great idol is not in the temple but in the banks (it has rightly been said that religious architecture has found the best replacement for cathedrals in the construction of bank headquarters, sometimes with very similar characteristics to old temples, with the sanctuary replaced by the vault).

Perhaps, in our Western world, there is no more powerful enemy of God than money. Perhaps there is no behavioural motivation more clearly elicited by our socio-cultural models. Without doubt, there is not a more decisive cause of death and destruction. The machinery of war, drugs, hunger, exploitation, the progressive decline into poverty of the Third World, north–south unbalance, great ecological disasters, etc., are all driven by that extremely powerful and terrible energy source which is the ambition for money.

If all this does not attract our deepest rejection, our indignation, and, it must be said without fear, our most intense aggressiveness, it means we are once again sickeningly sugar-coating the Gospel and using it to disguise and evade the unavoidably conflicting reality we live in. The option for the poor is necessarily something more than charitable assistance. If it is not joined with a solidarity that is both prophetic denunciation and determined courageous action against the causes of poverty, it means we are taking part in spiritual escapism.

Jesus expressed clearly his "violence" against the agents who, in their socio-cultural context of religious predominance, were causing the oppression of man. (Here we are using the term "violence" in order to evoke a special type of force, not necessarily physical, but of intensity, associated with the use of this term. We know that the word is used by Matthew (11: 12) with a controversial interpretation: "the violent" (*biátsetai)* can refer to those who suffer violence or to those who exert it. Therefore, it is possible to interpret that they "conquer" the Kingdom, laudably, or that they pretend to "get rid of it", in a reprehensible way. The verb *Apráxousin,* which comes next, accepts also both interpretations. This confusion and controversy in itself interestingly shows the double sense that, in fact, violence can have, as a positive or negative force, for the person: (Zerwick, 1960, p. 27).) Jesus' work for the Kingdom ran parallel to visible conflicts, opposition, and open struggle against all agents of domination. That violence and aggressiveness, we know very well from the Gospel, cannot be understood as mere destructiveness, and even less so as the use of physical or armed violence. But it is evident, unless we wish to close our eyes because of our unresolved problems with aggressiveness, that Jesus' behaviour is marked by continuous conflict with his environment and that he was not intimidated by fear or by a misconceived "goodness" or "docility". During his life he was true to "the kingdom of heaven suffers violence, and violent men take it by force" (Matthew 11: 12). His word was always blunt and potent, even sometimes adopting behaviour not far from provocation. Suffice to look, for instance, at the episode inside the synagogue in Nazareth, defying the narrow nationalism of his fellow countrymen, who ultimately wanted to throw him off a cliff (Luke 4: 24–30), or his irony with the scribes of the Pharisees calling them "righteous" in contrast with the "sinners" (Mark 2: 17). He said he did not come to bring peace, but a sword (Matthew 10: 34) and he himself even held a whip (John 2: 15). His transgressions of religious traditions and rules (Mark 2: 1–12, 18–22, 23–28, 3:1–6) were also a significant type of aggression directed at the imposed social behaviour patterns and those who represented them. Of course, from a psychoanalytical point of view, we have to consider aggression to be not only the tendency that leads to destructive action, but also any behaviour that somehow constrains other people, denying their wish or actually opposing them (Laplanche & Pontalis, 1973, "Aggression").

Jesus' denouncement, otherwise, was not done through the sort of ambiguous and generic analysis frequently carried out by our Church on the powers of this world. It was an open and manifest denunciation, clearly pointing a finger at all those who pretended to be, and, in fact, were seen as, saintly social benefactors. He used against them the hardest epithets: hypocrites, blind guides, dumb, whitewashed tombs, snakes, brood of vipers (Matthew 23). Regarding Jesus' denouncement of the rulers of the day, we have to recognise that he was not held back by a fear of conflict and aggressiveness that so many times paralyses his followers.

Yet, at the same time, we cannot forget that this Jesus of fighting character is the same one who proclaimed that the meek and the peacemakers are blessed (Matthew 5: 5–9), who called himself "gentle and humble in heart" (Matthew 11: 29–30), who, fulfilling the prophecy, did not break off a battered reed or put out a smouldering wick (Matthew 12: 15–21), who called for offering the other cheek (Matthew 5: 39–40), or harshly reprimanded those who asked for a fire to be brought down from heaven as a revenge (Luke 9: 51–55).

So (if we do not wish to make an intentionally biased reading, or even worse, a mutilation, of the texts, driven by ideology or by our traits), we will have to agree, based on Gospel data, that, in effect, the peace that Jesus brings "is not this world's peace". It is not the peace of systematic denial of any type of conflict. It is not the peace born from that massive negation of our aggressiveness. It is even less the peace stemming from complicity and hidden collusion with the perverse order of our world (Girardi, 1983, pp. 617–648). On the other hand, if we look at Jesus' manifestly pacifistic positions, we will have to agree that his violence is also not of this world. We will then need to be very attentive in order to understand and harmonise that peace with that violence, avoiding the idea that the assertion of one supposes the denial or elimination of the other. As we can see, important issues are implied in this hermeneutical problem. The whole matter, otherwise, sets us before that difficult problem that every human must face in working out and managing aggressiveness.

We purposefully ignore here everything related to the character of aggressiveness, whether innate, instinctive, biologic, or socio-culturally learnt. As we know, for Freud it has an original, not a secondary, character (as expressed in Freud, 1920g, pp. 7–64). Opposing this view are those who see aggressiveness as a consequence of frustration. However, this approach fudges the question. For instance, with the thought that, if it is instinctive, it is unalterable, and, because of that, perhaps we tone it down and shirk our responsibility for the violence around us. Or, on the other hand, if it is acquired, we dream of a mythical, pure man, soiled by others from "outside", from the "social-perverse". Thus, we obviate the fundamental problem: that aggressiveness is there with a certain irreducible, non-dispensable, character, and that it is there within ourselves, whether we like it or not. Because, even if it came solely out of frustration, the latter truly is our companion in a substantial way from the time we are born (Jeammet, 1989).

Our irreducible violence

As we have already said, the believer's usual road has been the denial of aggressiveness, with the resulting diversion on himself as feelings of guilt. However, another, more complex path is possible, by working through the aggressiveness and death drives, in articulation with love and with the life drives. It is not about closing our eyes towards our aggressive aspects, but of channelling them towards love and life. In that struggle between the "Heavenly Powers", Eros and Thanatos, in which the history of civilisation is played out (Freud, 1930a, p. 145), a Christian believer opts decidedly for Eros and makes all efforts to have Thanatos vanquished instead of illusorily denied. That will not be possible if, out of fear, we choose to ignore our aggressive powers.

In our personal histories, we have a series of unavoidable frustrations that surely are a source of aggressiveness. This poses an initial problem, that of acquiring enough capacity to tolerate frustrations. That is certainly a pedagogical problem of the first order. The aggressive response threshold is, in large measure, created by the tolerance threshold of frustration as narcissistic wound at the loss of the object. When that tolerance does not exist, the immediate reaction tends to be either to destroy the object that frustrates us, or else fall into sorrow or depression as a means of self-destruction.

However, in our life there are also many frustrations that, at least theoretically, would be perfectly avoidable (I have no money for food, the other does not let me be myself, others attack me). Against all those frustrations, aggressiveness should be converted into a source of energy, into entrepreneurial spirit, into a dynamic force for the person who asserts himself and does not run away from difficulty.

Understood in this way, aggressiveness must be recognised; it must have space and certain means of expression within our life. Among the most notable, no doubt, we can speak about the revolutionary fight and opposition against the agents of human frustration, as exemplified by Jesus of Nazareth, Gandhi, Martin Luther King, Oscar Romero, or Ignacio Ellacuría and his fellow martyrs in El Salvador. It is a matter of seeing how to use aggressiveness to work in favour of our life instincts; in the believer's case, as a means of realising the Kingdom of God.

On the other hand, this might serve as a way to avoid the pathology generally expressed either in an obsessive way converted into guilt, or on the paranoiac side, in which the denial of aggressiveness leads to the outer projection as persecutory delusions: "the others are evil and are after me".

This last type of behaviour has also been present during many instances of revolution, both inside and outside the realm of Christianity. The defence of "justice" has been found to be a great point, a perfect rationalisation, for the projection of unrecognised internal phantasies and for the displacement of aggressiveness from its original sources and objects towards others, seen as incarnations of those inner enemies. Obscure and ancient rancour or envy motivations might have been displaced to more tolerable categories such as class struggle, or action for justice. We should remember, however, that the aspiration to behave with absolutely "pure" motivations is a utopian ambition always worth pursuing, although never fully achievable. It would not be fair and honest, as has happened on occasion, to try to disqualify beneficent acts for the most deprived by questioning "purity of intention". Nevertheless, it is true that a certain dose of suspicion about his own real and true motivations would benefit more than one "revolutionary" activist, for their own good and for the very "revolution" they are supposed to be pursuing.

We all somehow carry inside us a ticking time bomb of varying size. It can explode inside us or we can quickly hurl it outside. That is the great danger. That potential, however, could also be wisely channelled in a way consistent with our life projects and our value system. We can use it in favour of life, in favour of our lives, in the form of a healthy sense of guilt that moves us towards change and conversion, or in service to others, denouncing injustice or any form of oppression. It is, thus, a violence for peace, for the establishment of a new society that progressively brings the Kingdom that God wants for men into reality.

Jesus' peace is not this world's peace. Neither is his violence, because it was always activated for the benefit of others and not for his own benefit. He did not use that sort of "ministry of defence" we all carry inside us, ready to mobilise against any affront or injury to our own rights. "If you seek me, let these go their way" (John 18: 8). For Jesus, the fight for human rights starts with the rights of others and not his own. It is not wounded narcissism that unleashes it, but a vilified love.

That love for the oppressed man, the poor, the marginalised, was always the trigger for his aggressiveness and his violence. That man is epitomised by the figure in the synagogue with the withered hand. Jesus healed him in the name of God, of that God who wants good for man over safeguarding the law. That could not be understood by those who had the law itself as God, through which they glorified themselves and martyred others. Jesus' behaviour, as described by Mark, is very enlightening in this respect. His indignation was immediate, casting upon them, the text says, "a look of anger" (*met' orgés*). Jesus is not intimidated by their power, and neither does he lessen his resolve.

But the text goes on to add something that helps us to understand the meaning and direction of Jesus' aggressiveness. Sadness accompanies it: "grieved" (*syllypoúmenos*) at their hardness of heart, he said to the man "Stretch out your hand" (Mark 3: 4). Bravely showing aggressiveness, indignation, and anger does not exclude the expression of compassion and pain for what we see as evil, and as a grave alienation of the other. Love controls and goes beyond aggression. But, at the same time, that compassion does not generate softness, complicity or passivity regarding matters that are harmful to the disadvantaged: Jesus then did "what should not be done". He did what was socially and politically forbidden. In his actions we can detect aggression, not sought after but undertaken none the less: thus, the man was freed. Those slighted "went out and immediately began conspiring with the Herodians against Him, as to how they might destroy Him" (Mark 3: 6).

Based on this, the believer and the whole Church should learn a lesson on the always difficult management of aggressiveness and how to put it at the service of a definitive fight for life and justice. The faith and love for a living God must simultaneously mobilise anger, indignation, aggressiveness, and violence against the god of death: money. Because, although we might find it hard to believe, we cannot serve two masters, and because serving one of them ultimately means turning against the other.

Epilogue

What does it mean, then, to believe after Freud? Above all, it means to believe. With the tremor one faces when daring to take a step into that unknown, also with the awareness of the many evils perpetrated throughout history in the name of belief. But faith after Freud, if it continues to be faith, knows how to stay determined and firm.

Because to believe after Freud does not mean to feel the need to, somewhat shamefully, dilute the identity and contents of that faith so that it conforms to previous psychoanalytic (or any other kind of) requirements, which are now granted the honour and glory. The unconscious, in spite of the fascination it is able to conjure, cannot be elevated to the altars. The proposal of a good relationship with it should not be proclaimed from the pulpit as a new "good word". Neither should religion feel the need to mutilate itself in accordance with some external requirement.

That firmness, however, should not be a maniacal defence against the horror of emptiness. Belief does not in any way guarantee the longed-for presence without fault or defect. Therefore, that faith does not prevent confronting that terrible situation at point zero, from which that first step can be an encounter with either all or nothing, the hopeful presence or the complaisant absence, sense or total nonsense, life or death as ultimate and final word. Because faith alone will not automatically shield us from the path towards unbelief, and neither will love shield us from the path to hate, nor hope towards despair, for ever.

So, to believe after Freud continues to mean having the experience (always with that necessarily ineffable character of the religious experience) of feeling grounded and embraced in God's symbolic magnitude with all the things it can offer to the different aspects of a person: as encouragement for growth, as the source of joy for life, and as a jumping-off point for understanding reality. Everything is experienced and accepted as a gift. Without arrogance, of course, but without guilt either, in the awareness that not everyone will join in an experience that could be joyously shared by all.

In the depths of that religious experience the mediation and the presence of unconscious structures of the psyche are recognised ("mysticism is the obscure self-perception of the realm outside the ego, the Id," Freud wrote in the final stages of his life (1941f)). The post-Freudian believer is not afraid of, or annoyed by, such a presence or mediation. He has renounced the pure, direct immediacy between his credo and his consciousness. He knows he is traversed by a discourse that speaks to him. And he believes that, in his faith, he is also being talked to by another presence that both lives in him and transcends him.

This conviction—which, at a certain level, never stops being so—avoids tangling itself in the pure infantile wish, so devastating, which tries to find security and a full guarantee of protection at all costs. To believe is just to risk reading reality, beyond the empirical and sensible, as a sign and symbol: reality as metaphor. But this reality, read thus in a different way, is not now magically transformed by that reading. That founding and protective God cannot, therefore, be taken as an "amenable" God in the face of the overwhelming and dreadful autonomy of reality. One will always be ready, then, to accept that, even with Him, one can also be drawn into the worst, into the utter senselessness of pain and of the unfathomable, just as Jesus was. Despite that, one will go on believing that God is present.

God is symbolically given the name of Father, without our ever being fully aware of all that we are saying or hiding when we do so. However, with it, we opt for the proclamation of the meaning. At the same time, that proclamation of God as our Father urges us not to yearn for any other type of paternity on earth.

The boldness of calling God Father is the result of both an "invention" and a "listening", an elaborated construction—"invention"—of the complex stratagems of the unconscious. The Word is heard, however, from a different place than our own wish. Therefore, faith will always be listening. Only in that way does it avoid becoming the mere expression of our own longing. Jesus, the Word spoken by the Father, confronts the simple affective creation about God—our "invention"—with what God says about Himself. A careful listening to the Word exorcises the mirages of the imaginary, and shows what God is and not what the believer desires. Mixing up God with his image is, thus, forbidden because the image is always of our own making.

God the Father, as spoken by Jesus, will be for us a permanent surprise, because that God has dismantled the most common and universal models that we are driven to draw up about him. The "invention" goes through a continual restructuring when it knows how to listen. In effect, that God the Father does not look at all like Jupiter. He has chosen to show His maximum power through utter weakness, not in order to incline us to an exaltation of failure, of the weak or the impotent, but just as an affirmation of everlasting love.

Everything has been said and done in the name of love. Freud, in particular, has taught us how many rotten roots love can grow from. Jesus did not speak much about it. His followers have elaborated it much more. With his life, Jesus clearly demonstrated that only through love can we recognise the force that, beyond narcissism and violence, may lead us to something better.

No Greek god, in spite of having loved so much and in such beautiful and terrible ways, would ever be seen compassionately kneeling down to wash his followers' feet. What could not be seen on Olympus, however, we have found as part of our history. And this gesture, having occurred in our own time and space, exerts an irresistible attraction, because we can infer the "salvation" of the human: the decentring of self as a requirement for reaching the plenitude and the full measure of oneself.

To believe that God is our Father means to profess He is so in just the same way that He was a Father to Jesus: He did not free him from his own responsibility or his death. This supposes, therefore, that belief is a way to find oneself in finitude, and by no means is a stratagem to break loose from it. It means owning that finitude that is ours, and abstaining from trying to turn God into the accomplice of the infinitude we long for. This means acquiring the only possible foundation for being faithful to ourselves from which we can strike up an honest relationship with Him. Because if, with Jesus' God the Father, we confess the triumph of life over death, it will not be to concede to that life—ours—the category of the unlimited.

In that finitude, an ample space for plenitude and joy, for surprise and discovery, can be perceived. The great beyond, as a possible gift in the definitive encounter, will not be expected as the fruit of need and, still less, of a demand. It has rightly been said that we do not believe in the soul's immortality, but in the resurrection of the dead.

And if the meaning is proclaimed, it will not be to claim the haughty pretension of having reached "the answer". Many taxing questions will remain open forever. We are, thus, invited to the healthy asceticism of renouncing total synthesis. The faith that confronts psychoanalysis learns to live and remain in the modesty of tentative formulations.

To believe after Freud also means the refusal of any type of religiousness that gives off the pestilence of rotten and dead flesh. We also know from psychoanalysis how much human flesh has been sacrificed at the altars of religion. Instinctual repression has often asked for God's signature in order to be executed, trying to send God into exile and repudiate in good part what He created and enlivened with His presence. We try to negate the God that "vegetates" in the plant, "senses" in the animal, and "understands" in the human being, and the God that—as beautifully as Ignatius of Loyola formulated—is "giving me being, animating me, giving me sensation and making me to understand". He did not exclude His presence from any part of us. We just have to perceive the beauty and gracefulness to be found throughout us. Bad is the faith that does not protect and promote joy and instead corrodes it with the woodworm of guilt, doubt, and remorse. Bad is the faith that places ethics at its centre. It is ungrateful, and, in addition, not elegant to God, who loves us regardless of our being more or less ethical.

To believe after Freud also means to recognise that faith is inseparable from the presence of others. From others faith came, traversing identifications and rejections. Faith is carried out with others, because only in intersubjectivity is faith free from the omnipotent aspiration to the imaginary. Faith invites others, as much to celebrate the shared gift as for the work in the fulfilment of a project. That project we call the Kingdom can easily appear delusional to others. For the Christian community, however, it just means participating in the dynamics that are heard pulsing under history's diverse beats. In consequence, within that history, they enlist themselves in battles of all sizes where human beings are brought down, marginalised, or rejected by others, or by mere contingencies of nature or history.

Believing after Freud means, therefore, to believe. Without diluting or mutilating its contents, with the purpose of "concordance" of loyalties. Inevitably, having come out of the unconscious, that faith will be experienced in a radically new way and, in the same measure, also thought about and told in a new way.

REFERENCES

Abraham, H. C., & Freud, E. L. (Eds.) (1965). *A Psychoanalytic Dialogue: The Letters of Sigmund Freud and Karl Abraham 1907–1926*. London: Hogarth.

Abraham, K. (1916). The spending of money in anxiety states. In: *Selected Papers of Karl Abraham* (pp. 200–302). London: Hogarth.

Adorno, T. W. (1975). Studies in the authoritarian personality. *Gesammelte Schriften, 9*(I): 143–509.

Ancona, L. (1983). Psicoanalisi e mondo católico. *Medicina e Morale, 3*: 241–253.

Ansbacher, H. L. (1948). Attitudes of German prisoners of war: a study of the dynamics of National-Socialistic followership. *Psychological Monographs: General and Applied, 62*: 1–42.

Anselmo de Canterbury (1929). *Cur Deus Homo*. Bonn: Sumptibus Petri Hanstein.

Aragó-Mitjans, J. M. (1965). *Psicología religiosa del niño*. Barcelona: Herder.

Asch, S. E. (1952). *Social Psychology*. Englewood Cliffs, NJ: Prentice-Hall.

Asch, S. E. (1956). Studies of independence and conformity. *Psychological Monographs, 70*: 416–436.

Assmann, J. (1997). *Moses the Egyptian: The Memory of Egypt in Western Monotheism*. Cambridge, MA: Harvard University Press.

Assoun, P. (2009). *Freud, la philosophie et les philosophes*. Paris: PUF.

Barande, R. (1973). *Education et psychanalyse*. Paris: Hachette.

Basaglia, F. (Ed.) (1969). *Morire di classe*. Turin: Einaudi.

Bastide, R. (1950). *Sociologie et psychanalyse*. Paris: PUF.

Beirnaert, L. (1964). *Expérience chrétienne et psychologie*. Paris: Epi.

Beirnaert, L. (1970). La teoría psicoanalítica y el mal moral. *Concilium, 56*: 364–375.

Beirnaert, L. (1987). *Aux frontières de l´acte analytique. La bible, saint Ignace, Freud et Lacan*. Paris: Seuil.

Bergler, E. (1951). *Money and Emotional Conflicts*. London: International Universities Press.

Bernstein, R. J. (1998). *Freud and the Legacy of Moses*. Cambridge: Cambridge University Press.

Bertolus, M., Ledoux, M., Ledoux, A., Lemaire, J., Lemaire, E., & Pohier, J. (1971). *La relation pastorale*. Paris: Cerf.

Bettelheim, B. (2006). Psychoanalysis and education. *School Review, 77*: 73–86.

Bourkes, J. G. (1913). *Der Unrat in Sitte, Brauch, Glauben and Gewohnheitsrecht der Völker*. Leipzig: Eichborn.

Bovet, P. (1925). *Le sentiment religieux et la psychologie de l'enfant*. Paris: Neuchatel.

Brown, J. A. C. (1964). *Freud and the Post-Freudians*. Harmondsworth: Penguin.

Brown, N. O. (1959). *Life against Death. The Psychoanalytic Meaning of History*. New York: Vintage.

Brown, R. E. (1979). *The Gospel According to John I–XII*. New York: Doubleday.

Cabarrús, C. (1990). La obediencia como problema latinoamericano. *Cuadernos de espiritualidad, 52*: 32–44.

Caparrós, A. (1975). *El carácter social según E. Fromm*. Salamanca: Sígueme.

Carr, D. M. (2003). *The Erotic Word. Sexuality, Spirituality and the Bible*. Oxford: Oxford University Press.

Carroll, M. P. (1987). Praying the rosary: the anal–erotic origins of a popular Catholic devotion. *Journal for the Scientific Study of Religion, 26*: 486–498.

Carter, W. (2001). *Matthew and the Margins*. New York: Orbis.

Caruso, P. (1969). *Conversazioni con Claude Lévi-Strauss, Michel Foucault, Jacques Lacan*. Milan: Mursia.

Castilho Pereira, W. C. (2004). *A formação religiosa em questão*. Pretropolis: Vozes.

Castillo, J. M. (1983). *El discernimiento cristiano*. Salamanca: Sígueme.

Castillo, J. M. (1986). *El seguimiento de Jesús*. Salamanca: Sígueme.

Castillo, J. M. (2009). *Dios y nuestra felicidad.* Bilbao: Desclée.
Castillo, J. M. (2010). *La humanización de Dios.* Madrid: Trotta.
Castillo, J. M. (2016). *La humanidad de Jesús.* Madrid: Trotta.
Cavanaugh, W. T. (2008). *Being Consumed: Economics and Christian Desire.* Grand Rapids, MI: Eerdmans.
Certeau, M. de (1988). *The Writing of History.* New York: Columbia University Press.
Champion, F., & Hervieu Léger, D. (1990). *De l'émotion en religion. Renouveaux et traditions.* Paris: Centurion.
Chasseguet-Smirgel, J. (1964). *La sexualité fémenine.* Paris: Payot.
Chevalier, J., & Gheerbrant, A. (1969). *Dictionnaire des symboles.* Paris: R. Lafont.
Cirlot, J. E. (1968). *Diccionario de símbolos.* Barcelona: Labor.
Cooper, D. (2006). *The Death of the Family.* London: Penguin.
Countryman, W. L. (1988). *Dirt, Greed and Sex: Sexual Ethics in the N. T. and their Implications for Today.* Filadelfia: Fortess.
Cullmann, O. (1956). *Immortalité de l'ame ou resurrection des morts? Le temoignage du Nouveau Testament.* Neuchatel: Delachaux.
D'Amore, A. (1978). *Hystorical Reflections on Psychoanalysis: 1920–1970.* New York: Brunner-Mazel.
Dalbiez, R. (1941). *Psychoanalytical Method and the Doctrine of Freud.* London: Longmans.
Deconchy, J. P. (1967). *Structure génétique de l'idée de Dieu.* Brussels: Lumen Vitae.
Demoulin, A., & Jarpard, J. M. (1965). *Perception symbolique et socialisation de l'attitude religieuse dans le rite.* Leuven: Université Catholique de Louven.
Dempsey, P. (1956). *Freud, Psychoanalysis, Catholicism.* Cork: Mercier.
Denzinger, H., & Hünermann, P. (2012). *Enchiridion Symbolorum.* San Francisco, CA: Ignatius Press.
Devereux, G. (1972). *Etnopsychanalyse complémentariste.* Paris: Flammarion.
Devereux, G. (1982). *Femme et mythe.* Paris: Flammarion.
Diéguez, M. de (1981). *L'idole monothéiste.* Paris: PUF.
Dolto, F. (1977a). *L'evangile au risque de la psychanalyse.* Paris: J. P. Delarge.
Dolto, F. (1977b). *Lorsque l'enfant paraît, Tome 1.* Paris: Seuil.
Domínguez-Morano, C. (1985). Aproximación psicoanalítica a la religiosidad tradicional andaluza. In: P. Castón (Ed.), *La religión en Andalucía* (pp.131–175). Seville: BCA.
Domínguez-Morano, C. (1991). *El psicoanálisis freudiano de la religión.* Madrid: Paulinas.

Domínguez-Morano, C. (1992). Psicoanálisis y antropología de la Religión en Andalucía. In: P. Gómez (Ed.), *Fiestas y religión en la cultura popular andaluza* (pp. 141–190). Granada: University of Granada.

Domínguez-Morano, C. (1996). Psicoanálisis clerical. In: J. I. González Faus, C. Domínguez-Morano, & A. Torres Queiruga (Eds.), *Clérigos en debate* (pp. 66–130). Madrid: PPC.

Domínguez-Morano, C. (2000). *Psicoanálisis y religión: diálogo interminable.* Madrid: Trotta.

Domínguez-Morano, C. (2001a). *Los registros del deseo.* Bilbao: Desclée.

Domínguez-Morano, C. (2001b). La vivencia mariana desde la perspectiva del psicólogo. *Ephemerides Mariologicae, LIII*: 97–116.

Domínguez-Morano, C. (2003). *Psicodinámica de los Ejercicios Ignacianos.* Bilbao/Santander: Mensajero/Sal Terrae.

Domínguez-Morano, C. (2006). *Experiencia cristiana y psicoanálisis.* Santander: Sal Terrae.

Domínguez-Morano, C. (2012). Manger ou boire: salud ou condemnation. Une analyse cinematographique. In: M. Vaucher, M. Durrer, & O. Revaz (Eds.), *Foi de cannibal* (pp. 357–392). Geneva: Labor et Fides.

Domínguez-Morano, C. (2016). *El otro de los místicos. Reflexiones desde el psicoanálisis.* Granada: Facultad de Teología.

Dominian, J. (1976). *Authority: A Christian Interpretation of the Psychological Solution of Authority.* London: Burns and Oates.

Drewermann, E. (1989). *Kleriker. Psychogramm eines Ideals.* Olten: Walter.

Duquoc, C. (1978). *Dieu different.* Paris: Cerf.

Engels, F. (1972). *The Origin of the Family, Private Property, and The State.* London: Penguin.

English, H. B., & English, A. C. (1958). *A Comprehensive Dictionary of Psychological and Psychoanalytical Terms: A Guide to Usage.* Oxford: Longmans.

Erikson, E. (1965). *Childhood and Society.* London: Hogarth.

Estrada, J. A. (1985). *La Iglesia, identidad y cambio.* Madrid: Trotta.

Estrada, J. A. (1988). *Del misterio de la Iglesia de Dios.* Salamanca: Sígueme.

Estrada, J. A. (2003). *La imposible teodicea.* Madrid: Trotta.

Estrada, J. A. (2008). *Religiosos en una sociedad secularizada.* Madrid: Trotta.

Fages, J. B. (1976). *Histoire de la psychanalyse après Freud.* Toulouse: Privat.

Fenichel, O. (1973). *The Psychoanalytic Theory of Neurosis.* New York: Norton.

Ferenczi, S. (1981). Ontogénesis del interés por el dinero. 1914. In: *O. C. II.* (pp. 183–191). Madrid: Espasa-Calpe.

Feuerbach, L. (1960). *Das Wesen des Christentums. S. W. VI.* Stuttgart: Frommann.

Fiddes, P. S. (1988). *The Creative Suffering of God*. Oxford: Oxford University Press.

Fitz, A. (1990). Religious and familial factors in the etiology of obsessive–compulsive disorder: a review. *Journal of Psychology and Theology, 18*: 141–147.

Font, J. (1999). *Religión, psicopatología y salud mental*. Barcelona: Paidós.

Foucault, M. (1972). *Histoire de la folie à l'âge classique*. Paris: Gallimard.

Franco, R. (1983). Sobre la genealogía de la obediencia religiosa. *Proyección, 30*: 3–21.

Freud, A. (1993). *The Ego and the Mechanisms of Defence*. London: Karnac.

Freud, A. (2011). *The Ego and the Mechanisms of Defence*. London: Karnac.

Freud, E. L. (Ed.). (1961). *Letters of Sigmund Freud 1873–1939*. London: Hogarth.

Freud, S. (1892–1893). A case of successful treatment by hypnotism. *S. E., 1*: 117–128. London: Hogarth.

Freud, S. (1893a). On the psychical mechanism of hysterical phenomena. *S. E., 2*: 1–17. London: Hogarth.

Freud, S. (1895). *Project for a Scientific Psychology*. *S. E., 1*: 283–397. London: Hogarth.

Freud, S. (1895d). *Studies on Hysteria*. *S. E.,* 2: 48–115. London: Hogarth.

Freud, S. (1900a). *The Interpretation of Dreams*. *S. E.,* 4–5. London: Hogarth.

Freud, S. (1901b). *The Psychopathology of Everyday Life*. *S. E., 6*: 1–279. London: Hogarth.

Freud, S. (1905a). On psychotherapy. *S. E., 7*: 255–268. London: Hogarth.

Freud, S. (1905c). *Jokes and their Relation to the Unconscious*. *S. E., 8*: 9–158. London: Hogarth.

Freud, S. (1905d). *Three Essays on the Theory of Sexuality*. *S. E., 7*: 125–245. London: Hogarth.

Freud, S. (1905e). *Fragment of an Analysis of a Case of Hysteria*. *S. E., 7*: 1–122. London: Hogarth.

Freud, S. (1907a). Delusions and dreams in Jensen's Gradiva. *S. E., 9*: 7–95. London: Hogarth.

Freud, S. (1907b). Obsessive actions and religious practices. *S. E., 9*: 115–127. London: Hogarth.

Freud, S. (1907c). The sexual enlightenment of children. *S. E., 9*: 1239–139. London: Hogarth.

Freud, S. (1908b). Character and anal erotism. *S. E., 9*: 167–175. London: Hogarth.

Freud, S. (1908c). On the sexual theories of children. *S. E., 9*: 205–226. London: Hogarth.

Freud, S. (1908d). 'Civilized' sexual morality and modern nervous illness. *S. E., 9*: 177–204. London: Hogarth.

Freud, S. (1908e). Creative writers and day-dreaming. *S. E., 9*: 141–153. London: Hogarth.

Freud, S. (1909c). Family romances. *S. E., 9*: 205–226. London: Hogarth.

Freud, S. (1909d). *Notes upon a Case of Obsessional Neurosis. S. E., 10*: 151–249. London: Hogarth.

Freud, S. (1910c). *Leonardo da Vinci and a Memory of his Childhood. S. E., 11*: 59–137. London: Hogarth.

Freud, S. (1910d). The future prospects of psycho-analytic therapy. *S. E., 11*: 139–151. London: Hogarth.

Freud, S. (1911c). *Psycho-Analytic Notes on an Autobiographical Account of a Case of Paranoia. S. E., 12*: 9–82. London: Hogarth.

Freud, S. (1911f). 'Great is Diana of the Ephesians'. *S. E., 22*: 342–344. London: Hogarth.

Freud, S. (1912–1913). *Totem and Taboo. S. E., 13*: 7–161. London: Hogarth.

Freud, S. (1913c). On beginning the treatment. *S. E., 12*: 121–144. London: Hogarth.

Freud, S. (1913f). The theme of the three caskets. *S. E., 12*: 289–302. London: Hogarth.

Freud, S. (1913k). Preface to Bourke's *Scatological Rites of All Nations. S. E., 12*: 335–337. London: Hogarth.

Freud, S. (1914b). The Moses of Michelangelo. *S. E., 13*: 211–238. London: Hogarth.

Freud, S. (1914c). On narcissism: an introduction. *S. E., 14*: 69–102. London: Hogarth.

Freud, S. (1914d). On the history of the psycho-analytic movement. *S. E., 14*: 7–66. London: Hogarth.

Freud, S. (1914f). Some reflections on schoolboy psychology. *S. E., 13*: 239–244. London: Hogarth.

Freud, S. (1915b). Thoughts for the times on war and death. *S. E., 14*: 273–300. London: Hogarth.

Freud, S. (1916–1917). *Introductory Lectures on Psycho-Analysis. S. E., 15*. London: Hogarth.

Freud, S. (1917c). On transformations of instinct as exemplified in anal erotism. *S. E., 17*: 128–131. London: Hogarth.

Freud, S. (1918a). The taboo of virginity. *S. E., 11*: 193–208. London: Hogarth.

Freud, S. (1918b). *From the History of an Infantile Neurosis. S. E., 17*: 7–122. London: Hogarth.

Freud, S. (1919a). Lines of advance in psycho-analytic therapy. *S. E., 17*: 157–168. London: Hogarth.

Freud, S. (1919g). Preface to Reik's *Ritual: Psycho-Analytic Studies. S. E., 17*: 259–263. London: Hogarth.

Freud, S. (1920d). Associations of a four-year-old child. *S. E., 18*: 266. London: Hogarth.

Freud, S. (1920g). *Beyond the Pleasure Principle. S. E., 18*: 1–64. London: Hogarth.

Freud, S. (1921c). *Group Psychology and the Analysis of the Ego. S. E., 18*: 65–143. London: Hogarth.

Freud, S. (1923a). Two encyclopaedia articles. *S. E., 18*: 235–259. London: Hogarth.

Freud, S. (1923b). *The Ego and the Id. S. E., 19*: 1–66. London: Hogarth.

Freud, S. (1923d). A seventeenth-century demonological neurosis. *S. E., 19*: 72–105. London: Hogarth.

Freud, S. (1923e). The infantile genital organization. *S. E., 19*: 141–145. London: Hogarth.

Freud, S. (1924c). The economic problem of masochism. *S. E., 19*: 155–170. London: Hogarth.

Freud, S. (1924f). A short account of psycho-analysis. *S. E., 19*: 190–209. London: Hogarth.

Freud, S. (1925d). An autobiographical study. *S. E., 20*: 52. London: Hogarth.

Freud, S. (1926d). *Inhibitions, Symptoms and Anxiety. S. E., 20*: 75–172. London: Hogarth.

Freud, S. (1926e). The question of lay analysis. *S. E., 20*: 177–250. London: Hogarth.

Freud, S. (1927c). *The Future of an Illusion. S. E., 21*: 1–56. London: Hogarth.

Freud, S. (1928a). A religious experience. *S. E., 21*: 169–172. London: Hogarth.

Freud, S. (1928b). Dostoevsky and parricide. *S. E., 21*: 177–196. London: Hogarth.

Freud, S. (1930a). *Civilization and its Discontents. S. E., 21*: 59–145. London: Hogarth.

Freud, S. (1930e). The Goethe prize. *S. E., 21*: 205–207. London: Hogarth.

Freud, S. (1932a). The acquisition and control of fire. *S. E., 22*: 183–193. London: Hogarth.

Freud, S. (1933a). *New Introductory Lectures on Psycho-Analysis. S.E., 22*: 1–182. London: Hogarth.

Freud, S. (1933b). Why war? *S. E., 22*: 195–215. London: Hogarth.

Freud, S. (1937d). Constructions in analysis. *S. E., 23*: 255–269 London: Hogarth.
Freud, S. (1939a). *Moses and Monotheism. S. E., 23*: 1–137. London: Hogarth.
Freud, S. (1940a). *An Outline of Psycho-Analysis. S. E., 23*: 23–207. London: Hogarth.
Freud, S. (1941f). Findings, ideas, problems. *S. E., 23*: 299–300. London: Hogarth.
Freud, S. (1942a/1906b). Psychopathic characters on the stage. *S. E., 7*: 305–310. London: Hogarth.
Freud, S. (1950a). *Extracts from the Fliess Papers*. 1892–1899: *S. E., I*: 177–392. London: Hogarth.
Fromm, E. (1955). *The Sane Society*. London: Routledge & Kegan Paul.
Fromm, E. (1982a). *To Have or To Be*. New York: HarperRow.
Fromm, E. (1982b). *Escape from Freedom*, New York: Farrar.
Fuchs, E. (1995). *Deseo y ternura. Fuentes e historia de una ética cristiana de la sexualidad y el matrimonio*. Bilbao: Desclée.
Gallimard, P. (1963). Les tentations de l'autorité. *Le supplement, 16*: 5–19.
García Callado, M. J. (1990). Falseamiento de la libertad y la obediencia. *Sal Terrae, 78*: 303–309.
García Reinoso, D. (1977). Culpa e ideología. *Clínica y análisis grupal, 5*: 94–111.
Gay, P. (1988). *Freud. A Life for Our Time*. New York: W. W. Norton.
Gemelli, A. (1952). *Psicología de la edad evolutiva*. Madrid: Razón y fe.
Girardi, G. (1983). Los cristianos y la paz: el proyecto de paz en la lucha ideológica de Jesús y en la Iglesia. *Misión abierta, 76*: 617–648.
Godin, A. (Ed.) (1961). *Child and Adult before God: Thought and Research*. Brussels: Lumen Vitae.
Godin, A. (1984). Cristianos de nacimiento: alienaciones psicológicas o liberación en el espíritu. *Concilium, 194*: 9–21.
Godin, A. (1986). *Psychologie des expériences religieuses: le désir et la realité*. Paris: Le Centurion.
Godin, A., & Hallez, M. (1964). Images parentales et paternité divine. In: A. Godin (Ed.), *De l'expérience à l'attitude religieuse* (pp. 81–114). Brussels: Lumen Vitae.
Goldman, R. (1964). *Religious Thinking from Childhood to Adolescence*. In: I. Acebo, T. León, & C. Domínguez-Morano (Eds.), *Mujeres en la iglesia* (pp. 69–139). Barcelona: Claret.
Gómez Acebo, I. (2012). Sexo, mujer y Biblia. In: R. M. Nogués, I. Gómez Acebo, T. León, & C. Domínguez-Morano (Eds.), *Mujeres en la iglesia* (pp. 143–207). Barcelona: Claret.

González Faus, J. I. (1982). *Clamor del Reino. Estudio sobre los milagros de Jesús*. Salamanca: Sigueme.

González Faus, J. I. (1990). La autoridad de Jesús. *Sal Terrae, 78*: 245–254.

González Faus, J. I. (2006). *Carta a un amigo agnóstico*. Barcelona: CyJ.

González Faus, J. I., Domínguez-Morano, C., & Torres Queiruga, A. (Eds.) (1996). *Clérigos en debate* (pp. 66–130). Madrid: PPC.

Grinberg, L. (1992). *Guilt and Depression*. London: Karnac.

Groddeck, G., & Freud, S. (1970). *Georg Groddeck–Sigmund Freud Briefwechsel*. Wiesbaden: Limes.

Grubrich-Simitis, I. (1991). *Freuds Moses-Studie als Tagtraum: Ein biographischer Essay*. Weinheim: Verlag Internationales Psychoanalyse.

Hartley, D. (1749). *An Enquiry into the Origin of the Human Appetite and Affections*. Lincoln, UK: W. Wood.

Hartmann, H. (1955). Note on a theory of sublimation. *Psychoanalytic Study of the Child, 10*: 9–29.

Heinzelman, K. (1980). *The Economics of The Imagination*. Boston, MA: University of Massachusetts Press.

Hierzenberger, G. (1969). *Der magische Rest. Ein Beitrag zur Entmagisierung des Christentums*. Düsseldorf: Patmos.

Hoffman, J. (2002). *The Divine Attributes*. Oxford: Blackwell.

Homans, P. (1970). *Theology after Freud: An Interpretative Inquiry*. Indianapolis, IN: Bobbs-Merrill.

Horney, K. (1937). *The Neurotic Personality of Our Time*. New York: Norton.

Humbert, A. (1970). Les péchés de sexualité dans le Nouveau Testament. *Moralia, VIII*: 149–183.

Ignacius de Loyola (1914). *Spiritual Exercises*. New York: Kennedy.

Jacobelli, M. C. (1990). *Il Risus Paschalis e il fondamento teologico del piacere sessuale*. Brescia: Queriniana.

Jeammet, J. (1989). *La haine nécessaire*. Paris: Gallimard.

Jeremías, J. (1965). *The Central Message of the New Testament*. London: SCM.

Jones, E. (1916). The theory of symbolism. *British Journal of Psychology, 9*(2): 181–229.

Jones, E. (1918). Anal–erotic character traits. *Journal of Abnormal Psychology, 13*(5) 261–284.

Jones, E. (1953–1957). *Sigmund Freud: Life and Work. Volume 1–3*. New York: Basic Books.

Jones, E. (1974). *Psycho-Myth, Psycho-History: Essays in Applied Psychoanalysis, Volumes I–II*. New York: Hillstone.

Jung, C. G. (1945). After the catastrophe. *C. W., 10*: 194–217. Princeton, NJ: Princeton University Press.

Jungmann, J. A. (1952). *Missarum Sollemnia*. Freiburg: Herder.

Kavanaugh, J. F. (2007). *Following Christ in a Consumer Society*. Maryknoll, NY: Orbis.

Kessler, H. (1985). *Sucht den Lebenden nicht bei den Toten*. Düsseldorf: Patmos.

Keynes, J. M. (1931). *Essays in Persuasion*. London: Macmillan.

Klein, M. (1937). *Love, Hate and Reparation*. London: Hogarth.

Klein, M. (1975). On the theory of anxiety and guilt. In: *The Writings of Melanie Klein, Vol. 3* (pp. 1946–1963). London: Hogarth.

Klein, M., & Riviere, J. (1964). *Love, Hate and Reparation*. New York: Norton.

Klein, M., Heiman, P., & Money-Kyrle, R. E. (1955). *New Directions in Psycho-Analysis*. New York: Basic Books.

Kosnik, A. (1977). *Human Sexuality. New Directions in American Catholic Thought*. New York: Paulist.

Krech, D., Crutchfield, R., & Ballachey, E. (1972). *Psicología social*. Madrid: Biblioteca Nueva.

Laboa, J. M. (1990). Los cristianos incómodos. *Sal Terrae, 78*: 291–302.

Lacan, J. (1978). *La Famille*. Barcelona: Argonauta.

Lagache, D. (1984). *De la fantaisie a`la sublimation: Oeuvres V*. Paris: PUF.

Lagache, D. (2013). *L´ unité de la psychologie*. Paris: PUF.

Laing, R. D. (1971). *The Politics of the Family and Other Essays*. London: Tavistock.

Laplanche, J. (1980). *Problématiques, III : La sublimation*. Paris: PUF.

Laplanche, J., & Pontalis, J. B. (1973). *The Language of Psychoanalysis*. London: Karnac.

Lebovici, S., & Soulé, M. (2007). *La connaissance de l'enfant par la psychanalyse*. Paris: PUF.

Legendre, L. (1974). *L'amour du censeur, essais sur l'ordre dogmatique*. París: Seuil.

León, T. (2012). Las mujeres en la iglesia: hermenéutica de una pertenencia y un exilio. In: R. M. Nogués, I. Gómez Acebo, T. León, & C. Domínguez-Morano (Eds.), *Mujeres en la iglesia* (pp. 143–207). Barcelona: Claret.

Levine, J. M., & Pavelchak, M. A. (1985). Conformity and obedience. In: S. Moscovici (Ed.), *Social Psychology* (pp. 25–50). Paris: PUF.

Lévi-Strauss, C. (1949). *Les structures élémentaires de la parenté*. Paris: PUF.

Lévi-Strauss, C. (1962). *La pensée sauvage*. Paris: Plon.

Lévi-Strauss, C. (1968). *Anthropologie structural*. Paris: Plon.

Lévi-Strauss, C. (1969). *Le totemism aujourd'hui*. Paris: PUF.

Loewald, H. W. (1988). *Sublimation. Inquiries into Theoretical Psychoanalysis*. New Haven, CT: Yale University Press.

López Azpitarte, E. (1981). *Moral del amor y de la sexualidad: praxis cristiana.* Madrid: Paulinas.

Lust, J. (1989). Freud, Hosea, and the murder of Moses. Notae et miscellanea. *Ephemerides Theologicae Lovanienses, LXV*: 81–93.

Magli, I. (1982). *Gesú du Nazaret, tabu e tramsgressione.* Milan: Rizzoli.

Magli, I. (1987). *La Madonna.* Milano: Rizzoli.

Malinowski, B. (1937). *Sex and Repression in Savage Society.* London: Kegan Paul.

Marconi, G. (2008). *Le donne di Giovanni.* Roma: Aracne.

Marcuse, H. (1957). La idea de progreso a la luz del psicoanálisis. In: W. Adorno & W. Dirks (Eds.), *Freud en la actualidad.* Barcelona: Barral.

Marcuse, H. (1971). La idea de progreso a la luz del psicoanálisis. In: W. Adorno & W. Dirks (Eds.), *Freud en la actualidad.* Barcelona: Barral.

Marcuse, H. (1987). *Eros and Civilization: A Philosophical Inquiry into Freud.* London: Routledge.

Marler, P. (1967). *Mechanisms of Animal Behavior.* Lincoln: Wiley.

Marty, P. (1998). *Les Mouvements individuels de vie et de mort.* Paris: Payot.

Masson, J. M. (1980). *The Oceanic Feeling. The Origins of Religious Sentiment in Ancient India.* Boston: Reidel.

Masson, J. M. (Ed.) (1985). *The Complete Letters of Sigmund Freud to Wilhelm Fliess 1887–1904.* Cambridge, MA: Harvard University Press.

Mateos, J., & Barreto, J. (1979). *El evangelio de Juan.* Madrid: Cristiandad.

Mateos, J., & Camacho, F. (1988). *El horizonte humano. La propuesta de Jesús,* Córdoba: El almendro.

Mead, M. (1952). *Sex and Temperament in Three Primitive Societies.* London: Routledge.

Meehl, P. E. (1954). *Clinical vs. Statistical Prediction.* Minneapolis, MN: University of Minnesota Press.

Meissner, M. D. (1984). *Psychoanalysis and Religious Experience.* New Haven, CT: Yale University Press.

Meissner, W. W. (1992). *Ignatius of Loyola. The Psychology of a Saint.* New Haven, CT: Yale University Press.

Mendel, G. (1968). *La révolte contre le père.* Paris: Payot.

Meng, H., & Freud, E. L. (Eds.) (1961). *Psychoanalysis and Faith: The Letters of Sigmund Freud & Oskar Pfister.* London: Hogarth.

Merleau-Ponty, M. (1975). *Phenomenology of Perception.* London: Routledge.

Milanesi, G., & Aletti, M. (1973). *Psicologia della religion.* Turin: Elle diCi.

Milgram, S. (1979). *Obedience to Authority: An Experimental View.* London: Tavistock.

Money-Kyrle, R. E. (1952). Psychoanalysis and ethics. *International Journal of Psychoanalysis, 33*: 225–234.

Moore, S. (1989). *Jesus the Liberator of Desire*. New York: Crossroad.
Morandi, F. (1983). Confessione psicoanalitica e confessione sacramentale. *Revista di Teologia Morale, XV*: 231–243.
Mounier, E. (1947). *Traité du caractère*. París: Seuil.
Muensterberger, W. (1976). *L´antropolgie psychanalytique depuis Totem et Tabu*. Paris: Payot.
Müller, A. (1966). *Obedience in the Church*. Westminster: Newman.
Munroe, R. (1955). *Schools of Psychoanalytic Thought: an Exposition, Critique and Attempt at Integration*. New York: Dryden.
Nédoncelle, M., Roger, A., Evdokimov, P., Congar, Y., Audinet, J., Rousseau, O., Dupuy, B., Chavasse, A., Conzemius, V., Latreille, A., & Geiselmann, J. R. (1960). *Le ecclésiologie du XIXe siècle*. Paris: Cerf.
Nelson, O. (1971). The concept of God and feelings toward parents. *Journal of Individual Psychology, 27*: 46–49.
Neumanns, E. (1956). *Die Grosse Mutter*. Zurich: Rhein.
Nietzsche, F. (1968). *Also sprach Zarathustra, Kritische Gesamtausgabe*. Berlin: Walter.
Parsons, M. (2003). Se défaire de la culpabilité. *Revue Française de Psychanalyse, 67*: 1619–1622.
Parsons, T. (1951). *The Social System*. London: Free Press.
Paul, R. A. (1996). *Moses and Civilization: The Meaning Behind Freud's Myth*. New Haven, CT: Yale University Press.
Pfister, O. (1927). *Die Pädagogik der Gegenwart in Selbstdarstellungen*. Leipzig: Felix Meiner.
Pfister, O. (1928). Die Illusion einer Zukunft. *Imago, 14*: 149–184.
Pfrimmer, T. (1982). *Freud lecteur de la bible*. Paris: PUF.
Pichot, A. (1993). *Histoire de la notion de vie*. Paris: Gallimard.
Pihlström, S. (2014). *Taking Evil Seriously*. London: Palgrave Macmillan.
Pinillos, J.-L. (1979). *Principios de psicología*. Madrid: Alianza.
Pintos, M. (1990). *La mujer en la Iglesia*. Madrid: Paulinas.
Pohier, J. (1967). *Psychologie et Théologie*. Paris: Cerf.
Pohier, J. (1972). *Au nom du Père. Recherches théologiques et psychanalytiques*. Paris: Cerf.
Pohier, J. (1977). *Quand je dis Dieu*. Paris: Seuil.
Pohier, J. (1985). *God in Fragments*. London: SCM.
Pontalis, J. B. (1968). *Après Freud*. Paris: Gallimard.
Pottmeyer, H. J. (1975). *Unfehlbarkeit und Souveränität*. Mainz: Grünewald.
Rahner, K. (1962). *Marginales sobre la pobreza y la obediencia*. Barcelona: Taurus.
Rahner, K. (1977). *Toleranz in der Kirche*. Freiburg: Herder.
Reich, W. (1942). *The Function of Orgasms*. New York: Orgone Institute.

Reich, W. (1945). *The Sexual Revolution*. New York: Orgone Institute.

Reich, W. (1953). *The Murder of Christ*. New York: Orgone Institute.

Rey, G. (1974). *Imagen materna del sacerdote*. Madrid: Studium.

Ricoeur, P. (1970). *De l'interpretation. Essais sur Freud*. Paris: Seuil.

Rinaudo, J. L. (2009). *TIC, Éducation et psychanalyse*. Paris: Hartman.

Rizzuto, A. M. (1979). *The Birth of the Living God: A Psychoanalytic Study*. Chicago, IL: University of Chicago Press.

Rizzuto, A. M. (1998). *Why Did Freud Reject God?* New Haven, CT: Yale University Press.

Rizzuto, A. M. (2003). Un Dios y dos géneros. In: C. Domínguez-Morano & R. Briones (Eds.), *Masculino-Femenino y hecho religioso* (pp. 147–161). Granada: Universidad de Granada.

Roazen, P. (1968). *Freud: Political and Social Thought*. New York: Knopf.

Rof Carballo, J. (1972). *Biología y Psicoanálisis*. Bilbao: Desclée de Brouwer.

Rof Carballo, J. (1987). *Violencia y ternura*. Madrid: Espasa Calpe.

Roheim, G. (1955). *Magic and Schizophrenia*. New York: International Universities Press.

Roheim, G. (1962). *The Panic of the Gods and Other Essays*. New York: Harper.

Rosolato, G. (1969). *Essais sur le symbolique*. Paris: Gallimard.

Roudinesco, E. (2014). *Sigmund Freud. En son temps et dans le nôtre*. Paris: Seuil.

Roudinesco, E., & Plon, M. (1997). *Dictionaire de la psychanalyse*. Paris: Fayard.

Rowe, W. L. (2008). *Divine Power, Goodness, and Knowledge*. Oxford: Scholarship.

Rubenstein, R. L. (1971). *L'imagination religieuse. Théologie juive et psychanalyse*. Paris: Gallimard.

Rüger, H. P. (1973). Mamônâs. *Zeitschrift für die neutestamentliche Wissenschaft, 64*: 127–131.

Ruitenbeek, H. M. (1962). *Psychoanalysis and Social Science*. New York: E. P. Dutton.

Ruitenbeek, H. M. (1964). *Psychoanalysis and Literature*. New York: E. P. Dutton.

Ruitenbeck, H. M. (1967). *The Male Myth*. New York: Dell.

Sales, M. (1983). Note sur l'ecclésiologie des Constitutions de la Compagnie de Jesus. *Cahiers de Spiritualité Ignatienne, 7*: 227–252.

Salvador Bertrán, G. (2009). *Familia*. Barcelona: Paidós.

Saussure, T. (2009). *L'Inconscient, nos croyences et la foi chrétienne*. Paris: Cerf.

Schillebeeckx, E. (1979). *Jesus, An Experiment in Christology*. London: Collins.

Schneider, M. (2004). *Le paradigme fémenin*. Paris: Flammarion.

Schreber, D. P. (2000). *Memoirs of My Nervous Illness*. New York: Review Books Classics.

Schur, M. (1972). *Freud: Living and Dying*. New York: International Universities Press.

Schüssler Fiorenza, E. (1983). *In Memory of Her: A Feminist Theological Reconstruction of Christian Origins*. New York: Crossroad.

Schützenberger, A. A. (1971). *Vocabulaire des techniques de groupe*. Paris: Epi.

Sesboüé, B. (1988). *Jésus-Christ l'unique médiateur. Essai sur le rédemption et le salut*. Paris: Desclée.

Siebenthal, W. (1956). *Schuldgefuhl and schuld bei psychiatrischen erkrankungen*. Zurich: Rascher.

Sillamy, N. (1980). *Dictionnaire encyclopédique de psychologie*. Paris: Bordas.

Simon, S. (1975). *Comprendre la sexualité aujourd'hui*. Paris: Flammarion.

Simpson, G. G. (1953). *The Major Features of Evolution*. New York: Columbia University Press.

Sobrino, J. (1990). *Iglesias ricas y pobres y el principio-misericordia*. Madrid: Evangelio y Liberación.

Strunk, O. (1959). Perceived relationship between parental and deity concepts. *Psychological Newsletter, 10*: 222–226.

Swidler, L. (2007). *Jesus Was a Feminist*. Plymouth: Sheed & Ward.

Tinbergen, N. (1953). *Social Behavior in Animals*. London: Methuen.

Tornos, A. (1987). *Acciones mágicas y sacramentos de fe*. Madrid: SM.

Torres Queiruga, A. (1986). *Creo en Dios Padre*. Santander: Sal Terrae.

Torri, R. (2014). *Deus analisado, os católicos e Freud*. São Paulo: Loyola.

Trías, E. (1991). Razón y superstición. *El País*, 28th March.

Urtubey, L. (1983). *Freud et le diable*. Paris: PUF.

Van Bunnen, C. (1964). *La buisson ardent; ses implications symboliques chez des enfants de 5 à 12 ans*. Brussels: Lumen Vitae.

Vande Kemp, H. (1984). *Psychology and Theology in Western Thought 1672–1965*. New York: Kraus.

Vasse, D. (1991). *L'Autre du désir et le Dieu de la foi*. Paris: Seuil.

Vergote, A. (1966). *Psychologie religieuse*. Brussels: Dessart.

Vergote, A. (1969). *Religious Man: Psychological Study of Religious Attitudes*. Dublin: Gill & Macmillan.

Vergote, A. (1978). *Dette et désir. Deux axes chretiéns et la dérive pathologique*. Paris: Seuil.

Vergote, A. (1983). *Religion, foi, incroyence*. Brussels: P. Mardaga.

Vergote, A. (1997). *La psychanalyse à l'épreuve de la sublimation*. Paris: Cerf.

Vergote, A., & Tamayo, A. (1980). *The Parental Figures and the Representation of God. A Psychological and Cross-Cultural Study*. The Hague: Mouton.

Vermes, G. (1977). *Jesus the Jew*. London: Collins.

Vermorel, H., & Vermorel, M. (1993). *Sigmund Freud et Romain Rolland. Correspondence 1923–1936*. Paris: PUF.

Wainwright, J. (2011). *The Lord Handbook of Philosophy of Religion*. Oxford: Oxford University Press.

Watson, J. B. (1913). Psychology as the behaviorist views it. *Psychological Review, 20*: 158–177.

Wolman, B. B. (1973). *Handbook of General Psychology*. Englewood Cliffs, NJ: Prentice-Hall.

Wolman, B. B., & Money, J. (Eds.) (1980). *Handbook on Human Sexuality*. Englewood Cliffs, NJ: Prentice-Hall.

Wyss, D. (1973). *Psychoanalytic Schools from the Beginning to the Present*. New York: Jason Aronson.

Yeruschalmi, Y. H. (1991). *Freud's Moses: Judaism Terminable and Interminable*. New York: Yale University Press.

Yourcenar, M. (1978). *Alexis, ou Le Traîté du Vain Combat*. Paris: Gallimard.

Zamora, J. A. (2004). *Th. W. Adorno. Pensar contra la barbarie*. Madrid: Trotta.

Zerwick, M. (1960). *Analysis philologica Novi Testamenti Graeci*. Rome: PIB.

Zilboorg, G. (1962). *Psychoanalysis and Religion*. New York: Farrar, Strauss & Cudahy.

INDEX